DEPARTMENT FOR EDUCATION AND SKILLS
NATIONAL ASSEMBLY FOR WALES
SCOTTISH EXECUTIVE
NORTHERN IRELAND DEPARTMENT OF EDUCATIO
HIGHER EDUCATION STATISTICS AGENCY
NORTHERN IRELAND DEPARTMENT FOR EMPLOY

CW01476553

EDUCATION AND TRAINING STATISTICS FOR THE UNITED KINGDOM

2001 EDITION

London: The Stationery Office

Contents

Introduction

This is the fifth edition of *Education and Training Statistics for the United Kingdom* and again provides an integrated overview of statistics on education and training in the UK. It largely follows the format of last year's volume, however, there have been a few of changes in the 2001 volume:

- In line with Tables 1.1 and 1.2, and in order to allow inter-country comparisons, Table 1.3 now uses PESA data from HM Treasury to show identifiable total managed expenditure on education services by country. This replaces the UK average spending per pupil in nursery & primary, and secondary schools data shown last year.

- Table 2.9 (Key Stage results) data for Wales includes those reaching or exceeding the KS expected standards in Welsh (and reading/writing at KS1).

- Due to a change in data reporting in DfES, the TEC delivered Government Supported Training Tables in Chapter 3 (Tables 3.10, 3.13, 3.14 and 3.15) together with Tables 4.6 and 5.2, report data for England only in this publication.

- Table 3.11 represents further education students in the first year of their course of study, rather than 'new entrants'.

- A new table (Table 3.26) reports participation in job-related training by disability status, from the Spring 2001 Labour Force Survey.

- Tables 4.2 and 4.3 have been expanded to give UK examinations data rather than GB data previously shown.

- Table 5.3 covers only destinations of full-time first degree home and **EU domiciled** higher education students and is not therefore directly comparable with previous years.

International Chapter
The international chapter (Chapter 7), reintroduced into last years' volume, reports data available from the Organisation for Economic Co-operation and Development (OECD) publication *Education at a Glance 2001*.

Regional Analyses
Where regional analyses are given they are on the basis of Government Office Regions (GORs). These have been the primary classification for the presentation of regional statistics since April 1997.

Contributions
The efforts of the statistics teams in DfES, National Assembly for Wales, Scottish Executive, Northern Ireland Department of Education and Northern Ireland Department for Employment and Learning, who have contributed data for the volume, are again greatly appreciated. In DfES the people responsible for bringing all the data together and producing the 2001 volume were Ken Bell, Paul Blackett, John Canlin, James Chapman, Martin Johnson, Adele Lingard and Dave Walton.

Chapter 1
Expenditure

CHAPTER 1: EXPENDITURE

Key Facts

- Total managed expenditure on education services by central and local government in the UK in 1999-00 was £40.9 billion, including £2.1 billion directly on under fives, £25.4 billion on schools, £4.6 billion on further education and £5.3 billion on higher education. £27.9 billion was spent by local education authorities and £13.0 billion by central government. **(Table 1.1)**

- Total managed expenditure on education services by central and local government in the UK in 1999-00 represented 4.5 per cent of Gross Domestic Product, compared with 4.9 per cent in 1995-96. **(Table 1.2)**

- In 1999-00, total managed expenditure on education services in the UK represented £685 per head of population, compared with £607 per head in 1995-96. Identifiable expenditure ranged from £659 per head in England to £935 per head in Northern Ireland. **(Table 1.3)**

CHAPTER 1: EXPENDITURE – LIST OF TABLES

EXPENDITURE
Total Managed Education Expenditure on services by function and economic category[1]

United Kingdom   Financial year 1 April 1999-31 March 2000   £ million

	Local education authorities	Central government	Total		Local education authorities	Central government	Total
Under fives				**Student support (inc mandatory awards & access funds)**			
Pay[2]	1,529.6	0.6	1,530.2	Pay[2]	.	7.1	7.1
Other current expenditure on goods and services[3]	466.9	1.0	468.0	Other current expenditure on goods and services[3]	.	28.7	28.7
Subsidies[4]	.	.	.	Subsidies[4]	.	721.2	721.2
Current grants to private sector[5]	.	123.7	123.7	Current grants to private sector[5]	796.4	418.5	1,214.9
Current transfers abroad[6]	.	.	.	Current transfers abroad[6]	.	0.1	0.1
Total current	**1,996.6**	**125.4**	**2,122.0**	**Total current**	**796.4**	**1,175.6**	**1,972.0**
Net capital expenditure on assets[7]	.	0.1	0.1	Net capital expenditure on assets[7]	.	.	.
Capital grants[8]	.	1.2	1.2	Capital grants[8]	.	.	.
Total capital	**.**	**1.3**	**1.3**	**Total capital**	**.**	**.**	**.**
Total under fives	**1,996.6**	**126.7**	**2,123.2**	**Total student support**	**796.4**	**1,175.6**	**1,972.0**
				Miscellaneous educational services, research and administration			
Schools				Pay[2]	343.8	145.8	489.5
Pay[2]	18,442.5	561.2	19,003.8	Other current expenditure on goods and services[3]	155.2	95.4	250.6
Other current expenditure on goods and services[3]	3,831.7	214.8	4,046.5	Subsidies[4]	.	.	.
Subsidies[4]	.	.	.	Current grants to private sector[5]	.	595.3	595.3
Current grants to private sector[5]	335.9	578.2	914.2	Current transfers abroad[6]	.	.	.
Current transfers abroad[6]	.	6.0	6.0	**Total current**	**499.0**	**836.4**	**1,335.4**
Total current	**22,610.1**	**1,360.3**	**23,970.4**	Net capital expenditure on assets[7]	42.8	8.2	51.0
Net capital expenditure on assets[7]	1,387.9	24.2	1,412.1	Capital grants[8]	1.3	23.3	24.6
Capital grants[8]	4.6	54.4	58.9	**Total capital**	**44.1**	**31.5**	**75.6**
Total capital	**1,392.5**	**78.5**	**1,471.0**	**Total miscellaneous etc**	**543.1**	**867.9**	**1,411.0**
Total schools	**24,002.6**	**1,438.8**	**25,441.5**				
Further Education				**GRAND TOTALS**			
Pay[2]	454.4	13.5	467.9	Pay[2]	20,770.4	738.4	21,508.8
Other current expenditure on goods and services[3]	76.5	51.2	127.6	Other current expenditure on goods and services[3]	4,541.5	396.1	4,937.7
Subsidies[4]	.	.	.	Subsidies[4]	.	721.2	721.2
Current grants to private sector[5]	2.1	3,901.3	3,903.4	Current grants to private sector[5]	1,134.4	10,820.5	11,954.9
Current transfers abroad[6]	.	.	.	Current transfers abroad[6]	.	8.2	8.2
Total current	**532.9**	**3,966.0**	**4,499.0**	**Total current**	**26,446.3**	**12,684.4**	**39,130.6**
Net capital expenditure on assets[7]	45.4	-1.6	43.8	Net capital expenditure on assets[7]	1,476.2	30.8	1,507.1
Capital grants[8]	4.2	65.2	69.4	Capital grants[8]	10.0	241.0	251.0
Total capital	**49.6**	**63.6**	**113.2**	**Total capital**	**1,486.2**	**271.8**	**1,758.1**
Total further education	**582.6**	**4,029.7**	**4,612.2**	**TOTAL Education Expenditure**	**27,932.5**	**12,956.2**	**40,888.7**
Higher Education							
Pay[2]	.	10.2	10.2				
Other current expenditure on goods and services[3]	11.3	5.0	16.3				
Subsidies[4]	.	.	.				
Current grants to private sector[5]	.	5,203.4	5,203.4				
Current transfers abroad[6]	.	2.0	2.0				
Total current	**11.3**	**5,220.6**	**5,231.9**				
Net capital expenditure on assets[7]	.	.	.				
Capital grants[8]	.	96.9	96.9				
Total capital	**.**	**96.9**	**96.9**				
Total higher education	**11.3**	**5,317.6**	**5,328.9**				

Source: HM Treasury – Public Expenditure Statistical Analysis

1 Total Managed Expenditure on services is a definition of aggregate public spending based on the national accounts aggregate TME. It is the consolidated sum of current and capital expenditure of central and local government, and public corporations, but excludes net public service pension payments in Annually Managed Expenditure (AME), debt interest payments and other accounting adjustments.
2 Pay and pension costs.
3 Including general administrative expenses and purchases of other goods and services which are not of a capital nature.
4 Payments to producers designed to reduce their prices.
5 Including grants to households, and from the Further and Higher Education Funding Councils to further education colleges and higher education institutions for their pay and other running costs.
6 Including net payments to European Institutions, payments from UK's development assistance, subscriptions to international organisations and pensions paid to overseas residents.
7 Comprising expenditure on new construction, the purchase of land, buildings and other physical assets, less the proceeds from sales of similar assets and the value of net changes in the level of stocks.
8 Grants to the private sector, nationalised industries and other public corporations.

1.2 EXPENDITURE
Summary of Total Managed Expenditure on education services[1] – time series

United Kingdom		Financial Year 1 April to 31 March			£ million
	1995-96[2]	1996-97[2]	1997-98[2]	1998-99[2]	1999-00
Local education authorities					
Current	23,962.4	24,386.6	24,360.2	26,101.7	26,446.3
Capital	1,202.1	1,114.4	1,186.3	1,369.5	1,486.2
Total	**25,164.5**	**25,501.0**	**25,546.5**	**27,471.2**	**27,932.5**
Central Government					
Current	9,702.6	10,469.1	11,461.5	11,149.6	12,684.4
Capital	705.8	173.1	165.9	140.6	271.8
Total	**10,408.4**	**10,642.2**	**11,627.4**	**11,290.1**	**12,956.2**
All public authorities					
Current	33,665.1	34,855.7	35,821.7	37,251.3	39,130.6
Capital	1,907.9	1,287.5	1,352.2	1,510.0	1,758.1
Total	**35,572.9**	**36,143.2**	**37,173.9**	**38,761.3**	**40,888.7**
Gross Domestic Product (GDP, cash)[3]	729,001	772,918	824,396	868,809	914,856
Education expenditure as a percentage of GDP	**4.9**	**4.7**	**4.5**	**4.5**	**4.5**
GDP deflator[3]	89.302	92.121	94.960	97.614	100.000
GDP in real terms[4]	816,330	839,029	868,150	890,041	914,856
Total education expenditure in real terms[4]	**39,834.3**	**39,234.6**	**39,146.9**	**39,708.6**	**40,888.7**

Sources: HM Treasury – Public Expenditure Statistical Analysis; Office for National Statistics

1 Total Managed Expenditure on services is a definition of aggregate public spending based on the national accounts aggregate TME. It is the consolidated sum of current and capital
expenditure of central and local government, and public corporations, but excludes net public service pension payments in Annually Managed Expenditure (AME), debt interest
payments and other accounting adjustments.

2 Includes revised data.

3 Source: Office for National Statistics – September 2001 National Accounts release.

4 At 1999-00 prices.

1.3 EXPENDITURE

Identifiable[1] total managed expenditure on education services[2] by country 1995-96 to 1999-00

	Financial Year 1 April to 31 March				cash £ million
	1995-96	1996-97	1997-98	1998-99	1999-00
By country					
England	28,314	28,908	29,721	31,115	32,766
Scotland	4,075	3,980	4,099	4,023	4,417
Wales	1,799	1,819	1,884	1,935	2,004
Northern Ireland	1,377	1,428	1,462	1,509	1,583
United Kingdom	**35,565**	**36,135**	**37,166**	**38,762**	**40,770**

					£ per head[3]
By country					
England	579	589	603	629	659
Scotland	793	776	800	821	863
Wales	617	623	644	660	682
Northern Ireland	832	855	870	896	935
United Kingdom	**607**	**614**	**630**	**654**	**685**

Sources: HM Treasury – Public Expenditure Statistical Analysis

1 A small amount of expenditure cannot be disaggregated to individual country level. Therefore, the figures in this table are slightly different from those shown in Table 1.2.

2 Total Managed Expenditure on services is a definition of aggregate public spending based on the national accounts aggregate TME. It is the consolidated sum of current and capital expenditure of central and local government, and public corporations, but excludes net public service pension payments in Annually Managed Expenditure (AME), debt interest payments and other accounting adjustments.

3 Comparisons of expenditure per head between countries should be made with caution e.g. different countries have different proportions of young people within their population.

Chapter 2
Schools

CHAPTER 2: SCHOOLS

Key Facts

- There were 10.1 million full-time and part-time pupils in 34.7 thousand schools in 2000/01, compared with 9.3 million pupils in 34.6 thousand schools in 1990/91. **(Tables 2.1, 2.2, 2.3)**

- There were 301 thousand full-time and part-time pupils with statements of Special Educational Needs (SEN) in 2000/01, representing 3.0% of all pupils, with 64% of SEN pupils with statements being educated in mainstream schools. **(Table 2.4)**

- There were 502 thousand full-time qualified teachers in the United Kingdom in 1999/00, of which two-thirds were female. Eighty-six per cent of full-time teachers were employed in maintained nursery, primary and secondary schools. **(Table 2.5)**

- There were an average 44 pupils per maintained mainstream nursery school in 2000/01, 231 pupils per primary school and 903 pupils per secondary school. **(Table 2.6)**

- The average class size in primary schools in the United Kingdom in 2000/01 was 26.4 pupils. The average class size in secondary schools in England and Wales was 22.1 pupils. **(Table 2.7)**

- The average size of one-teacher classes in primary and secondary schools in England in 2000/01 was 26.7 pupils and 22.0 pupils respectively. **(Table 2.7)**

- The average pupil/teacher ratio in nursery schools in 2000/01 was 26.5. In primary schools the pupil/teacher ratio was 22.3 and in secondary schools it was 16.5. The average pupil/teacher ratio for all schools was 17.9 compared to 17.3 in 1990/91. **(Table 2.8)**

- 70% of boys and 80% of girls in England achieved Level 4 or above in the 2001 Key Stage 2 English test. 72% of boys and 82% of girls in Wales achieved Level 4 or above. **(Table 2.9)**

- 71% of boys and 70% of girls in England achieved Level 4 or above in the 2001 Key Stage 2 Maths test. 73% of boys and 76% of girls in Wales achieved Level 4 or above. **(Table 2.9)**

CHAPTER 2: SCHOOLS - LIST OF TABLES

2.1

SCHOOLS
Number of schools or departments[1] by type – time series

United Kingdom

Numbers

	Academic years				
	1990/91	1995/96	1998/99[2]	1999/00[3]	2000/01[4]
UNITED KINGDOM					
Public sector mainstream					
Nursery[5]	1,364	1,486	2,369	2,864	3,228
Primary	24,135	23,441	23,125	23,036	22,902
Secondary[6]	4,790	4,463	4,418	4,405	4,337
of which					
middle deemed secondary	491	400	377	377	316
modern	171	113	124	148	145
Grammar	222	231	237	234	231
Technical	3	1	7	4	3
Comprehensive	3,696	3,509	3,465	3,439	3,443
of which 6th form colleges	116	.	.	.	.
Other	207	209	208	203	199
Non-maintained mainstream	2,508	2,436	2,482	2,457	2,414
Special – maintained	}	1,456	1,428	1,426	1,401
	} 1,830				
– non maintained	}	109	94	97	97
Pupil referral units	.	315	325	325	338
ALL SCHOOLS	34,627	33,706	34,241	34,610	34,717
ENGLAND					
Public sector mainstream					
Nursery	566	547	520	514	506
Primary	19,047	18,480	18,234	18,158	18,069
Secondary[6]	3,897	3,594	3,560	3,550	3,481
of which					
middle deemed secondary	491	400	377	377	316
modern	171	113	124	148	145
Grammar	152	160	165	162	159
Technical	3	1	7	4	3
Comprehensive	3,042	2,876	2,844	2,822	2,825
of which 6th form colleges	114	.	.	.	.
Other	38	44	43	37	33
Non-maintained mainstream	2,289	2,266	2,231	2,204	2,205
Special – maintained	}	1,191	1,148	1,134	1,113
	} 1,380				
– non maintained	}	72	61	63	62
Pupil referral units	.	291	298	295	308
ALL SCHOOLS	27,179	26,441	26,052	25,918	25,744
WALES					
Public sector mainstream					
Nursery	54	52	46	42	41
Primary	1,717	1,681	1,660	1,644	1,631
Secondary[6,7]	230	228	229	228	229
of which 6th form colleges	2	.	.	.	.
Non-maintained mainstream	71	62	54	55	54
Special (maintained)	61	54	48	47	45
Pupil referral units	.	24	27	30	30
ALL SCHOOLS	2,133	2,101	2,064	2,046	2,030
SCOTLAND					
Public sector mainstream					
Nursery[5]	659	796	1,712	2,213	2,586
Primary	2,372	2,332	2,291	2,293	2,278
Secondary[7]	424	405	392	389	389
Non-maintained mainstream[1]	131	87	175	176	129
Special – maintained	343	164	185	195	195
– non maintained	.	37	33	34	35
ALL SCHOOLS	3,929	3,821	4,788	5,300	5,612
NORTHERN IRELAND					
Grant aided mainstream					
Nursery[8]	85	91	91	95	95
Primary[9]	999	948	940	941	924
Secondary	239	236	237	238	238
of which					
Grammar	70	71	72	72	72
Other (Secondary intermediate)	169	165	165	166	166
Non-maintained mainstream	17	21	22	22	26
Special (maintained)	46	47	47	50	48
ALL SCHOOLS	1,386	1,343	1,337	1,346	1,331

Sources: Department for Education and Skills; National Assembly for Wales; Scottish Executive; Northern Ireland Department of Education

1 For 1998/99 and 1999/00, non-maintained mainstream schools in Scotland with more than one department have been counted once for each department e.g. a school with nursery, primary and secondary departments has been counted 3 times. The 2000/01 figure shows primary and secondary only.
2 Includes revised nursery schools data for Scotland.
3 Revised to include 1999/00 data for Wales and updated nursery schools and non-maintained special schools data for Scotland.
4 Provisional.
5 Nursery schools figures for Scotland prior to 1998/99 only include data for Local Authority pre-schools. Data thereafter include partnership pre-schools.
6 From 1993/94, excludes sixth form colleges in England and Wales which were reclassified as further education colleges on 1 April 1993.
7 All secondary schools are classed as Comprehensive.
8 Excludes voluntary and private pre-school education centres (304 in total in 2000/01).
9 From 1995/96, includes Preparatory Departments in Grammar Schools (22 in total in 2000/01).

SCHOOLS
Full-time and part-time pupils by age[1], gender[2] and school type, 2000/01[3]

United Kingdom | Thousands

| | Maintained schools[4] | | | | | | | | Non-maintained | | | |
| | | Primary Schools | | | | | | | | | | |
Age at 31 August 2000[10]	Nursery Schools[5,6]	Nursery Classes	Other Classes[7]	Total Primary Schools	Secondary Schools	Special schools	Pupil Referral Units[8]	All maintained schools	Special schools	Other Schools[9]	All non-maintained schools	All schools
All												
2-4[11,12]	152.2	30.3	73.0	956.9	-	6.9	-	1,116.0	0.1	71.2	71.2	1,187.2
5	-	-	696.1	696.1	-	4.2	-	700.3	0.1	32.6	32.7	733.0
6	-	-	712.0	712.0	-	4.9	-	716.9	0.1	33.5	33.6	750.6
7	-	-	714.1	714.1	-	5.7	0.1	719.8	0.1	34.9	35.0	754.8
8	-	-	739.0	739.0	-	6.5	0.1	745.7	0.2	37.6	37.8	783.4
9	-	-	712.6	712.6	31.3	7.3	0.2	751.4	0.2	39.4	39.6	791.0
10	-	-	698.8	698.8	35.8	7.9	0.2	742.8	0.3	40.8	41.2	783.9
11	-	-	68.1	68.1	643.6	9.8	0.2	721.8	0.5	49.0	49.5	771.3
12	-	-	-	-	721.7	11.0	0.6	733.3	0.6	50.0	50.7	784.0
13	-	-	-	-	701.8	11.5	1.2	714.4	0.7	49.3	50.0	764.4
14	-	-	-	-	683.5	11.5	2.3	697.2	0.8	50.4	51.2	748.4
15	-	-	-	-	664.4	11.6	4.7	680.7	0.9	50.3	51.2	731.9
16	-	-	-	-	240.7	3.9	0.1	244.7	0.5	41.3	41.7	286.5
17	-	-	-	-	177.2	3.1	-	180.2	0.3	38.0	38.4	218.6
18	-	-	-	-	14.4	1.9	-	16.3	0.2	5.6	5.8	22.1
19 and over	-	-	-	-	2.5	-	-	2.6	0.1	2.1	2.2	4.8
Total[11]	152.2	30.3	4,413.7	5,297.7	3,916.9	107.7	9.7	9,484.2	5.7	626.1	631.8	10,116.0
of which												
England	45.0	..	..	4,406.2	3,231.8	91.0	9.3	7,783.3	4.6	586.2	590.8	8,374.1
Wales	2.4	24.4	261.4	285.8	210.4	3.8	0.4	502.8	-	9.5	9.5	512.3
Scotland[6]	98.8	-	425.2	425.2	319.1	8.3	.	851.5	1.1	29.2	30.3	881.8
Northern Ireland[5]	6.0	6.0	174.5	180.4	155.6	4.7	.	346.6	-	1.2	1.2	347.9
Males[2]												
2-4[11,12]	79.2	15.5	37.5	489.7	-	4.4	-	573.3	-	35.6	35.6	608.9
5	-	-	356.3	356.3	-	2.9	-	359.3	-	16.3	16.3	375.6
6	-	-	363.8	363.8	-	3.4	-	367.2	0.1	17.0	17.1	384.3
7	-	-	364.6	364.6	-	4.0	0.1	368.7	0.1	17.7	17.8	386.5
8	-	-	377.7	377.7	-	4.5	0.1	382.4	0.1	19.3	19.4	401.7
9	-	-	363.2	363.2	15.9	5.1	0.1	384.3	0.2	20.3	20.5	404.8
10	-	-	356.3	356.3	18.4	5.4	0.2	380.3	0.2	21.2	21.4	401.7
11	-	-	34.9	34.9	327.1	6.7	0.2	368.9	0.4	25.0	25.4	394.3
12	-	-	-	-	365.9	7.6	0.5	374.1	0.5	25.9	26.4	400.4
13	-	-	-	-	356.8	8.0	1.0	365.7	0.5	25.4	25.9	391.6
14	-	-	-	-	347.4	7.8	1.8	357.0	0.6	26.0	26.6	383.6
15	-	-	-	-	336.1	7.8	3.3	347.2	0.6	25.9	26.6	373.8
16	-	-	-	-	114.7	2.3	-	117.0	0.3	21.5	21.8	138.9
17	-	-	-	-	82.6	1.8	-	84.4	0.2	20.2	20.4	104.8
18	-	-	-	-	7.7	1.1	-	8.8	0.1	3.2	3.3	12.1
19 and over	-	-	-	-	1.1	-	-	1.2	0.1	1.2	1.3	2.4
Total[11]	79.2	15.5	2,254.5	2,706.6	1,973.7	72.8	7.4	4,839.7	4.0	321.9	325.8	5,165.5
Females[2]												
2-4[11,12]	73.0	14.9	35.5	467.2	-	2.4	-	542.7	-	35.6	35.6	578.4
5	-	-	339.7	339.7	-	1.3	-	341.1	-	16.3	16.3	357.4
6	-	-	348.2	348.2	-	1.6	-	349.7	-	16.5	16.6	366.3
7	-	-	349.4	349.4	-	1.7	-	351.2	-	17.2	17.2	368.4
8	-	-	361.3	361.3	-	2.0	-	363.3	0.1	18.3	18.4	381.7
9	-	-	349.5	349.5	15.4	2.2	-	367.1	0.1	19.1	19.1	386.2
10	-	-	342.5	342.5	17.5	2.5	-	362.5	0.1	19.6	19.7	382.2
11	-	-	33.2	33.2	316.5	3.1	-	352.9	0.2	23.9	24.1	377.0
12	-	-	-	-	355.7	3.4	0.1	359.2	0.2	24.1	24.3	383.5
13	-	-	-	-	345.0	3.5	0.2	348.7	0.2	23.9	24.1	372.8
14	-	-	-	-	336.1	3.6	0.5	340.2	0.2	24.4	24.6	364.8
15	-	-	-	-	328.3	3.8	1.4	333.5	0.3	24.3	24.6	358.1
16	-	-	-	-	126.0	1.6	0.1	127.7	0.2	19.7	19.9	147.6
17	-	-	-	-	94.6	1.2	-	95.8	0.1	17.9	18.0	113.8
18	-	-	-	-	6.7	0.8	-	7.5	0.1	2.4	2.5	10.0
19 and over	-	-	-	-	1.4	-	-	1.4	0.1	0.9	0.9	2.3
Total[11]	73.1	14.9	2,159.3	2,591.0	1,943.2	34.9	2.4	4,644.6	1.8	304.2	305.9	4,950.5

Sources: Department for Education and Skills; National Assembly for Wales; Scottish Executive; Northern Ireland Department of Education

1 Figures for Scotland are estimates using proportions of the stage rolls.
2 In Scotland gender split is not collected by age but has been estimated according to figures collected in September 1999. In Northern Ireland a gender split is not collected by age but is available by year group and so this is used as a proxy. For example pupils in Year 1 are counted as age 4, pupils in Year 2 are counted as age 5 etc.
3 Provisional.
4 Grant-aided schools in Northern Ireland.
5 Excludes 3,957 children at voluntary and private pre-school centres in Northern Ireland in places funded under the Pre-School Expansion Programme which began in 1998/99.
6 Nursery schools figures for Scotland include pre-school education centres.
7 Includes reception pupils in primary classes and, in Northern Ireland, pupils in preparatory departments of grammar schools.
8 England and Wales only. Figures exclude dually registered pupils.
9 Age 2-4 includes pupils less than 2 years of age in England.
10 1 July for Northern Ireland and 31 December for Scotland.
11 A spilt between nursery classes and other classes in primary schools is not available for 2-4 year olds in England. Figures are included in the Total Primary Schools column only.
12 Includes the so-called rising five's (i.e. those pupils who became 5 during the autumn term).

SCHOOLS
Full-time and part-time pupils by gender and school type – time series

United Kingdom
Thousands

| | | Maintained Schools[1] | | | | | | | Non-maintained | | | |
| | Nursery schools[2,3] | Primary Schools | | | Secondary schools[5] | Special schools | Pupil Referral Units[6] | All maintained schools | Special schools | Other schools | All non-maintained schools | All schools |
		Nursery classes	Other classes[4]	Total Primary Schools								
1990/91												
All	**104.9**		**4,954.5**	**4,954.5**	**3,473.3**	**107.7**	**.**	**8,640.4**	**6.4**	**613.4**	**619.7**	**9,260.2**
Males	54.0		2,529.4	2,529.4	1,753.6	70.6	.	4,407.7	4.2	323.8	328.0	4,735.6
Females	50.9		2,425.1	2,425.1	1,719.7	37.1	.	4,232.8	2.2	289.6	291.8	4,524.5
1995/96												
All	**84.3**	**366.7**	**4,968.6**	**5,335.2**	**3,676.2**	**107.7**	**..**	**9,203.3**	**6.7**	**602.9**	**609.7**	**9,813.0**
Males	43.5	187.8	2,535.4	2,723.2	1,853.0	71.6	..	4,691.3	4.6	314.7	319.3	5,010.5
Females	40.8	178.8	2,433.2	2,612.0	1,823.2	36.1	..	4,512.1	2.2	288.3	290.4	4,802.5
1998/99[7]												
All	**79.0**	**379.8**	**5,026.0**	**5,405.7**	**3,793.3**	**109.8**	**8.9**	**9,396.7**	**5.7**	**617.3**	**623.0**	**10,019.7**
Males	40.9	194.5	2,565.1	2,759.6	1,910.6	73.8	6.7	4,791.5	3.9	317.9	321.9	5,113.4
Females	38.1	185.3	2,460.9	2,646.2	1,882.6	36.0	2.2	4,605.2	1.8	299.3	301.1	4,906.3
1999/00[8]												
All[9]	**143.5**	**344.9**	**4,990.1**	**5,335.0**	**3,861.1**	**108.6**	**8.8**	**9,457.0**	**5.8**	**618.3**	**624.1**	**10,081.1**
Males	73.7	176.2	2,548.3	2,724.5	1,943.3	73.2	6.7	4,821.4	4.0	318.0	322.0	5,143.4
Females	68.2	168.7	2,441.8	2,610.5	1,917.7	35.4	2.2	4,634.0	1.8	300.3	302.0	4,936.1
2000/01[10,11]												
All	**152.2**	**30.3**	**4,413.7**	**5,297.7**	**3,916.9**	**107.7**	**9.7**	**9,484.2**	**5.7**	**626.1**	**631.8**	**10,116.0**
Males	79.2	15.5	2,254.5	2,706.6	1,973.7	72.8	7.4	4,839.7	4.0	321.9	325.8	5,165.5
Females	73.1	14.9	2,159.3	2,591.0	1,943.2	34.9	2.4	4,644.6	1.8	304.2	305.9	4,950.5

Source: Department for Education and Skills; National Assembly for Wales; Scottish Executive; Northern Ireland Department of Education

1 Grant aided schools in Northern Ireland.
2 For 1990/91 and from 1999/00, nursery schools includes some nursery classes in primary schools for Scotland. From 1999/00 nursery schools figures for Scotland include pre-school education centres.
3 Includes children at voluntary and private pre-school centres (3,957 in 2000/01) in Northern Ireland in places funded under the Pre-School Expansion Programme which began in 1998/99.
4 Includes reception pupils in primary schools and, in Northern Ireland, pupils in preparatory departments of grammar schools.
5 From 1993/94 excludes sixth form colleges in England and Wales which were reclassified as Further Education colleges from 1 April 1993.
6 England and Wales only. Figures for England exclude dually registered pupils, but these are included for Wales in 1998/99.
7 Includes 1997/98 nursery schools and non-maintained nursery schools data for Scotland.
8 Revised to include 1999/00 data for Wales.
9 Includes some nursery schools figures for Scotland which cannot be split by gender.
10 Provisional.
11 A spilt between nursery classes and other classes in primary schools is not available for 2 - 4 year olds in England. Figures are included in the Total Primary Schools column only.

2.4 SCHOOLS
Full-time and part-time pupils with Special Educational Needs (SEN)[1] by type of school, 2000/01[2]

United Kingdom

Thousands and percentages

	UK	England[3]	Wales	Scotland	N Ireland
ALL SCHOOLS					
Total Pupils	10,109.9	8,374.1	512.3	871.7	351.9
SEN pupils with statements	300.8	258.2	17.0	16.7	8.8
Incidence(%)[4]	*3.0*	*3.1*	*3.3*	*1.9*	*2.5*
MAINTAINED SCHOOLS[5]					
Nursery[6,7]					
Total Pupils	146.1	45.0	2.4	88.8	9.9
SEN pupils with statements	1.1	0.6	-	0.4	0.1
Incidence(%)[4]	*0.8*	*1.3*	*1.0*	*0.5*	*0.6*
Placement(%)[8]	*0.4*	*0.2*	*0.1*	*2.6*	*0.6*
Primary[9]					
Total Pupils	5,297.7	4,406.2	285.8	425.2	180.4
SEN pupils without statements[10]	996.6	927.0	58.1	11.5	-
SEN pupils with statements	88.2	75.3	6.2	4.2	2.5
Pupils with statements – Incidence(%)[4]	*1.7*	*1.7*	*2.2*	*1.0*	*1.4*
Pupils with statements – Placement(%)[8]	*29.3*	*29.1*	*36.3*	*25.0*	*28.7*
Secondary					
Total Pupils	3,916.9	3,231.8	210.4	319.1	155.6
SEN pupils without statements[10]	628.5	586.3	32.4	9.8	-
SEN pupils with statements	96.2	82.1	6.7	5.0	2.4
Pupils with statements – Incidence(%)[4]	*2.5*	*2.5*	*3.2*	*1.6*	*1.5*
Pupils with statements – Placement(%)[8]	*32.0*	*31.8*	*39.5*	*30.1*	*26.8*
Special[11,12]					
Total Pupils	107.7	91.0	3.8	8.3	4.7
SEN pupils with statements	101.6	87.4	3.7	6.7	3.9
Incidence(%)[4]	*94.3*	*96.1*	*97.2*	*80.4*	*82.9*
Placement(%)[8]	*33.8*	*33.9*	*21.5*	*39.9*	*43.9*
Pupil Referral Units[11,13]					
Total Pupils	9.7	9.3	0.4	.	.
SEN pupils with statements	1.9	1.8	0.1	.	.
Incidence(%)[4]	*20.0*	*19.4*	*34.0*	.	.
Placement(%)[8]	*0.6*	*0.7*	*0.9*	.	.
OTHER SCHOOLS					
Independent					
Total Pupils	626.1	586.2	9.5	29.2	1.3
SEN pupils with statements[10]	6.9	6.6	0.3	-	..
Incidence(%)[4]	*1.1*	*1.1*	*3.0*	*0.1*	*..*
Placement(%)[8]	*2.3*	*2.6*	*1.7*	*0.3*	*..*
Non-maintained Special[11]					
Total Pupils	5.7	4.6	.	1.1	.
SEN pupils with statements	4.8	4.5	.	0.3	.
Incidence(%)[4]	*85.1*	*96.1*	.	*31.8*	.
Placement(%)[8]	*1.6*	*1.7*	.	*2.1*	.

Sources: Department for Education and Skills; National Assembly for Wales; Scottish Executive; Northern Ireland Department of Education

1 For Scotland, pupils with a Record of Needs.

2 Provisional.

3 Estimates have been made for January 2001 because the data for SEN are known to be incomplete.

4 Incidence of pupils – the number of pupils with statements within each school type expressed as a proportion of the total number of pupils on roll in each school type.

5 Grant-Aided schools in Northern Ireland.

6 Nursery schools figures for Scotland are for 1999/00.

7 Includes pupils in Voluntary and Private Pre-School Centres in Northern Ireland funded under the Pre-School Expansion Programme which began in 1998/99.

8 Placement of pupils – the number of pupils with statements within each school type expressed as a proportion of the number of pupils with statements in all schools.

9 Includes nursery classes (except for Scotland, where they are included with Nursery schools) and reception classes in primary schools.

10 UK totals are slight undercounts as data are not collected for Northern Ireland.

11 England and Wales figures exclude dually registered pupils.

12 Including general and hospital special schools.

13 England and Wales only.

2.5

SCHOOLS
Qualified teachers by type of school and gender — time series

		(i) Full-time teachers			Thousands
	Public sector mainstream schools		Non-maintained mainstream schools	All Special schools	Total All Schools
	Nursery and Primary	Secondary[1]			
All teachers					
Great Britain					
1990/91	200.3	223.2	44.9	18.2	**486.6**
1995/96	203.3	212.2	48.6	16.6	**480.6**
1996/97[2]	202.8	211.4	48.2	16.3	**478.7**
1997/98[2]	201.3	209.8	49.1	16.0	**476.2**
United Kingdom					
1998/99[2]	210.8	221.7	50.5	16.7	**499.7**
1999/00[3]	211.1	223.0	51.2	16.6	**502.0**
of which:					
England & Wales[4]	181.4	190.3	48.4	13.8	**433.9**
Scotland	21.5	22.6	2.7	2.1	**48.9**
Northern Ireland[3]	8.1	10.2	0.1	0.7	**19.2**
Males					
Great Britain					
1990/91	35.8	116.0	20.6	5.8	**178.2**
1995/96	33.8	103.4	21.1	5.3	**163.5**
1996/97[2]	33.0	101.7	20.6	5.1	**160.4**
1997/98[2]	31.9	99.4	20.7	5.0	**157.1**
United Kingdom					
1998/99[2]	33.0	103.4	20.8	5.1	**162.4**
1999/00[3]	32.6	102.9	21.1	5.0	**161.6**
of which:					
England & Wales[4]	29.6	87.8	19.9	4.4	**141.8**
Scotland	1.5	10.9	1.1	0.4	**13.9**
Northern Ireland[3]	1.5	4.3	-	0.1	**5.9**
Females					
Great Britain					
1990/91	164.5	107.1	24.3	12.4	**308.4**
1995/96	169.5	108.8	27.4	11.3	**317.0**
1996/97[2]	169.8	109.7	27.6	11.2	**318.3**
1997/98[2]	169.3	110.3	28.5	11.0	**319.1**
United Kingdom					
1998/99[2]	177.8	118.3	29.6	11.6	**337.3**
1999/00[3]	178.5	120.1	30.2	11.6	**340.4**
of which:					
England & Wales[4]	151.8	102.5	28.5	9.4	**292.2**
Scotland	20.1	11.7	1.6	1.6	**35.0**
Northern Ireland[3]	6.6	5.9	0.1	0.6	**13.2**

		(ii) Part-time teachers[5]			Thousands
	Public sector mainstream schools		Non-maintained mainstream schools	All Special schools	Total All Schools
	Nursery and Primary	Secondary[1]			
All teachers					
Great Britain					
1990/91	..	..	..	..	**30.0**
1995/96	18.7	17.6	8.9	1.5	**46.7**
1996/97	17.8	15.7	9.4	1.4	**44.3**
1997/98	18.0	16.2	10.7	1.4	**46.4**
United Kingdom					
1998/99[2]	19.7	16.8	9.8	1.5	**47.8**
1999/00[3]	20.0	17.3	10.2	1.6	**49.0**

Sources: Department for Education and Skills; National Assembly for Wales; Scottish Executive; Northern Ireland Department of Education

1 From 1993/94 excludes sixth form colleges in England and Wales which were reclassified as further education colleges on 1 April 1993.

2 Includes revised data for England and Wales.

3 Provisional. Includes 1998/99 data for Northern Ireland.

4 A gender breakdown of public sector teachers in England and Wales is only available from the Database of Teachers Records (DTR) where some in service teachers may
be shown as not in service because their service details are not recorded. Complete coverage of teachers in England and Wales is available from the Form 618G
survey, and published in "Statistics of Education: Teachers England and Wales".

5 Full-time equivalents of part-time teachers.

SCHOOLS

Schools, and pupils by size of school[1] or department[2], by school type, 2000/01[3]

United Kingdom — (i) Number of schools — Numbers

	25 and under	26 to 50	51 to 100	101 to 200	201 to 300	301 to 400	401 to 600	601 to 800	801 to 1,000	1,001 to 1,500	1,501 and over	Total
United Kingdom												
Public sector mainstream												
Nursery[4,5]	1,388	867	966	307	4	.	.	.	.	.	.	3,532
Primary[6]	319	1,108	2,695	5,592	7,107	3,456	2,360	243	21	1	.	22,902
Secondary[7]	7	8	13	46	91	174	586	830	942	1,388	252	4,337
Pupil referral units	218	66	33	19	.	2	.	.	.	.	.	338
Non-maintained mainstream[2,8]	224	222	318	584	356	243	204	117	74	71	1	2,414
Special	173	332	608	356	27	2	.	.	.	.	.	1,498
All schools	**2,329**	**2,603**	**4,633**	**6,904**	**7,585**	**3,877**	**3,150**	**1,190**	**1,037**	**1,460**	**253**	**35,021**
England												
Public sector mainstream												
Nursery	1	46	302	156	1	.	.	.	.	.	.	506
Primary	59	558	1,883	4,312	6,070	2,921	2,048	201	17	.	.	18,069
Secondary	.	1	3	26	65	123	446	665	741	1,189	222	3,481
Pupil referral units	201	61	26	18	.	2	.	.	.	.	.	308
Non-maintained mainstream[8]	175	190	292	551	335	223	195	105	70	68	1	2,205
Special	66	247	524	317	19	2	.	.	.	.	.	1,175
All schools	**502**	**1,103**	**3,030**	**5,380**	**6,490**	**3,271**	**2,689**	**971**	**828**	**1,257**	**223**	**25,744**
Wales												
Public sector mainstream												
Nursery	3	15	21	2	.	.	.	.	.	.	.	41
Primary	41	184	270	500	431	136	67	2	.	.	.	1,631
Secondary	.	.	.	1	3	6	35	50	48	70	16	229
Pupil referral units	17	5	7	1	.	.	.	.	.	.	.	30
Non-maintained mainstream	13	8	7	8	6	6	1	5	.	.	.	54
Special	1	11	22	10	1	.	.	.	.	.	.	45
All schools	**75**	**223**	**327**	**522**	**441**	**148**	**103**	**57**	**48**	**70**	**16**	**2,030**
Scotland												
Public sector mainstream												
Nursery[4]	1,086	792	565	140	3	.	.	.	.	.	.	2,586
Primary	198	266	319	539	471	301	172	12	.	.	.	2,278
Secondary	7	7	8	12	9	11	45	66	111	102	11	389
Non-maintained mainstream[2]	25	17	14	23	14	14	8	7	4	3	.	129
Special	101	66	47	12	4	.	.	.	.	.	.	230
All schools	**1,417**	**1,148**	**953**	**726**	**501**	**326**	**225**	**85**	**115**	**105**	**11**	**5,612**
Northern Ireland												
Grant aided mainstream												
Nursery[5]	298	14	78	9	.	.	.	.	.	.	.	399
Primary[6]	21	100	223	241	135	98	73	28	4	1	.	924
Secondary[7]	.	.	2	7	14	34	60	49	42	27	3	238
Non-maintained mainstream	11	7	5	2	1	.	.	.	.	.	.	26
Special	5	8	15	17	3	.	.	.	.	.	.	48
All schools	**335**	**129**	**323**	**276**	**153**	**132**	**133**	**77**	**46**	**28**	**3**	**1,635**

Sources: Department for Education and Skills; National Assembly for Wales; Scottish Executive; Northern Ireland Department of Education

1 School size on a pupil headcount basis.

2 Non-maintained mainstream schools in Scotland with more than one department have been counted once for each department e.g. a school with primary and secondary department has been counted twice.

3 Provisional.

4 Nursery schools figures for Scotland include pre-school education centres.

5 Northern Ireland figures include 304 Voluntary and Private Pre-School Centres including 3,957 pupils, funded under the Pre-School Expansion Programme which began in 1998/99.

6 Includes 24 preparatory departments attached to Grammar Schools in Northern Ireland.

7 Includes Voluntary Grammar Schools in Northern Ireland.

8 Includes City Technology Colleges.

9 Includes pupils in nursery classes in primary schools in Scotland.

10 Includes pupils in nursery classes and reception classes, except for Scotland - see footnote (9).

11 Figures for Wales include dually registered pupils.

SCHOOLS

Schools, and pupils by size of school[1] or department[2], by school type, 2000/01[3]

United Kingdom					(ii) Number of pupils							Thousands
	25 and under	26 to 50	51 to 100	101 to 200	201 to 300	301 to 400	401 to 600	601 to 800	801 to 1,000	1,001 to 1,500	1,501 and over	Total
United Kingdom												
Public sector mainstream												
Nursery[4,5,9]	19.0	31.2	67.3	37.7	0.9	-	-	-	-	-	-	156.2
Primary[6,10]	5.5	43.2	204.6	860.1	1,724.8	1,193.0	1,085.9	161.0	18.4	1.2	-	5,297.7
Secondary[7]	0.1	0.3	1.0	7.3	23.4	61.6	296.1	583.1	845.5	1,672.8	425.7	3,916.9
Pupil referral units[11]	2.3	2.2	2.4	2.6	-	0.6	-	-	-	-	-	10.2
Non-maintained mainstream[8]	3.1	8.5	23.5	86.8	87.2	83.5	98.9	82.4	66.1	83.0	2.9	626.1
Special	2.4	13.1	44.7	46.5	6.1	0.7	-	-	-	-	-	113.4
All schools	**32.4**	**98.7**	**343.5**	**1,041.1**	**1,842.4**	**1,339.5**	**1,480.9**	**826.5**	**930.0**	**1,757.0**	**428.6**	**10,120.5**
England												
Public sector mainstream												
Nursery	-	1.9	23.1	19.8	0.2	-	-	-	-	-	-	45.0
Primary[10]	1.1	22.2	144.1	667.6	1,473.0	1,008.0	942.0	133.2	14.8	-	-	4,406.2
Secondary	-	0.1	0.2	4.2	16.7	43.3	226.0	467.0	665.6	1,434.2	374.5	3,231.8
Pupil referral units	2.1	2.1	2.0	2.5	-	0.6	-	-	-	-	-	9.3
Non-maintained mainstream[8]	2.4	7.2	21.7	82.0	82.4	76.6	94.8	74.1	62.5	79.5	2.9	586.2
Special	1.1	10.0	38.6	41.0	4.3	0.7	-	-	-	-	-	95.6
All schools	**6.7**	**43.4**	**229.6**	**817.2**	**1,576.7**	**1,129.3**	**1,262.9**	**674.3**	**742.9**	**1,513.6**	**377.3**	**8,374.1**
Wales												
Public sector mainstream												
Nursery	0.1	0.6	1.5	0.3	-	-	-	-	-	-	-	2.4
Primary[10]	0.8	7.1	20.4	74.8	103.5	46.7	30.9	1.4	-	-	-	285.8
Secondary	-	-	-	0.1	0.8	2.2	17.6	35.5	42.5	85.0	26.8	210.4
Pupil referral units[11]	0.2	0.2	0.4	0.1	-	-	-	-	-	-	-	0.9
Non-maintained mainstream	0.2	0.3	0.5	1.3	1.3	2.1	0.5	3.4	-	-	-	9.5
Special	-	0.5	1.6	1.5	0.2	-	-	-	-	-	-	3.8
All schools	**1.3**	**8.6**	**24.5**	**78.0**	**105.8**	**51.1**	**49.0**	**40.3**	**42.5**	**85.0**	**26.8**	**512.8**
Scotland												
Public sector mainstream												
Nursery[4,9]	15.2	28.4	37.9	16.7	0.7	-	-	-	-	-	-	98.8
Primary	3.2	9.9	23.6	82.8	115.5	104.2	78.1	7.9	-	-	-	425.2
Secondary	0.1	0.3	0.6	1.8	2.3	3.9	23.1	46.5	99.9	121.9	18.8	319.1
Non-maintained mainstream	0.3	0.7	1.0	3.3	3.3	4.8	3.6	4.9	3.6	3.6	-	29.2
Special	1.2	2.4	3.4	1.6	0.9	-	-	-	-	-	-	9.4
All schools	**20.0**	**41.7**	**66.5**	**106.2**	**122.7**	**112.9**	**104.8**	**59.2**	**103.4**	**125.5**	**18.8**	**881.8**
Northern Ireland												
Grant aided mainstream												
Nursery[5]	3.7	0.4	4.8	1.0	-	-	-	-	-	-	-	9.9
Primary[6,10]	0.4	3.9	16.5	34.9	32.7	34.0	34.8	18.4	3.6	1.2	-	180.4
Secondary[7]	-	-	0.1	1.2	3.6	12.1	29.4	34.2	37.5	31.7	5.6	155.6
Non-maintained mainstream	0.2	0.3	0.3	0.3	0.2	-	-	-	-	-	-	1.2
Special	0.1	0.3	1.2	2.4	0.7	-	-	-	-	-	-	4.7
All schools	**4.4**	**4.9**	**22.8**	**39.7**	**37.2**	**46.2**	**64.3**	**52.7**	**41.1**	**32.9**	**5.6**	**351.8**

Sources: Department for Education and Skills; National Assembly for Wales; Scottish Executive; Northern Ireland Department of Education

See previous page for footnotes.

2.7 SCHOOLS
Average class size[1], by Government Office Region[2] – time series

United Kingdom | Numbers

	One teacher classes		All classes[3]	
	Primary	Secondary[4]	Primary	Secondary[4]
1990/91				
Great Britain	..	..	26.4	21.0
North East	26.0	20.6	26.5	21.6
North West	27.1	20.4	27.5	21.1
Yorkshire and the Humber	25.9	20.5	26.4	21.2
East Midlands	26.1	20.1	26.5	20.9
West Midlands	26.3	20.6	26.8	21.1
Eastern	26.0	20.9	26.4	21.7
London	25.8	20.7	26.2	21.4
South East	26.7	20.7	27.1	21.4
South West	26.4	20.9	26.7	21.4
England	26.3	20.6	26.8	21.3
Wales	..	19.5	24.8	21.0
Scotland	..	..	24.7	18.5
1995/96				
Great Britain	..	..	27.1	21.6
North East	27.1	22.0	27.2	22.5
North West	27.7	21.8	28.0	22.0
Yorkshire and the Humber	27.6	21.9	27.9	22.1
East Midlands	27.6	21.6	27.8	21.9
West Midlands	27.3	21.8	27.6	22.0
Eastern	26.6	21.3	26.8	21.6
London	27.0	21.7	27.3	22.0
South East	27.3	21.4	27.4	21.6
South West	27.3	21.8	27.4	22.0
England	27.3	21.7	27.5	21.9
Wales	..	..	25.9	20.2
Scotland	..	..	24.8	19.5
1998/99				
United Kingdom	..	..	27.1	21.9[5]
North East	26.7	22.3	26.9	22.6
North West	27.7	21.8	27.9	22.0
Yorkshire and the Humber	27.7	22.2	27.9	22.3
East Midlands	27.6	21.8	27.7	22.0
West Midlands	27.2	22.0	27.2	22.0
Eastern	27.1	21.3	27.2	21.7
London	27.3	21.8	27.5	22.1
South East	27.7	21.7	27.8	21.8
South West	27.7	22.0	27.8	22.2
England	27.5	21.9	27.6	22.0
Wales	..	..	25.6	20.7
Scotland	24.9	..	24.9	..
Northern Ireland	..	..	24.3[6]	..

Source: Department for Education and Skills; National Assembly for Wales; Scottish Executive; Northern Ireland Department of Education

1 Maintained schools only.
2 Government Office Regions in England and each UK country.
3 Includes classes where more than one teacher may be present.
4 Figures throughout the table exclude sixth form colleges in England and Wales, which were reclassified as further education colleges from 1 April 1993.
5 England and Wales.
6 Excludes preparatory departments attached to Grammar schools, but includes reception pupils integrated into P1.
7 Revised to include 1999/00 data for Wales.
8 Provisional.

CONTINUED
SCHOOLS
Average class size[1], by Government Office Region[2] – time series

United Kingdom   Numbers

	One teacher classes		All classes[3]	
	Primary	Secondary[4]	Primary	Secondary[4]
1999/00				
United Kingdom	..	..	26.8	22.1[5]
North East	26.2	22.1	26.3	22.2
North West	27.1	22.0	27.3	22.1
Yorkshire and the Humber	27.2	22.3	27.4	22.4
East Midlands	27.4	22.1	27.5	22.3
West Midlands	26.9	22.0	27.1	22.1
Eastern	26.8	21.7	26.9	21.9
London	27.3	22.0	27.5	22.2
South East	27.3	21.9	27.4	22.0
South West	27.3	22.2	27.4	22.3
England	27.1	22.0	27.3	22.2
Wales	..	..	25.2	21.0[7]
Scotland	24.5	..	24.6	..
Northern Ireland	..	..	24.1[6]	..
2000/01[8]				
United Kingdom	..	..	26.4	22.1[5]
North East	25.8	22.1	25.9	22.2
North West	26.7	22.0	26.8	22.1
Yorkshire and the Humber	26.6	22.1	26.8	22.3
East Midlands	26.7	22.1	26.8	22.2
West Midlands	26.5	21.9	26.6	22.1
Eastern	26.4	21.8	26.5	22.0
London	27.0	22.1	27.2	22.2
South East	27.0	22.0	27.1	22.0
South West	26.7	22.2	26.8	22.3
England	26.7	22.0	26.8	22.1
Wales	..	..	24.8	21.3
Scotland	24.3	..	24.4	..
Northern Ireland	..	..	23.9[6]	..

Source: Department for Education and Skills; National Assembly for Wales; Scottish Executive; Northern Ireland Department of Education

See previous page for footnotes.

SCHOOLS

2.8

Pupil/teacher[1] ratios[2] by type of school and Government Office Region[3] — time series

United Kingdom

Numbers

	Public sector mainstream			Non-maintained mainstream schools	Pupil Referral Units	Special schools		All schools[6]
	Nursery Schools	Primary Schools[4]	Secondary Schools[5]			Maintained	Non-maintained	
1990/91								
United Kingdom	21.6	22.0	15.2	10.7	.	5.9	..	17.3
North East	19.3	22.3	15.6	12.5	.	6.1	4.7	18.0
North West	19.3	22.8	15.4	12.6	.	5.7	5.0	18.1
Yorkshire and the Humber	18.1	21.9	15.5	11.6	.	5.8	4.7	17.6
East Midlands	19.1	22.4	15.2	10.5	.	5.7	5.4	17.5
West Midlands	24.0	22.4	15.5	10.6	.	6.3	3.9	17.7
Eastern	18.7	22.4	16.2	10.7	.	5.8	5.0	17.6
London	16.9	20.6	15.3	11.6	.	5.1	4.8	16.6
South East	18.1	22.8	16.2	9.9	.	7.0	4.8	17.0
South West	19.2	22.4	16.0	9.8	.	6.5	4.9	17.2
England	19.1	22.2	15.7	10.8	.	6.0	4.8	17.4
Wales	20.6	22.3	15.4	9.8	.	6.3	.	18.2
Scotland	25.7	19.5	12.2	10.5	.	4.5	..	15.2
Northern Ireland	24.7	22.9	14.7	11.0	.	6.9	.	18.1
1995/96[5]								
United Kingdom	21.3	22.7	16.1	10.3	..	6.3	.	18.0
North East	21.3	23.7	17.1	11.9	5.7	7.1	5.0	19.3
North West	20.0	23.7	16.6	11.7	4.1	5.8	4.5	18.9
Yorkshire and the Humber	18.7	23.8	17.0	11.3	4.6	6.5	3.8	19.2
East Midlands	19.2	24.1	16.8	10.1	2.9	6.2	5.2	18.9
West Midlands	23.3	23.5	16.7	10.4	3.1	7.1	3.6	18.7
Eastern	19.3	22.7	16.5	10.1	4.3	6.6	4.1	17.9
London	16.4	21.6	15.8	10.8	5.2	5.5	5.5	17.0
South East	17.0	23.0	16.7	9.4	3.9	7.1	4.7	17.2
South West	20.4	23.6	17.1	9.4	4.1	6.9	4.9	18.2
England	19.2	23.2	16.6	10.2	4.3	6.7	4.6	18.2
Wales	19.5	22.5	16.0	10.1	..	6.7	.	18.7
Scotland	24.3	19.5	12.9	11.0	.	4.8	3.7	15.5
Northern Ireland[7]	24.1	20.7	14.8	10.9	.	6.7	.	17.2
1998/99[5,7,8]								
United Kingdom[7]	20.6	22.9	16.5	10.0	..	6.4	.	18.2
North East	19.6	23.5	17.4	11.7	4.8	7.3	4.9	19.2
North West	19.0	23.9	16.8	11.3	4.7	6.5	5.0	19.0
Yorkshire and the Humber	18.5	24.1	17.5	11.1	4.9	6.7	3.7	19.6
East Midlands	17.8	24.2	17.3	10.0	4.1	6.2	5.1	19.2
West Midlands	22.3	23.6	17.0	10.1	4.2	7.0	3.6	18.8
Eastern	19.0	23.3	16.9	9.6	5.1	6.9	4.5	18.2
London	16.3	22.3	16.1	10.5	5.4	5.9	5.7	17.3
South East	16.4	23.6	17.1	9.2	4.6	7.0	4.7	17.5
South West	19.6	24.0	17.5	9.5	4.2	6.9	5.2	18.5
England	18.4	23.5	17.0	10.0	4.5	6.7	4.7	18.4
Wales	18.4	22.3	16.5	9.8	..	6.8	.	18.8
Scotland[8]	23.1	19.4	13.0	10.4	.	4.4	3.3	15.4
Northern Ireland[7]	23.7	20.5	14.9	10.0	.	6.5	.	17.1

Sources: Department for Education and Skills; National Assembly for Wales; Scottish Executive; Northern Ireland Department of Education

1 Qualified teachers only for all countries.
2 Includes full-time equivalents of part-time pupils and teachers.
3 Government Office Regions in England and each UK country.
4 Includes preparatory departments attached to grammar schools in Northern Ireland.
5 From 1993/94 excludes sixth form colleges in England and Wales which were reclassified as further education colleges from 1 April 1993.
6 Excludes Pupil Referral Units as information on teachers is not collected for Wales.
7 Includes revised data.
8 Includes 1997/98 nursery data for Scotland.
9 Provisional.
10 Nursery schools figures for Scotland include pre-school education centres and are not therefore directly comparable with figures prior to 1999/00.

CONTINUED
SCHOOLS
Pupil/teacher[1] ratios[2] by type of school and Government Office Region[3] – time series

United Kingdom

Numbers

| | Public sector mainstream | | | Non-maintained mainstream schools | Pupil Referral Units | Special schools | | All schools[6] |
	Nursery Schools	Primary Schools[4]	Secondary Schools[5]			Maintained	Non-maintained	
1999/00[5,10]								
United Kingdom	24.2	22.7	16.6	9.9	..	6.3	.	18.1
North East	20.0	23.1	17.3	11.7	5.7	7.2	5.1	19.1
North West	18.7	23.4	16.8	11.0	4.6	6.4	4.8	18.8
Yorkshire and the Humber	18.0	23.7	17.5	10.9	4.8	6.7	3.7	19.4
East Midlands	17.1	24.0	17.5	9.8	4.3	6.2	5.0	19.1
West Midlands	21.9	23.5	17.1	9.9	4.3	7.0	3.3	18.7
Eastern	17.8	23.1	17.2	9.6	2.7	6.9	5.0	18.2
London	16.3	22.3	16.5	10.6	4.2	5.8	5.8	17.4
South East	16.3	23.2	17.3	8.9	4.4	7.0	4.5	17.3
South West	18.1	23.7	17.7	9.2	4.3	6.7	5.2	18.4
England	18.1	23.3	17.2	9.9	4.3	6.6	4.6	18.3
Wales[7]	17.3	21.9	16.7	9.8	..	6.7	.	18.7
Scotland[10]	31.3	19.1	12.9	10.3	.	4.2	3.1	15.4
Northern Ireland[7]	25.3	20.3	14.7	8.8	.	6.2	.	16.9
2000/01[5,9,10]								
United Kingdom	26.5	22.3	16.5	9.7	..	6.3	.	17.9
North East	19.9	22.6	17.0	11.4	4.4	7.1	5.0	18.6
North West	18.1	22.9	16.6	10.7	6.8	6.4	4.9	18.4
Yorkshire and the Humber	16.9	23.1	17.3	10.9	5.5	6.3	4.3	19.1
East Midlands	16.7	23.5	17.3	9.9	4.1	6.2	5.3	18.9
West Midlands	21.2	23.1	17.0	9.9	3.4	7.0	3.5	18.5
Eastern	17.0	22.8	17.4	9.3	2.8	6.9	5.2	18.1
London	16.4	22.5	16.6	10.4	4.7	6.0	5.5	17.5
South East	15.9	22.9	17.4	8.9	4.0	6.9	4.8	17.2
South West	17.5	23.0	17.5	9.0	4.6	6.4	5.3	18.0
England	17.7	22.9	17.1	9.7	4.4	6.6	4.8	18.1
Wales	17.3	21.5	16.6	9.6	..	6.8	.	18.4
Scotland[10]	35.8	19.0	13.0	10.1	.	4.2	3.3	15.6
Northern Ireland	24.4	20.1	14.5	9.3	.	5.9	.	16.6

Sources: Department for Education and Skills; National Assembly for Wales; Scottish Executive; Northern Ireland Department of Education

See previous page for footnotes.

SCHOOLS
Proportion of pupils reaching or exceeding expected standards, by key stage, subject and gender – time series

England, Wales and Northern Ireland   Percentages

	England				Wales				Northern Ireland			
	Tests		Teacher assessment		Tests		Teacher assessment		Tests		Teacher assessment	
	Boys	Girls	Boys	Girls	Boys	Girls	Boys	Girls	Boys	Girls	Boys	Girls
1996												
Key Stage 1[1]												
English	.	.	74	84	.	.	73	84	..	..	..	..
Reading	73	83	73	83	72	83	72	84	..	..	..	..
Writing	74	85	71	82	72	84	70	82	..	..	..	..
Maths	81	84	80	83	80	84	78	84	..	..	..	..
Science	.	.	83	85	.	.	81	85	..	..	..	..
Key Stage 2[2]												
English	50	65	53	68	48	65	53	68	..	..	..	..
Maths	54	54	58	62	56	56	60	64	..	..	..	..
Science	61	63	64	67	64	66	66	70	..	..	..	..
Key Stage 3[3]												
English	48	66	51	70	47	65	48	68	..	..	..	..
Maths	56	58	60	64	53	56	58	62	..	..	..	..
Science	57	56	59	61	55	55	57	60	..	..	..	..
1997												
Key Stage 1[1]												
English	.	.	75	85	.	.	75	86	..	..	..	..
Reading	75	85	75	85	74	85	75	85	..	..	..	..
Writing	75	85	72	83	74	85	72	83	..	..	..	..
Maths	82	85	82	86	82	86	82	86	..	..	..	..
Science	.	.	84	86	.	.	82	86	..	..	..	..
Key Stage 2[2]												
English	57	70	57	70	57	70	58	71	..	..	..	..
Maths	63	61	63	65	63	64	64	68	..	..	..	..
Science	68	69	68	70	70	73	70	74	..	..	..	..
Key Stage 3[3]												
English	48	67	52	70	48	68	51	69	..	..	..	..
Maths	60	60	62	65	58	58	60	64	..	..	..	..
Science	61	60	60	63	61	60	60	64	..	..	..	..
1998												
Key Stage 1[1]												
English	.	.	76	86	.	.	75	85	.	.	91	95
Reading	75	85	76	85	74	84	74	84	..	..	..	..
Writing	76	86	73	84	74	85	72	83	..	..	..	..
Maths	83	86	83	87	82	87	82	86	.	.	92	94
Science	.	.	85	87	.	.	84	87	.	.	.	.
Key Stage 2[2]												
English	57	73	58	72	56	74	57	73	.	.	61	73
Maths	59	58	64	66	60	62	63	68	.	.	69	75
Science	70	69	70	72	69	69	69	73	.	.	.	.
Key Stage 3[3]												
English	56	73	53	71	53	72	52	72	62	79	..	..
Maths	60	59	62	65	60	60	62	65	63	69	..	..
Science	57	55	60	63	56	54	59	62	65	70	..	..

Sources: Department for Education and Skills; National Assembly for Wales; Northern Ireland Department of Education

1 Percentage of pupils achieving level 2 or above.
2 Percentage of pupils achieving level 4 or above.
3 Percentage of pupils achieving level 5 or above.
4 Includes revised figures.
5 Figures for England and Wales are provisional.

CONTINUED
SCHOOLS
Proportion of pupils reaching or exceeding expected standards, by key stage, subject and gender – time series

England, Wales and Northern Ireland   Percentages

	England				Wales				Northern Ireland			
	Tests		Teacher assessment		Tests		Teacher assessment		Tests		Teacher assessment	
	Boys	Girls	Boys	Girls	Boys	Girls	Boys	Girls	Boys	Girls	Boys	Girls
1999												
Key Stage 1[1]												
English	.	.	78	87	.	.	76	87	.	.	92	96
Reading	78	86	78	86	75	86	76	86	..	..	..	..
Writing	78	88	75	85	76	87	73	85	..	..	..	..
Welsh	.	.	.	.	84	91	83	91	.	.	.	.
Reading	.	.	.	.	77	87	76	87	.	.	.	.
Writing	.	.	.	.	71	84	69	83	.	.	.	.
Maths	85	88	84	88	84	88	83	88	.	.	93	95
Science	.	.	85	88	.	.	84	88	.	.	.	.
Key Stage 2[2]												
English	65	76	62	74	63	74	61	73	.	.	64	75
Welsh	.	.	.	.	59	72	57	70	.	.	.	.
Maths	69	69	69	70	67	67	68	70	.	.	71	77
Science	79	78	75	76	77	77	75	76	.	.	.	.
Key Stage 3[3]												
English	55	73	55	73	54	70	54	71	58	77	65	80
Welsh	.	.	.	.	63	79	64	79	.	.	.	.
Maths	62	62	63	66	60	60	62	64	68	72	68	75
Science	55	55	59	62	55	55	59	60	63	68	67	73
2000[4]												
Key Stage 1[1]												
English	.	.	80	88	.	.	77	88	.	.	92	97
Reading	79	88	80	88	77	87	77	87	..	..	..	..
Writing	80	89	77	87	78	88	75	87	..	..	..	..
Welsh	.	.	.	.	84	91	82	91	.	.	.	.
Reading	.	.	.	.	76	88	76	87	.	.	.	.
Writing	.	.	.	.	68	83	67	83	.	.	.	.
Maths	89	91	87	89	88	92	85	90	.	.	94	96
Science	.	.	87	89	.	.	86	90	.	.	.	.
Key Stage 2[2]												
English	70	79	65	76	67	80	63	76	.	.	66	77
Welsh	.	.	.	.	61	75	60	74	.	.	.	.
Maths	72	71	71	73	67	71	69	73	.	.	73	78
Science	84	85	78	80	79	82	76	80	.	.	.	.
Key Stage 3[3]												
English	55	73	56	73	51	68	54	72	59	79	65	81
Welsh	.	.	.	.	61	78	62	81	.	.	.	.
Maths	64	65	65	68	60	61	63	66	64	70	69	75
Science	61	58	60	63	60	58	60	62	64	69	67	74
2001[5]												
Key Stage 1[1]												
English	.	.	81	89	.	.	79	89	.	.	..	..
Reading	80	88	80	88	79	88	79	88	..	..	..	..
Writing	82	90	79	88	79	89	76	88	..	..	..	..
Welsh	.	.	.	.	82	91	82	91	.	.	.	.
Reading	.	.	.	.	75	85	74	85	.	.	.	.
Writing	.	.	.	.	69	83	68	82	.	.	.	.
Maths	90	92	87	90	90	93	87	91	.	.	.	.
Science	.	.	88	90	.	.	87	91	.	.	.	.
Key Stage 2[2]												
English	70	80	67	78	72	82	67	79	.	.	..	..
Welsh	.	.	.	.	65	78	62	76	.	.	.	.
Maths	71	70	73	74	73	76	72	76	.	.	.	.
Science	87	88	81	83	81	83	78	83	.	.	.	.
Key Stage 3[3]												
English	56	73	57	74	53	71	54	72	..	..	..	..
Welsh	.	.	.	.	63	78	63	78	.	.	.	.
Maths	65	67	67	70	60	63	63	67	..	..	..	..
Science	66	66	63	66	63	64	62	64	..	..	..	..

Sources: Department for Education and Skills; National Assembly for Wales; Northern Ireland Department of Education

See previous page for footnotes

Chapter 3
Post Compulsory Education and Training
(a) Institutions and Staff
(b) Participation Rates
(c) Students and Starters
(d) Job Related Training

CHAPTER 3: POST- COMPULSORY EDUCATION AND TRAINING

Key Facts

(a) INSTITUTIONS AND STAFF

- There were 90 universities, 60 other higher education institutions and 499 further education colleges (of which 105 were 6th form colleges) in the UK in 2000/01. **(Table 3.1)**

- There were 76 thousand full-time higher education lecturers and 55 thousand full-time further education lecturers in the United Kingdom in 1999/00. **(Table 3.1)**

(b) PARTICIPATION RATES

- 70% of 16 year olds and 56% of 17 year olds were in post-compulsory education either at school or in full-time further education in 1998/99. **(Table 3.2)**

- In Spring 2001 15% of people of working age had received job-related training in the last four weeks. Employees were more likely to receive job-related training than the self-employed, the unemployed or the economically inactive. **(Table 3.3)**

(c) STUDENTS AND STARTERS

- There were almost 4.1 million further education students in the United Kingdom during the academic year 1999/00, of which nearly three quarters were part time. **(Table 3.5)**

- There were just over 2 million higher education students in the United Kingdom in the academic year 2000/01, of which nearly 800,000 were part time. Around 400,000 were known to be postgraduate students, 1 million first degree students and around 650,000 on other undergraduate courses. **(Table 3.6)**

- The most popular subjects studied were social sciences and business and financial studies, each with just over 100,000 full-time first degree students enrolled. **(Table 3.6)**

- In 2000/01 24,700 students from Greece were in full-time higher education in the UK, the highest of any overseas country. **(Table 3.7)**

- There were 3.5 million further education students in the first year of their course of study in 1999/00 of which almost 2.7 million were part time. **(Table 3.11)**

- There were nearly 950,000 new entrants to higher education in 2000/01, of which just over 40% were part-time. **(Table 3.12)**

TEC Delivered Government-Supported Training Programmes

(i) Work-Based Training for Young People (WBTYP)

Modern Apprenticeships (MAs)

- There were 84,600 new starts on Advanced Modern Apprenticeship schemes (AMAs) in England in 2000-01, a slight increase on the 1999-00 figure of 84,100. **(Table 3.13)**

- The overall number of participants in AMAs decreased by almost 6% between March 2000 and March 2001 to 123,800, but still represented nearly half of work-based training for young people participants. **(Table 3.10)**

Foundation Modern Apprenticeships (FMAs)

- There were 103,700 new starts on Foundation Modern Apprenticeships (FMAs) in 2000-01, almost three times the figure in 1998-99 (36,800). **(Table 3.13)**

- FMA participants accounted for a third of work-based training for young people participants in March 2001. **(Table 3.10)**

- Female starts on FMAs in 2000-01 (54% of total) outnumbered Male starts (46%). **(Table 3.14)**

Other Training (OT)

- As a result of increases in other schemes for young people, the number of new starts on Other Training (OT) programmes in England in 2000-01 fell to 57,000, over a quarter less than the number of new starts in 1999-00. **(Table 3.13)**

- The proportion of starts on OT with a disability, and the proportion identified as having literacy or numeracy needs fell by one percentage point each to 6% and 18% respectively in 2000-01. The proportion of ethnic minority starts, however, rose to 13% in 2000-01, an increase of six percentage points since 1997-98. **(Table 3.14)**

(ii) Work-Based Learning for Adults

- As at March 2001, there were 32,200 participants in Work-Based Learning for Adults in England, compared to 33,400 the previous year and 114,700 in March 1991. **(Table 3.10)**

- There were 108,300 starts on Work-Based Learning for Adults in England in 2000-01 compared to 102,700 in 1999-00, but still significantly lower than recruitment in 1990-91. This long-term fall in starts reflects the fall in unemployment during this period. **(Table 3.13)**

- The proportion of starts from ethnic minority groups rose from 19% in 1999-00 to 21% in 2000-01. 21% of those who joined WBLA programmes in 2000-01 had disabilities, the same as the previous year, while those with literacy/numeracy needs increased by two percentage points to 15%. **(Table 3.15)**

- 19% of starts on WBLA in 2000-01 had been unemployed for more than 3 years before joining, two percentage points lower than in 1999-00. **(Table 3.15)**

(d) JOB RELATED TRAINING

- In Spring 2001 people in the London region (16.3%) were more likely to have received job-related training in the last four weeks than people in any other region. People in Northern Ireland (11.5%) were least likely to receive training. **(Table 3.16)**

- 21.2% of Black or Black British employees, 15.4% of those of Asian or Asian British origin, and 20.0% of Chinese employees had received job-related training compared with 16.2% of White employees. **(Table 3.17)**

- People with high levels of qualifications were much more likely than those with low or no qualifications to have received job-related training. **(Table 3.17)**

- In Spring 2001, 8.1% of employees had received off-the-job training in the last four weeks, 5.1% had received only on-the-job training and 3.2% had received both types of training. **(Table 3.17)**

- Employees in public administration, education and health were more likely than employees in other industries to have received job-related training. Those employed in agriculture, forestry and fishing were least likely to have received training. **(Table 3.18)**

- Much of the job-related training received by employees is of short duration; in Spring 2001, a third of the training received by employees lasted for less than a week. **(Table 3.21)**

- The economically inactive tend to receive job-related training that is of a longer duration than the training received by employees. **(Table 3.21)**

- A Further Education college or university is the most common location for off-the-job training. The employer's premises are another common location for employees' off-the-job training. **(Table 3.22)**

- In Spring 2001, young employees receiving training *in the last week* spent more hours in job-related training than older employees. Males spent more hours in training than females. **(Table 3.23)**

- In Spring 2001, 33.2% of employees in temporary employment had undertaken job-related training *in the last thirteen weeks* compared to 30.5% of permanent employees. 31.8% of full-time employees had undertaken job-related training compared with 26.6% of part-time employees. **(Table 3.24)**

- In Spring 2001, 30.6% of employees had received job-related training *in the last thirteen weeks*, 16.4% had received job-related training *in the last four weeks*, and 8.8% had received job-related training *in the last week*. 29.9% of employees had never been offered training by their current employer. **(Table 3.25)**

- In Spring 2001, 24.4% of employees who were classed as both DDA disabled and work-limiting disabled had received job-related training *in the last thirteen weeks*, compared with 30.6% of all employees. **(Table 3.26)**

CHAPTER 3: POST-COMPULSORY EDUCATION AND TRAINING – LIST OF TABLES

(a) INSTITUTIONS AND STAFF

3.1 Number of further and higher education institutions by type, and lecturers by gender – time series

(b) PARTICIPATION RATES

3.2 16 and 17 year olds participating in post-compulsory education and government supported training – time series

3.3 Participation in job-related training in the last four weeks – time series

3.4 Participation in job-related training in the last four weeks by economic activity and age, 2001

(c) STUDENTS AND STARTERS

3.5 Students in further education by country of study, mode of study, gender and subject group, during 1999/00

3.6 Students in higher education by type of course, mode of study, gender and subject group, 2000/01

3.7 Full-time higher education students from overseas, by type of course, gender and country, 2000/01 and time series

3.8 Students in further education by country of study, mode of study, gender and age, during 1999/00

3.9 Students in higher education by level, mode of study, gender and age, 2000/01

3.10 Participants in TEC Delivered Government-Supported Training programmes by region (England) – time series

3.11 Further education students in the first year of their course of study by country of study, mode of study, gender and age, 1999/00

3.12 New entrants to higher education by level, mode of study, gender and age, 2000/01

3.13 Starts in TEC Delivered Government-Supported Training programmes by region (England) – time series

3.14 Work-Based Training for Young People: characteristics of starts (England) – time series

3.15 Work-Based Learning for Adults: characteristics of starts (England) – time series

(d) JOB RELATED TRAINING

3.16 Participation in job-related training in the last four weeks by economic activity and region, 2001

3.17 Participation by employees in job-related training in the last four weeks by type of training and a range of personal characteristics, 2001

3.18 Participation by employees in job-related training in the last four weeks by a range of economic characteristics, 2001

3.19 Participation by employees in job-related training in the last four weeks by type of training and a range of economic characteristics, 2001

3.20 Participation by employees in job-related training in the last four weeks by region and a range of personal and economic characteristics, 2001

3.21 Length of job-related training, 2001

3.22 Location of off-the-job training, 2001

3.23 Hours spent on job-related training in the last week, 2001

3.24 Participation by employees in job-related training in the last thirteen weeks by a range of personal and economic characteristics – time series

3.25 Employees of working age in the United Kingdom – summary of job-related training received, 2001

3.26 Participation by employees in job-related training in the last thirteen weeks by disability status and a range of personal characteristics, 2001

POST-COMPULSORY EDUCATION AND TRAINING – INSTITUTIONS AND STAFF

3.1

Number of further and higher education institutions by type, and lecturers by gender – time series

United Kingdom (i) Number of establishments of further and higher education Numbers

		Academic years				
	1990/91	1995/96	1995/96	1998/99	1999/00	2000/01[1]
UNITED KINGDOM						
Universities (including Open University)[2]		48	89	88	88	90
Other higher education institutions	}		66	58	58	60
	}	588				
Further education colleges	}		543	523	516	499
of which 6th form colleges		.	110	107	105	105
ENGLAND						
Universities (including Open University)[2]		37	72	70	70	72
Other higher education institutions	}		50	47	47	46
	}	460				
Further education colleges	}		453	435	428	411
of which 6th form colleges		.	110	107	105	105
WALES						
Universities[2]		1	2	2	2	2
Other higher education institutions	}		5	4	4	6
	}	38				
Further education colleges	}		26	24	24	24
SCOTLAND						
Universities[2]		8	13	14	14	14
Other higher education institutions	}		9	5	5	6
	}	64				
Further education colleges	}		47	47	47	47
NORTHERN IRELAND						
Universities		2	2	2	2	2
Colleges of Education		2	2	2	2	2
Further education colleges		24	17	17	17	17

United Kingdom (ii) Number of full-time lecturers, by gender Thousands

	Academic years				
	1990/91	1995/96[3]	1998/99[3]	1999/00[1]	2000/01
All					
Further and Higher Education Institutions	122	136	130	131	..
of which					
Further Education Institutions(FEIs)[4,5]	..	60[6]	55	55	..
Higher Education Institutions(HEIs)[2,7,8]	..	76	75	76	..
Males					
Further and Higher Education Institutions	89	90	83	83	..
of which					
Further Education Institutions(FEIs)[4,5]	..	34[6]	30	30	..
Higher Education Institutions(HEIs)[2,7,8]	..	55	53	53	..
Females					
Further and Higher Education Institutions	33	46	47	48	..
of which					
Further Education Institutions(FEIs)[4,5]	..	26[6]	25	25	..
Higher Education Institutions(HEIs)[2,7,8]	..	21	22	23	..

Sources: Department for Education and Skills; National Assembly for Wales; Scottish Executive; Northern Ireland Department for Employment and Learning

1 Provisional.
2 From 1993/94 includes former polytechnics and colleges which became universities as a result of the Further and Higher Education Act 1992.
3 Includes revised data.
4 Figures for England relate to staff whose primary role is teaching, and do not include other staff whose primary role is supporting teaching and learning or other.
5 Scotland figures include full-time equivalent (rather than headcount) staff in academic departments only. Cross-college staff are excluded.
6 Excludes Wales.
7 Excludes the Open University.
8 Non-clinical academic staff paid wholly by the institution.

3.2

United Kingdom   Percentages[2]

	1995/96									
	16 year olds					17 year olds				
		In further education[3]		Government-supported training (GST)	All in full-time education and GST[4]		In further education[3]		Government-supported training (GST)	All in full-time education and GST[4]
	At school	Full-time	Part-time			At school	Full-time	Part-time		
Region of study										
United Kingdom	37.3	33.6	8.4	..	..	28.1	29.1	9.9	..	..
North East	24.3	37.8	8.5	19.0	80.0	18.0	30.6	11.2	18.8	66.4
North West	24.0	42.3	9.0	14.5	78.9	19.5	34.7	10.6	15.5	68.0
Yorkshire and the Humber	29.9	35.6	9.1	13.7	77.4	22.4	29.0	10.6	15.3	65.2
East Midlands	35.6	30.8	8.3	12.4	77.5	27.4	27.4	9.7	14.6	67.9
West Midlands	30.1	38.2	8.7	12.9	79.7	24.1	33.1	10.2	12.7	68.6
Eastern	39.6	34.9	5.9	9.1	82.8	31.4	30.7	7.9	11.3	72.4
London	39.1	36.7	4.5	5.4	80.8	28.6	33.7	6.0	6.7	68.4
South East	38.8	37.5	5.0	6.3	81.9	31.1	32.4	6.6	8.5	71.2
South West	38.8	36.8	6.7	9.8	84.0	31.1	31.5	7.9	11.7	73.2
England	33.8	37.1	7.1	10.8	80.4	26.4	31.8	8.7	12.2	69.2
Wales	37.3	33.2	10.1	11.8	82.2	27.9	27.9	8.5	14.6	70.3
Scotland[5,6]	66.5	8.8	19.0	10.4	85.8	40.1	9.6	19.9	13.8	63.4
Northern Ireland	46.1	29.9	11.2	..	..	35.4	28.8	14.3	..	..

	1996/97									
	16 year olds					17 year olds				
		In further education[3]		Government-supported training (GST)	All in full-time education and GST[4]		In further education[3]		Government-supported training (GST)	All in full-time education and GST[4]
	At school	Full-time	Part-time			At school	Full-time	Part-time		
Region of study										
United Kingdom	37.5	33.3	8.1	..	..	28.4	29.4	10.0	..	..
North East	25.3	36.3	8.7	17.8	78.8	18.7	31.2	10.6	19.1	68.5
North West	23.8	41.2	9.5	13.5	77.0	19.1	34.5	10.7	15.4	67.7
Yorkshire and the Humber	30.0	34.4	10.1	13.6	76.7	23.3	29.4	11.3	14.8	66.2
East Midlands	36.0	30.9	8.1	11.5	77.6	28.6	26.7	9.5	12.7	67.0
West Midlands	30.9	35.9	9.2	11.0	76.6	23.4	31.6	10.6	13.2	67.1
East	40.4	34.5	6.5	7.4	81.8	31.1	29.7	7.9	10.2	70.2
London	38.7	35.3	4.7	5.2	78.7	28.6	32.7	6.1	6.8	67.6
South East	38.8	36.1	5.1	5.9	80.3	30.6	31.2	6.4	8.2	69.4
South West	38.6	36.0	6.5	8.5	82.0	31.0	30.5	8.1	10.7	71.1
England	34.0	35.9	7.4	9.8	78.8	26.4	31.1	8.8	11.8	68.3
Wales	37.3	33.9	11.1	10.6	81.9	28.0	28.9	9.3	14.8	71.7
Scotland[5]	66.7	9.9	11.0	4.6	81.2	40.5	10.4	14.9	16.2	67.1
Northern Ireland	45.7	29.2	11.5	..	..	36.9	28.5	13.8	..	..

Source: Department for Education and Skills; National Assembly for Wales; Scottish Executive; Northern Ireland Department of Education

1 Excluding higher education.

2 As a percentage of the estimated 16 year old and 17 year old population respectively.

3 Including sixth form colleges and a small element of further education in higher education institutions in England.

4 Figures for England exclude overlap between full-time education and government-supported training.

5 The estimates of 16 year olds at school exclude those pupils who leave school in the Winter term at the minimum statutory school-leaving age.

6 Figures shown for government supported training are not directly comparable with later years.

7 Including a small element of further education in higher education institutions in England.

8 Participation in part-time FE should not be aggregated with full-time FE or schools activity due to the unquantifiable overlap with these activities.

3.2 POST-COMPULSORY EDUCATION AND TRAINING – PARTICIPATION RATES

16 and 17 year olds participating in post-compulsory education[1] and government supported training – time series

United Kingdom

Percentages[2]

1997/98

	16 year olds					17 year olds				
		In further education[3,7]		Government-supported training (GST)	All in full-time education and GST[4]		In further education[3,7]		Government-supported training (GST)	All in full-time education and GST[4]
	At school	Full-time	Part-time			At school	Full-time	Part-time		
Region of study										
United Kingdom	37.9	32.5	8.0	..	..	28.2	28.2	9.2	..	..
North East	25.4	34.9	7.4	17.9	77.6	19.5	29.7	9.4	17.8	66.6
North West	24.3	40.8	8.5	13.3	77.4	19.4	33.9	10.2	14.7	67.5
Yorkshire and the Humber	30.9	33.6	9.1	12.8	76.3	23.4	27.6	11.0	14.7	64.9
East Midlands	36.7	29.7	7.9	11.2	76.7	29.1	25.9	9.3	13.2	67.1
West Midlands	30.7	35.4	8.3	11.0	76.0	24.5	30.7	10.3	12.4	66.7
East	40.2	33.1	5.7	7.0	79.9	32.0	28.4	7.4	9.2	68.9
London	39.7	35.0	4.4	5.4	79.7	28.9	32.2	6.0	6.2	67.0
South East	39.7	35.2	4.7	5.8	80.4	30.6	29.7	6.1	7.7	67.5
South West	38.4	34.4	6.1	9.0	80.9	30.9	29.7	7.5	10.5	70.4
England	34.4	35.1	6.7	9.7	78.5	26.8	30.1	8.4	11.2	67.4
Wales	36.8	31.8	12.6	16.6	85.3	28.2	27.2	9.7	15.1	70.5
Scotland[5]	68.1	10.9	12.6	9.1	88.1	38.8	10.9	15.2	15.8	65.5
Northern Ireland[8]	45.0	27.5	17.8	..	..	36.6	28.2	13.2	..	..

1998/99

	16 year olds					17 year olds				
		In further education[3,7]		Government-supported training (GST)	All in full-time education and GST[4]		In further education[3,7]		Government-supported training (GST)	All in full-time education and GST[4]
	At school	Full-time	Part-time			At school	Full-time	Part-time		
Region of study										
United Kingdom	38.0	32.4	7.2	..	..	28.7	27.7	9.0	..	..
North East	25.9	35.3	7.8	13.9	73.4	19.8	29.0	9.4	15.8	63.1
North West	24.5	40.5	8.4	12.3	73.6	19.8	33.5	9.9	14.7	63.8
Yorkshire and the Humber	29.6	33.9	9.7	13.1	73.6	23.8	27.6	11.6	14.7	62.3
East Midlands	37.2	29.4	7.4	10.6	74.8	29.8	24.9	9.2	13.3	64.9
West Midlands	31.1	36.4	7.9	9.8	74.6	24.7	30.3	10.0	11.6	63.7
East	40.9	33.2	5.0	6.4	78.0	32.6	27.9	7.1	8.2	65.6
London	39.4	34.6	4.2	4.5	77.7	29.8	31.7	5.8	5.9	66.5
South East	39.3	34.9	4.5	5.9	78.4	31.7	29.8	6.1	8.2	67.7
South West	39.2	33.8	5.8	8.2	78.6	31.1	28.7	7.9	12.0	68.5
England	34.5	35.0	6.5	8.9	76.1	27.4	29.6	8.4	11.1	65.3
Wales	37.7	31.0	7.6	16.1	84.9	28.4	26.3	9.4	15.7	70.4
Scotland[5]	67.4	11.2	11.0	9.4	88.0	37.6	10.9	13.4	14.9	63.4
Northern Ireland[8]	46.5	27.9	13.3	..	..	37.0	25.9	13.7	..	..

Source: Department for Education and Skills; National Assembly for Wales; Scottish Executive; Northern Ireland Department of Education

See previous page for footnotes.

POST COMPULSORY EDUCATION AND TRAINING: PARTICIPATION RATES

3.3

Participation in job-related training[1] in the last four weeks – time series

United Kingdom: People of working age[2]

Thousands and percentages[3]

	1991	1996[4]	1999[4]	2000[4]	2001[4]
Numbers (thousands)					
All People					
All	4,471	4,656	5,087	5,196	5,327
Males	2,385	2,353	2,510	2,516	2,539
Females	2,086	2,303	2,577	2,680	2,788
Employees[5,6]					
All	3,268	3,271	3,723	3,833	3,934
Males	1,745	1,643	1,830	1,872	1,855
Females	1,522	1,628	1,893	1,961	2,079
Self-employed[6,7]					
All	185	199	229	238	237
Males	128	126	144	140	146
Females	57	73	85	98	91
ILO unemployed[8]					
All	142	196	166	166	153
Males	78	117	92	87	80
Females	64	80	75	79	72
Economically inactive[9]					
All	561	811	839	841	889
Males	251	361	357	349	387
Females	310	449	482	491	502
Percentages[3]					
All People					
All	12.7	13.1	14.1	14.3	14.6
Males	13.0	12.6	13.2	13.2	13.3
Females	12.5	13.5	15.0	15.5	16.0
Employees[5,6]					
All	14.9	14.8	15.9	16.1	16.4
Males	14.7	14.1	14.7	14.7	14.4
Females	15.1	15.6	17.3	17.8	18.5
Self-employed[6,7]					
All	5.7	6.4	7.6	8.1	8.0
Males	5.1	5.4	6.4	6.4	6.6
Females	7.5	9.7	11.4	13.0	12.3
ILO unemployed[8]					
All	5.7	8.5	9.6	10.4	11.0
Males	4.9	7.6	8.4	8.8	9.4
Females	7.0	10.2	11.6	12.8	13.5
Economically inactive[9]					
All	8.0	10.4	10.7	10.9	11.2
Males	11.6	12.6	11.9	11.7	12.4
Females	6.4	9.1	10.0	10.3	10.5

Source: Labour Force Survey, Spring of each year[10]

1 Job-related training includes both on and off-the-job training.
2 Working age is defined as males aged 16-64 and females aged 16-59.
3 Expressed as a percentage of the total number of people in each group.
4 Due to a change in the LFS questionnaire, data from Summer 1994 onwards are not comparable with earlier figures.
5 Employees are those in employment excluding the self-employed, unpaid family workers and those on government employment and training programmes.
6 The split into employees and self-employed is based on respondents' own assessment of their employment status.
7 Self-employed are those in employment excluding employees, unpaid family workers and those on government employment and training programmes.
8 Unemployed according to the International Labour Office (ILO) definition.
9 Economically inactive are those who are neither in employment nor ILO unemployed and includes students.
10 Users of these data should read the LFS entry in Annex A, as it contains important information about the LFS and the concepts and definitions used.

3.4 POST COMPULSORY EDUCATION AND TRAINING: PARTICIPATION RATES

Participation in job-related training[1] in the last four weeks by economic activity and age, 2001

United Kingdom: People of working age[2]

Thousands and percentages[3]

	Thousands				Percentages[3]		
	All	Males	Females		All	Males	Females
All people							
All	5,327	2,539	2,788		14.6	13.3	16.0
16-19	675	354	321		23.2	23.8	22.6
20-24	913	459	455		25.8	25.5	26.2
25-29	657	312	345		16.8	15.6	18.0
30-39	1,381	662	719		14.6	13.8	15.5
40-49	1,064	455	609		13.3	11.3	15.3
50-64	637	297	339		7.3	5.9	9.1
Employees[4,5]							
All	3,934	1,855	2,079		16.4	14.4	18.5
16-19	335	174	161		23.8	24.8	22.9
20-24	546	267	279		23.5	21.7	25.6
25-29	526	257	269		17.9	16.0	20.2
30-39	1,140	563	577		16.8	15.3	18.5
40-49	872	362	510		15.4	12.6	18.2
50-64	515	231	284		10.4	8.4	13.0
Self-employed[5,6]							
All	237	146	91		8.0	6.6	12.3
16-19	*	*	*		*	*	*
20-24	*	*	*		*	*	*
25-29	17	*	*		9.0	*	*
30-39	62	34	28		7.5	5.7	12.6
40-49	90	56	35		10.3	8.8	14.4
50-64	60	42	19		6.2	5.4	9.1
ILO unemployed[7]							
All	153	80	72		11.0	9.4	13.5
16-19	30	16	14		12.6	11.1	15.0
20-24	32	19	13		14.4	13.8	15.3
25-29	18	10	*		11.7	10.7	*
30-39	33	16	17		9.5	8.2	11.3
40-49	25	11	14		10.4	8.0	13.9
50-64	15	*	*		7.8	*	*
Economically inactive[8]							
All	889	387	502		11.2	12.4	10.5
16-19	249	121	128		21.6	21.6	21.6
20-24	317	160	157		35.4	44.8	29.2
25-29	88	32	56		14.4	20.9	12.3
30-39	130	40	90		8.9	12.3	8.0
40-49	65	21	44		5.5	5.8	5.4
50-64	39	13	26		1.5	0.9	2.1

Source: Labour Force Survey, Spring 2001[9]

1 Job-related training includes both on and off-the-job training.
2 Working age is defined as males aged 16-64 and females aged 16-59.
3 Expressed as a percentage of the total number of people in each group.
4 Employees are those in employment excluding the self-employed, unpaid family workers and those on government employment and training programmes.
5 The split into employees and self-employed is based on respondents' own assessment of their employment status.
6 Self-employed are those in employment excluding employees, unpaid family workers and those on government employment and training programmes.
7 Unemployed according to the International Labour Office (ILO) definition.
8 Economically inactive are those who are neither in employment nor ILO unemployed.
9 Users of these data should read the LFS entry in Annex A, as it contains important information about the LFS and the concepts and definitions used.

3.5 Students in further education[1] by country of study, mode of study[2], gender and subject group, during 1999/00[3]

United Kingdom   (i) Home and Overseas Students   Thousands

	United Kingdom		England[3]		Wales		Scotland[4]		Northern Ireland	
	Full-time	Part-time	Full-time	Part-time	Full-time	Part-time	Full-time	Part-time	Full-time	Part-time
All										
Medicine & Dentistry	-	-	-	-	-	-	-	-	-	-
Subjects Allied to Medicine	100.2	157.8	97.7	145.8	-	-	1.1	10.3	1.4	1.8
Biological Sciences	1.0	2.3	0.8	0.2	-	-	0.2	2.1	-	-
Vet. Science, Agriculture & related	35.4	155.6	33.8	145.7	-	-	1.5	9.4	0.1	0.5
Physical Sciences	13.6	6.6	13.6	5.4	-	-	-	0.9	-	0.3
Mathematical and Computing Sciences	127.7	351.0	123.3	276.4	-	-	2.8	63.8	1.6	10.8
Engineering & Technology	49.8	111.6	42.2	86.9	-	-	5.6	20.7	1.9	4.0
Architecture, Building & Planning	26.3	49.2	20.6	39.8	-	-	3.1	7.8	2.6	1.6
Social Sciences	16.6	72.0	10.8	46.3	-	-	5.1	23.0	0.7	2.6
Business & Financial Studies	99.3	277.0	87.3	220.4	-	-	6.9	43.8	5.1	12.7
Librarianship & Info Science	8.4	21.6	7.3	12.1	-	-	0.7	9.1	0.4	0.4
Languages	21.3	83.5	20.6	66.3	-	0.1	0.6	15.1	-	1.9
Humanities	6.4	9.9	6.2	7.0	-	-	0.2	2.8	-	-
Creative Arts & Design	68.4	75.7	60.7	54.5	0.1	-	5.1	17.9	2.5	3.3
Education[5]	17.7	44.8	15.0	26.7	-	0.4	2.1	15.2	0.6	2.5
Combined, general	148.7	207.1	141.4	156.5	0.2	4.2	3.3	31.7	3.8	14.8
Unknown	295.6	1,389.6	250.6	1,212.8	45.0	176.8	-	-	-	-
All subjects	**1,036.3**	**3,015.2**	**932.0**	**2,502.7**	**45.3**	**181.5**	**38.2**	**273.7**	**20.7**	**57.3**
Males										
Medicine & Dentistry	-	-	-	-	-	-	-	-	-	-
Subjects Allied to Medicine	32.8	61.4	32.6	56.3	-	-	0.1	5.0	0.1	0.2
Biological Sciences	0.4	0.9	0.3	-	-	-	0.1	0.8	-	-
Vet. Science, Agriculture & related	15.7	56.3	14.9	51.3	-	-	0.8	4.8	-	0.3
Physical Sciences	9.6	3.9	9.6	3.3	-	-	-	0.4	-	0.1
Mathematical and Computing Sciences	60.5	129.3	57.4	100.1	-	-	1.9	25.6	1.3	3.5
Engineering & Technology	46.4	102.1	39.3	81.0	-	-	5.3	17.4	1.8	3.6
Architecture, Building & Planning	25.0	45.3	19.5	37.2	-	-	2.9	6.5	2.6	1.6
Social Sciences	2.2	10.6	1.4	5.9	-	-	0.8	4.5	0.1	0.2
Business & Financial Studies	43.3	100.2	39.4	80.9	-	-	2.2	16.1	1.7	3.3
Librarianship & Info Science	4.3	8.4	3.7	4.6	-	-	0.4	3.7	0.2	0.1
Languages	8.8	29.3	8.5	23.0	-	-	0.3	5.5	-	0.7
Humanities	3.0	4.1	2.9	3.1	-	-	0.1	1.1	-	-
Creative Arts & Design	24.9	14.5	22.5	9.4	-	-	1.7	4.7	0.8	0.4
Education[5]	10.7	16.9	9.1	9.4	-	0.1	1.2	6.4	0.4	0.9
Combined, general	71.6	80.9	68.0	58.4	0.1	1.5	1.7	15.2	1.8	5.8
Unknown	159.0	586.9	138.1	514.2	21.0	72.7	-	-	-	-
All subjects	**518.2**	**1,251.1**	**466.9**	**1,038.2**	**21.1**	**74.3**	**19.5**	**117.8**	**10.8**	**20.7**
Females										
Medicine & Dentistry	-	-	-	-	-	-	-	-	-	-
Subjects Allied to Medicine	67.4	96.4	65.1	89.5	-	-	1.0	5.3	1.3	1.6
Biological Sciences	0.6	1.4	0.5	0.2	-	-	0.1	1.2	-	-
Vet. Science, Agriculture & related	19.7	99.3	18.9	94.4	-	-	0.6	4.6	0.1	0.3
Physical Sciences	4.0	2.7	4.0	2.0	-	-	-	0.5	-	0.1
Mathematical and Computing Sciences	67.1	221.7	65.9	176.3	-	-	0.9	38.2	0.3	7.2
Engineering & Technology	3.4	9.5	3.0	5.9	-	-	0.4	3.3	0.1	0.4
Architecture, Building & Planning	1.3	3.9	1.1	2.5	-	-	0.2	1.3	-	0.1
Social Sciences	14.4	61.4	9.5	40.5	-	-	4.3	18.6	0.7	2.4
Business & Financial Studies	56.0	176.7	47.9	139.5	-	-	4.7	27.7	3.4	9.5
Librarianship & Info Science	4.1	13.2	3.6	7.5	-	-	0.3	5.4	0.2	0.3
Languages	12.5	54.2	12.2	43.3	-	-	0.3	9.6	-	1.3
Humanities	3.4	5.7	3.3	4.0	-	-	0.1	1.8	-	-
Creative Arts & Design	43.5	61.2	38.3	45.1	-	-	3.4	13.2	1.7	2.9
Education[5]	7.0	27.9	5.9	17.3	-	0.3	0.9	8.7	0.2	1.6
Combined, general	77.1	126.2	73.4	98.0	0.1	2.7	1.6	16.5	2.0	9.0
Unknown	136.5	802.7	112.5	698.6	24.0	104.1	-	-	-	-
All subjects	**518.1**	**1,764.1**	**465.1**	**1,464.5**	**24.2**	**107.1**	**18.8**	**155.9**	**10.0**	**36.5**

Sources: Department for Education and Skills; National Assembly for Wales; Scottish Executive; Northern Ireland Department for Employment and Learning

1 Further education figures are whole year counts and differ from the higher education tables which use annual snapshots. Data for Northern Ireland however, are collected on a snapshot basis.
2 Full-time includes sandwich, and for Scotland, short full-time. Part-time comprises both day and evening, including block release (except for Scotland) and open/distance learning.
3 Provisional. Includes estimated breakdowns by subjects for students in further education institutions in England but excludes approximately 175,650 aggregate return students in further education institutions in England since the information cannot be broken down in this way. External institutions and specialist designated colleges are also excluded.
4 Figures for Scotland further education institutions are enrolments rather than headcounts. Due to a reclassification of subject groupings, subject categories for Scotland cannot be directly compared with previous years.
5 Including ITT and INSET.
6 Includes estimated breakdowns for further education students in higher education institutions.

3.5 POST COMPULSORY EDUCATION AND TRAINING: STUDENTS AND STARTERS

Students in further education[1] by country of study, mode of study[2], gender and subject group, during 1999/00[3]

United Kingdom   (ii) of which Overseas Students   Thousands

	United Kingdom		England[3]		Wales		Scotland[4]		Northern Ireland	
	Full-time	Part-time	Full-time	Part-time	Full-time	Part-time	Full-time	Part-time	Full-time	Part-time
All										
Medicine & Dentistry	-	-	-	-	-	-	-	-	-	-
Subjects Allied to Medicine	0.6	2.0	0.6	1.9	-	-	-	0.1	0.1	-
Biological Sciences	-	-	-	-	-	-	-	-	-	-
Vet. Science, Agriculture & related	0.5	2.4	0.5	2.0	-	-	-	0.3	-	-
Physical Sciences	0.1	0.1	0.1	-	-	-	-	-	-	-
Mathematical and Computing Sciences	2.1	2.3	2.0	2.0	-	-	-	0.2	-	0.1
Engineering & Technology	1.0	1.2	0.9	0.9	-	-	-	0.1	-	0.1
Architecture, Building & Planning	0.2	0.7	0.1	0.6	-	-	-	-	-	-
Social Sciences	0.1	0.4	-	0.2	-	-	-	0.1	-	0.1
Business & Financial Studies	1.4	2.8	1.2	2.4	-	-	-	0.3	0.2	0.1
Librarianship & Info Science	0.6	0.5	0.5	0.5	-	-	-	0.1	-	-
Languages	6.7	16.3	6.5	14.4	-	-	0.3	1.9	-	-
Humanities	-	-	-	-	-	-	-	-	-	-
Creative Arts & Design	1.0	0.6	0.8	0.5	-	-	-	-	0.1	0.1
Education[5]	0.1	0.2	0.1	0.1	-	-	-	0.1	-	-
Combined, general	2.9	3.0	2.8	2.8	-	-	-	-	0.1	0.2
Unknown	9.8	54.9	9.7	54.7	0.1	0.3	-	-	-	-
All subjects	**27.1**	**87.5**	**25.9**	**83.1**	**0.2**	**0.3**	**0.4**	**3.2**	**0.6**	**0.9**
of which European Union[6]	9.0	17.0	8.3	13.7	0.1	0.2	0.1	2.2	0.6	0.9
Other Europe[6]	1.2	4.8	1.2	4.6	-	-	-	0.2	-	-
Commonwealth[6]	3.1	4.0	3.0	3.6	-	-	-	0.5	-	-
Other Countries[6]	13.8	61.6	13.5	61.2	0.1	-	0.2	0.4	-	-
Males										
Medicine & Dentistry	-	-	-	-	-	-	-	-	-	-
Subjects Allied to Medicine	0.2	0.7	0.2	0.6	-	-	-	0.1	-	-
Biological Sciences	-	-	-	-	-	-	-	-	-	-
Vet. Science, Agriculture & related	0.2	0.9	0.2	0.7	-	-	-	0.2	-	-
Physical Sciences	0.1	-	0.1	-	-	-	-	-	-	-
Mathematical and Computing Sciences	0.9	1.0	0.9	0.8	-	-	-	0.2	-	-
Engineering & Technology	0.9	1.1	0.8	0.8	-	-	-	0.1	-	0.1
Architecture, Building & Planning	0.2	0.6	0.1	0.6	-	-	-	-	-	-
Social Sciences	-	0.1	-	-	-	-	-	-	-	-
Business & Financial Studies	0.6	1.5	0.6	1.2	-	-	-	0.2	-	-
Librarianship & Info Science	0.2	0.2	0.2	0.2	-	-	-	-	-	-
Languages	2.6	4.2	2.5	3.5	-	-	0.1	0.7	-	-
Humanities	-	-	-	-	-	-	-	-	-	-
Creative Arts & Design	0.3	0.1	0.3	0.1	-	-	-	-	-	-
Education[5]	0.1	0.1	-	-	-	-	-	-	-	-
Combined, general	1.1	1.1	1.1	1.0	-	-	-	-	-	-
Unknown	5.5	20.5	5.5	20.4	-	0.1	-	-	-	-
All subjects	**12.9**	**32.1**	**12.5**	**29.9**	**0.1**	**0.1**	**0.2**	**1.8**	**0.2**	**0.3**
of which European Union[6]	3.6	5.8	3.4	4.3	-	0.1	0.1	1.1	0.2	0.3
Other Europe[6]	0.4	0.9	0.4	0.9	-	-	-	0.1	-	-
Commonwealth[6]	1.8	2.1	1.7	1.7	-	-	-	0.4	-	-
Other Countries[6]	7.1	23.2	6.9	23.0	-	-	0.1	0.2	-	-
Females										
Medicine & Dentistry	-	-	-	-	-	-	-	-	-	-
Subjects Allied to Medicine	0.4	1.3	0.4	1.3	-	-	-	-	0.1	-
Biological Sciences	-	-	-	-	-	-	-	-	-	-
Vet. Science, Agriculture & related	0.3	1.4	0.3	1.3	-	-	-	0.1	-	-
Physical Sciences	-	-	-	-	-	-	-	-	-	-
Mathematical and Computing Sciences	1.2	1.4	1.1	1.3	-	-	-	-	-	0.1
Engineering & Technology	0.1	0.1	0.1	0.1	-	-	-	-	-	-
Architecture, Building & Planning	-	-	-	-	-	-	-	-	-	-
Social Sciences	0.1	0.3	-	0.2	-	-	-	-	-	0.1
Business & Financial Studies	0.8	1.3	0.7	1.2	-	-	-	0.1	0.2	0.1
Librarianship & Info Science	0.4	0.4	0.4	0.3	-	-	-	-	-	-
Languages	4.1	12.1	4.0	11.0	-	-	0.1	1.1	-	-
Humanities	-	-	-	-	-	-	-	-	-	-
Creative Arts & Design	0.7	0.5	0.5	0.4	-	-	-	-	0.1	0.1
Education[5]	-	0.1	-	0.1	-	-	-	-	-	-
Combined, general	1.8	1.9	1.7	1.8	-	-	-	-	-	0.1
Unknown	4.3	34.4	4.2	34.3	0.1	0.2	-	-	-	-
All subjects	**14.1**	**55.4**	**13.5**	**53.2**	**0.1**	**0.2**	**0.2**	**1.5**	**0.4**	**0.6**
of which European Union[6]	5.4	11.2	4.9	9.4	0.1	0.1	0.1	1.1	0.4	0.6
Other Europe[6]	0.8	3.8	0.8	3.7	-	-	-	0.1	-	-
Commonwealth[6]	1.3	1.9	1.3	1.9	-	-	-	-	-	-
Other Countries[6]	6.7	38.4	6.5	38.2	-	-	0.1	0.2	-	-

Sources: Department for Education and Skills; National Assembly for Wales; Scottish Executive; Northern Ireland Department for Employment and Learning

See previous page for footnotes.

3.6 POST COMPULSORY EDUCATION AND TRAINING: STUDENTS AND STARTERS

Students in higher[1] education by type of course, mode of study,[2] gender and subject group, 2000/01[3,4]

United Kingdom (i) Home and Overseas Students Thousands

| | Postgraduate level | | | | | | First degree | | Other Undergraduate | | Total higher education students[5] | |
| | PHD's & equivalent | | Masters and Others | | Total Postgraduate | | | | | | | |
	Full-time	Part-time	Full-time	Part-time	Full-time	Part-time	Full-time	Part-time	Full-time	Part-time	Full-time[5]	Part-time[5]
All												
Medicine & Dentistry	2.3	3.5	2.9	5.3	5.2	8.8	30.0	0.1	0.2	0.1	**35.3**	**9.0**
Subjects Allied to Medicine	1.8	2.0	3.2	16.0	5.0	18.0	53.3	23.7	56.1	44.4	**114.5**	**86.1**
Biological Sciences	6.0	3.7	4.1	4.8	10.1	8.4	65.1	3.0	2.5	1.7	**77.7**	**13.2**
Vet. Science, Agriculture & related	0.9	0.6	1.2	1.2	2.1	1.8	10.3	0.4	4.7	2.2	**17.2**	**4.4**
Physical Sciences	6.1	3.2	4.5	3.2	10.7	6.3	44.9	2.0	1.5	2.8	**57.1**	**11.1**
Mathematical and Computing Sciences	2.4	1.6	10.1	8.0	12.4	9.6	72.3	5.5	18.4	22.5	**103.0**	**37.6**
Engineering & Technology	5.8	4.2	9.4	9.7	15.2	13.9	73.0	7.0	13.0	28.5	**101.3**	**49.5**
Architecture, Building & Planning	0.4	0.6	4.2	5.3	4.6	5.9	20.2	5.6	3.7	9.8	**28.5**	**21.3**
Social Sciences	4.1	4.4	21.1	20.8	25.2	25.3	109.2	10.8	11.6	24.3	**145.9**	**60.3**
Business & Financial Studies	1.4	2.2	19.0	44.6	20.4	46.8	107.8	11.4	34.0	75.8	**162.3**	**134.1**
Librarianship & Info Science	0.2	0.3	3.1	3.4	3.3	3.7	18.1	0.8	2.6	1.4	**23.9**	**5.8**
Languages	2.3	2.5	4.5	4.2	6.8	6.8	56.5	3.1	4.0	16.2	**67.2**	**26.1**
Humanities	2.3	2.7	3.8	5.6	6.1	8.4	31.4	2.8	0.7	9.1	**38.2**	**20.3**
Creative Arts & Design	0.6	0.9	5.5	3.8	6.1	4.7	79.3	3.2	15.8	7.0	**101.1**	**14.9**
Education[6]	0.9	3.9	25.4	38.6	26.3	42.5	43.0	4.6	3.3	15.7	**72.6**	**62.8**
Combined, general	0.6	0.8	2.4	29.4	3.0	30.2	99.2	9.8	14.1	173.6	**116.3**	**213.6**
Unknown[5]	-	-	-	0.4	-	0.4	8.4	2.0	5.0	17.4	**14.1**	**21.0**
All subjects	**38.1**	**37.2**	**124.5**	**204.4**	**162.6**	**241.6**	**922.0**	**95.7**	**191.2**	**452.6**	**1,276.3**	**791.0**
Males												
Medicine & Dentistry	1.0	2.0	1.3	2.5	2.3	4.5	13.6	0.1	0.1	-	**15.9**	**4.6**
Subjects Allied to Medicine	0.8	0.8	1.1	4.1	1.8	4.9	12.6	2.8	8.5	4.3	**23.0**	**12.0**
Biological Sciences	2.6	1.7	1.6	1.6	4.2	3.2	24.2	1.1	1.2	0.6	**29.6**	**5.0**
Vet. Science, Agriculture & related	0.5	0.4	0.7	0.6	1.1	1.0	3.8	0.2	2.3	1.2	**7.3**	**2.3**
Physical Sciences	4.1	2.2	2.6	1.9	6.7	4.1	27.5	1.1	0.9	1.6	**35.1**	**6.8**
Mathematical and Computing Sciences	1.8	1.2	7.1	5.3	8.9	6.5	55.0	4.1	13.7	13.1	**77.6**	**23.7**
Engineering & Technology	4.6	3.6	7.5	8.4	12.1	12.0	61.5	6.4	11.3	26.3	**85.0**	**44.7**
Architecture, Building & Planning	0.3	0.4	2.5	3.5	2.8	3.9	14.5	4.5	3.0	8.4	**20.4**	**16.8**
Social Sciences	2.2	2.4	9.3	8.6	11.4	11.0	43.1	4.2	2.7	5.3	**57.2**	**20.4**
Business & Financial Studies	0.9	1.5	10.7	24.5	11.6	25.9	50.9	4.9	14.6	30.2	**77.1**	**61.0**
Librarianship & Info Science	0.1	0.1	1.1	1.2	1.2	1.3	6.9	0.2	1.3	0.5	**9.4**	**2.1**
Languages	1.0	1.1	1.5	1.4	2.4	2.5	15.6	0.9	1.3	6.4	**19.3**	**9.8**
Humanities	1.4	1.6	1.8	2.6	3.2	4.2	14.6	1.1	0.3	3.3	**18.1**	**8.6**
Creative Arts & Design	0.3	0.5	2.3	1.6	2.5	2.1	31.9	1.0	7.6	2.5	**42.0**	**5.6**
Education[6]	0.4	1.8	7.5	11.3	7.9	13.1	9.9	1.1	1.7	4.7	**19.5**	**18.9**
Combined, general	0.3	0.5	1.3	16.9	1.6	17.4	42.6	3.5	5.8	74.4	**50.0**	**95.3**
Unknown[5]	-	-	-	0.2	-	0.2	3.8	0.6	2.5	7.8	**6.6**	**9.2**
All subjects	**22.1**	**21.6**	**59.8**	**96.3**	**81.9**	**117.9**	**432.1**	**37.9**	**78.8**	**190.3**	**593.1**	**346.7**
Females												
Medicine & Dentistry	1.3	1.6	1.6	2.8	2.9	4.4	16.4	-	0.1	0.1	**19.4**	**4.4**
Subjects Allied to Medicine	1.0	1.2	2.1	11.9	3.2	13.1	40.7	20.9	47.6	40.1	**91.5**	**74.1**
Biological Sciences	3.4	2.0	2.6	3.2	6.0	5.2	40.9	1.9	1.3	1.1	**48.1**	**8.2**
Vet. Science, Agriculture & related	0.4	0.3	0.6	0.6	1.0	0.9	6.5	0.2	2.4	1.0	**9.9**	**2.1**
Physical Sciences	2.0	1.0	1.9	1.3	3.9	2.3	17.5	0.8	0.6	1.2	**22.0**	**4.3**
Mathematical and Computing Sciences	0.5	0.4	3.0	2.7	3.5	3.1	17.2	1.4	4.7	9.4	**25.4**	**13.9**
Engineering & Technology	1.2	0.7	1.9	1.3	3.1	1.9	11.5	0.7	1.7	2.2	**16.3**	**4.8**
Architecture, Building & Planning	0.2	0.2	1.6	1.8	1.8	2.0	5.7	1.1	0.6	1.5	**8.1**	**4.5**
Social Sciences	1.9	2.0	11.9	12.2	13.8	14.3	66.1	6.7	8.9	19.0	**88.7**	**39.9**
Business & Financial Studies	0.5	0.7	8.3	20.2	8.8	20.9	56.9	6.5	19.5	45.6	**85.2**	**73.0**
Librarianship & Info Science	0.1	0.1	2.0	2.2	2.1	2.3	11.2	0.5	1.2	0.9	**14.5**	**3.8**
Languages	1.3	1.4	3.1	2.8	4.4	4.3	40.9	2.2	2.7	9.8	**48.0**	**16.3**
Humanities	0.9	1.2	1.9	3.0	2.9	4.2	16.8	1.7	0.4	5.9	**20.1**	**11.7**
Creative Arts & Design	0.3	0.4	3.3	2.2	3.6	2.6	47.4	2.1	8.2	4.6	**59.2**	**9.3**
Education[6]	0.5	2.1	17.9	27.3	18.4	29.4	33.1	3.5	1.6	11.0	**53.1**	**43.9**
Combined, general	0.3	0.4	1.1	12.4	1.4	12.8	56.6	6.3	8.3	99.2	**66.3**	**118.3**
Unknown[5]	-	-	-	0.2	-	0.2	4.6	1.4	2.5	9.7	**7.5**	**11.8**
All subjects	**15.9**	**15.6**	**64.8**	**108.1**	**80.7**	**123.7**	**489.9**	**57.9**	**112.3**	**262.2**	**683.2**	**444.4**

Sources: Department for Education and Skills; National Assembly for Wales; Scottish Executive; Northern Ireland Department for Employment and Learning

1 Higher education institutions include Open University students. Part-time figures include dormant modes, those writing up at home and on sabbaticals, which are not included in HESA SFR48.

2 Full-time includes sandwich, and for Scotland, short full-time. Part-time comprises both day and evening, including block release (except for Scotland) and open/distance learning.

3 Provisional. Figures for higher education students in further education institutions (except for Northern Ireland) relate to 1999/00. Includes estimated breakdowns by subjects for students in further education institutions in England.

4 Figures for students (other than in Scotland further education institutions) are snapshots counted at a particular point in the year [December for UK HE institutions and FE institutions in Wales, November for FE institutions in England and Northern Ireland]. Students starting courses after these dates will not therefore be counted. Figures for Scotland, however, are whole year (not snapshot) enrolments (rather than headcounts) for 1999/00.

5 Includes data for FE institutions in Wales which cannot be split by level.

6 Including ITT and INSET.

7 Numbers in grouped countries do not sum to overall student numbers due to overlaps.

3.6 POST COMPULSORY EDUCATION AND TRAINING: STUDENTS AND STARTERS

Students in higher[1] education by type of course, mode of study,[2] gender and subject group, 2000/01[3,4]

United Kingdom   (ii) of which Overseas Students   Thousands

| | Postgraduate level | | | | | | First degree | | Other Undergraduate | | Total higher education students[5] | |
| | PHD's & equivalent | | Masters and Others | | Total Postgraduate | | | | | | | |
	Full-time	Part-time	Full-time	Part-time	Full-time	Part-time	Full-time	Part-time	Full-time	Part-time	Full-time[5]	Part-time[5]
All												
Medicine & Dentistry	0.6	0.5	1.2	0.6	1.9	1.1	2.6	-	0.1	-	**4.6**	**1.1**
Subjects Allied to Medicine	0.5	0.3	0.8	1.3	1.3	1.7	3.5	0.7	3.9	0.6	**8.6**	**2.9**
Biological Sciences	1.5	0.7	1.2	0.5	2.7	1.2	4.4	0.1	0.4	0.1	**7.4**	**1.5**
Vet. Science, Agriculture & related	0.4	0.3	0.7	0.3	1.1	0.6	0.9	0.1	0.3	0.1	**2.3**	**0.7**
Physical Sciences	1.8	0.8	1.6	0.7	3.4	1.5	2.3	0.1	0.4	0.1	**6.1**	**1.7**
Mathematical and Computing Sciences	1.2	0.5	3.9	1.1	5.0	1.7	6.5	0.4	0.9	0.3	**12.4**	**2.5**
Engineering & Technology	3.2	1.6	5.8	1.7	9.0	3.3	15.7	0.6	1.7	0.7	**26.4**	**4.6**
Architecture, Building & Planning	0.2	0.2	1.7	0.6	1.9	0.8	2.9	0.2	0.5	0.1	**5.3**	**1.1**
Social Sciences	2.3	1.6	9.2	2.5	11.5	4.1	11.5	0.3	1.6	0.4	**24.6**	**4.8**
Business & Financial Studies	0.9	0.7	12.8	6.5	13.8	7.2	16.2	0.8	3.1	1.1	**33.1**	**9.1**
Librarianship & Info Science	0.1	0.1	1.1	0.4	1.2	0.5	1.7	0.1	0.1	-	**3.0**	**0.7**
Languages	1.0	1.0	2.3	1.1	3.3	2.0	3.8	0.3	3.1	2.4	**10.3**	**4.8**
Humanities	1.1	0.8	1.5	0.4	2.6	1.2	1.1	0.1	0.5	0.2	**4.2**	**1.5**
Creative Arts & Design	0.3	0.2	2.3	0.4	2.5	0.5	7.6	0.1	0.8	0.2	**11.0**	**0.8**
Education[6]	0.5	1.1	2.4	2.7	2.9	3.8	1.2	0.5	0.2	0.4	**4.3**	**4.7**
Combined, general	0.2	0.2	1.3	0.9	1.5	1.0	8.6	0.3	9.3	2.0	**19.4**	**3.3**
Unknown[5]	-	-	-	-	-	-	0.4	-	0.4	0.4	**0.8**	**0.4**
All subjects	**15.7**	**10.5**	**49.8**	**21.9**	**65.5**	**32.4**	**90.8**	**4.7**	**27.5**	**9.0**	**183.8**	**46.1**
of which European Union[7]	5.0	3.2	18.1	7.4	23.1	10.6	45.9	1.9	14.2	4.2	**83.3**	**16.8**
Other Europe[7]	1.2	0.8	3.4	1.9	4.6	2.7	7.9	0.3	0.9	0.5	**13.4**	**3.5**
Commonwealth[7]	3.1	2.1	10.5	4.9	13.6	7.0	22.0	1.1	4.2	1.2	**39.8**	**9.3**
Other Countries[7]	6.5	4.5	18.6	8.2	25.1	12.7	17.8	1.5	8.2	3.2	**51.1**	**17.4**
Males												
Medicine & Dentistry	0.4	0.3	0.6	0.4	1.0	0.6	1.2	-	0.1	-	**2.2**	**0.6**
Subjects Allied to Medicine	0.2	0.2	0.3	0.5	0.6	0.7	1.0	0.2	0.9	0.1	**2.5**	**1.0**
Biological Sciences	0.7	0.4	0.5	0.2	1.2	0.5	1.4	0.1	0.1	0.1	**2.7**	**0.6**
Vet. Science, Agriculture & related	0.2	0.2	0.4	0.2	0.6	0.4	0.4	-	0.2	-	**1.2**	**0.5**
Physical Sciences	1.2	0.5	0.9	0.5	2.0	1.0	1.3	-	0.3	0.1	**3.5**	**1.1**
Mathematical and Computing Sciences	0.9	0.4	2.7	0.8	3.6	1.2	4.6	0.3	0.6	0.2	**8.8**	**1.8**
Engineering & Technology	2.5	1.3	4.7	1.5	7.3	2.8	13.2	0.5	1.4	0.6	**21.9**	**4.0**
Architecture, Building & Planning	0.2	0.2	0.9	0.5	1.1	0.6	1.7	0.1	0.3	0.1	**3.0**	**0.8**
Social Sciences	1.3	0.9	4.6	1.4	5.9	2.3	5.4	0.2	0.6	0.1	**11.9**	**2.6**
Business & Financial Studies	0.6	0.5	7.3	4.2	7.9	4.7	8.1	0.4	1.6	0.6	**17.6**	**5.7**
Librarianship & Info Science	-	-	0.4	0.1	0.4	0.2	0.5	-	-	-	**1.0**	**0.2**
Languages	0.4	0.4	0.6	0.4	1.0	0.8	0.9	0.1	0.9	0.9	**2.8**	**1.8**
Humanities	0.7	0.5	0.7	0.2	1.3	0.7	0.5	0.1	0.2	0.1	**2.0**	**0.8**
Creative Arts & Design	0.1	0.1	0.8	0.2	0.9	0.2	2.6	0.1	0.3	0.1	**3.8**	**0.4**
Education[6]	0.2	0.6	0.6	1.0	0.9	1.5	0.3	0.2	-	0.2	**1.2**	**2.0**
Combined, general	0.1	0.1	0.7	0.5	0.8	0.6	3.8	0.1	3.5	0.6	**8.2**	**1.3**
Unknown[5]	-	-	-	-	-	-	0.2	-	0.2	0.2	**0.3**	**0.2**
All subjects	**9.9**	**6.4**	**26.7**	**12.4**	**36.6**	**18.8**	**46.9**	**2.6**	**11.3**	**3.9**	**94.7**	**25.3**
of which European Union[7]	2.9	1.8	9.5	4.1	12.4	5.9	23.5	1.0	5.4	1.8	**41.3**	**8.7**
Other Europe[7]	0.7	0.5	1.7	1.0	2.4	1.5	3.7	0.1	0.4	0.2	**6.5**	**1.8**
Commonwealth[7]	2.1	1.4	6.4	3.0	8.5	4.4	12.1	0.6	2.0	0.6	**22.7**	**5.6**
Other Countries[7]	4.3	2.9	9.5	4.6	13.7	7.5	9.1	0.9	3.5	1.4	**26.3**	**9.7**
Females												
Medicine & Dentistry	0.3	0.2	0.6	0.3	0.9	0.5	1.4	-	0.1	-	**2.4**	**0.5**
Subjects Allied to Medicine	0.3	0.2	0.4	0.8	0.7	1.0	2.5	0.5	3.0	0.5	**6.2**	**1.9**
Biological Sciences	0.8	0.4	0.7	0.3	1.5	0.7	3.0	0.1	0.3	0.1	**4.7**	**0.8**
Vet. Science, Agriculture & related	0.1	0.1	0.3	0.1	0.4	0.2	0.5	-	0.1	-	**1.1**	**0.2**
Physical Sciences	0.6	0.3	0.7	0.3	1.3	0.6	1.0	-	0.2	-	**2.6**	**0.6**
Mathematical and Computing Sciences	0.3	0.1	1.2	0.3	1.4	0.4	1.8	0.1	0.3	0.1	**3.5**	**0.7**
Engineering & Technology	0.6	0.2	1.1	0.2	1.7	0.5	2.5	0.1	0.3	0.1	**4.6**	**0.6**
Architecture, Building & Planning	0.1	0.1	0.7	0.2	0.8	0.2	1.2	-	0.2	-	**2.2**	**0.3**
Social Sciences	1.0	0.7	4.6	1.2	5.6	1.8	6.1	0.2	1.0	0.2	**12.6**	**2.2**
Business & Financial Studies	0.3	0.2	5.5	2.4	5.9	2.6	8.1	0.3	1.5	0.5	**15.5**	**3.4**
Librarianship & Info Science	-	-	0.7	0.3	0.7	0.3	1.2	0.1	0.1	-	**2.0**	**0.4**
Languages	0.6	0.6	1.7	0.7	2.3	1.3	3.0	0.2	2.2	1.5	**7.5**	**3.0**
Humanities	0.4	0.3	0.8	0.2	1.3	0.5	0.6	-	0.3	0.1	**2.2**	**0.7**
Creative Arts & Design	0.1	0.1	1.5	0.2	1.6	0.3	5.1	0.1	0.5	0.1	**7.2**	**0.5**
Education[6]	0.3	0.6	1.8	1.7	2.0	2.3	1.0	0.2	0.2	0.2	**3.1**	**2.7**
Combined, general	0.1	0.1	0.6	0.3	0.7	0.4	4.8	0.2	5.8	1.3	**11.3**	**1.9**
Unknown[5]	-	-	-	-	-	-	0.2	-	0.2	0.2	**0.5**	**0.2**
All subjects	**5.8**	**4.0**	**23.1**	**9.5**	**28.9**	**13.6**	**44.0**	**2.1**	**16.2**	**5.1**	**89.1**	**20.8**
of which European Union[7]	2.1	1.4	8.6	3.3	10.7	4.7	22.5	0.9	8.8	2.4	**42.0**	**8.0**
Other Europe[7]	0.5	0.3	1.7	0.9	2.2	1.2	4.2	0.2	0.5	0.3	**6.9**	**1.7**
Commonwealth[7]	1.0	0.7	4.1	1.9	5.1	2.6	9.9	0.4	2.2	0.6	**17.2**	**3.6**
Other Countries[7]	2.2	1.6	9.1	3.7	11.3	5.3	8.7	0.7	4.8	1.9	**24.8**	**7.8**

Sources: Department for Education and Skills; National Assembly for Wales; Scottish Executive; Northern Ireland Department for Employment and Learning

See previous page for footnotes.

3.7 POST COMPULSORY EDUCATION AND TRAINING: STUDENTS AND STARTERS

Full-time higher education students from overseas, by type of course, gender and country, 2000/01[1,2] and time series

United Kingdom

Thousands

2000/01 RANK	1999/00 RANK	TOP FIFTY NAMED COUNTRIES	1980/81 All	1999/00 All	Males	Females	2000/01[1,2] All	Males	Females	PhD	Masters	Total post-graduate	First degree	Other under-graduate	Total Higher Education
1	(1)	Greece	2.5	25.1	15.2	9.9	24.7	14.9	9.8	1.1	8.1	9.3	14.9	0.5	24.7
2	(2)	Germany	1.3	11.4	5.5	5.9	11.3	5.4	5.9	0.9	1.9	2.9	5.5	2.9	11.3
3	(3)	France	0.7	11.3	5.6	5.7	11.1	5.4	5.6	0.6	2.2	2.8	5.2	3.1	11.1
4	(4)	Irish Republic	0.5	11.2	4.4	6.8	9.8	3.8	6.0	0.4	1.2	1.6	6.0	2.1	9.8
5	(9)	China	0.2	5.0	2.5	2.5	9.1	4.6	4.5	0.9	4.0	5.0	3.0	1.1	9.1
6	(6)	USA	2.9	8.7	3.7	5.0	8.8	3.7	5.1	0.9	2.3	3.2	1.4	4.2	8.8
7	(5)	Malaysia	13.3	8.9	5.2	3.7	8.0	4.5	3.4	0.7	1.3	2.0	5.8	0.2	8.0
8	(7)	Spain	0.2	6.4	3.0	3.4	6.3	2.9	3.3	0.4	1.1	1.4	2.7	2.1	6.3
9	(8)	Hong Kong	7.2	5.2	2.8	2.5	5.6	2.9	2.7	0.1	0.9	1.0	4.2	0.3	5.6
10	(11)	Japan	0.3	4.8	1.7	3.2	5.0	1.8	3.2	0.3	1.6	2.0	1.9	1.1	5.0
11	(10)	Italy	0.1	4.9	2.3	2.6	4.9	2.3	2.6	0.7	1.1	1.7	1.9	1.2	4.9
12	(15)	India	0.9	3.1	2.1	0.9	3.8	2.7	1.1	0.4	1.9	2.3	1.2	0.4	3.8
13	(12)	Singapore	1.6	4.0	2.5	1.6	3.8	2.2	1.5	0.2	0.6	0.8	2.9	0.1	3.8
14	(13)	Norway	0.5	3.8	1.6	2.1	3.5	1.5	2.0	0.1	0.5	0.6	2.8	0.2	3.5
15	(14)	Sweden	0.1	3.5	1.3	2.2	3.5	1.2	2.2	0.1	0.4	0.5	2.5	0.5	3.5
16	(17)	Taiwan	..	3.0	1.3	1.8	3.4	1.4	2.0	0.4	2.0	2.3	0.9	0.2	3.4
17	(16)	Cyprus	1.5	3.1	1.6	1.4	3.2	1.7	1.5	0.1	0.7	0.9	2.3	0.1	3.2
18	(18)	Finland	-	2.4	0.8	1.6	2.3	0.8	1.5	0.1	0.3	0.3	1.6	0.4	2.3
19	(21)	Thailand	0.2	2.0	0.9	1.1	2.2	1.0	1.2	0.4	1.2	1.6	0.5	0.1	2.2
20	(28)	Zimbabwe	0.9	1.6	0.7	0.9	2.1	0.9	1.2	0.1	0.2	0.2	0.4	1.5	2.1
21	(22)	Kenya	1.1	2.0	1.0	1.0	2.1	1.1	1.0	0.1	0.4	0.5	1.5	0.1	2.1
22	(19)	Canada	0.7	2.2	1.0	1.2	2.1	0.9	1.2	0.4	0.9	1.3	0.4	0.4	2.1
23	(20)	Belgium	0.1	2.0	1.0	1.0	2.1	1.0	1.0	0.1	0.4	0.5	1.3	0.3	2.1
24	(24)	Nigeria	5.2	1.8	1.0	0.8	2.1	1.1	0.9	0.1	0.7	0.8	1.1	0.1	2.1
25	(25)	Portugal	0.2	1.8	1.0	0.9	1.9	1.0	0.9	0.3	0.4	0.7	1.0	0.2	1.9
26	(26)	South Korea	0.1	1.7	1.0	0.7	1.9	1.1	0.8	0.3	0.7	1.0	0.7	0.1	1.9
27	(23)	Netherlands	0.1	1.9	0.9	1.0	1.8	0.8	1.0	0.1	0.4	0.5	0.9	0.3	1.8
28	(29)	Pakistan	0.8	1.5	1.2	0.3	1.6	1.3	0.3	0.1	0.7	0.9	0.6	0.1	1.6
29	(27)	Denmark	-	1.6	0.7	0.9	1.5	0.6	0.9	0.1	0.3	0.4	0.8	0.3	1.5
30	(30)	Turkey	0.7	1.3	0.7	0.6	1.4	0.8	0.6	0.2	0.6	0.8	0.5	0.1	1.4
31	(33)	Sri Lanka	1.2	1.0	0.6	0.4	1.1	0.7	0.4	0.1	0.3	0.4	0.7	0.1	1.1
32	(38)	Russia	..	0.9	0.4	0.5	1.1	0.5	0.6	0.2	0.3	0.5	0.6	0.1	1.1
33	(40)	Mexico	0.4	0.9	0.6	0.3	1.1	0.7	0.4	0.4	0.6	1.0	0.1	0.1	1.1
34	(31)	Austria	-	1.1	0.5	0.6	1.1	0.5	0.6	0.1	0.2	0.3	0.5	0.3	1.1
35	(37)	Mauritius	0.4[3]	0.9	0.5	0.4	1.1	0.6	0.5	-	0.2	0.2	0.6	0.2	1.1
36	(32)	Switzerland	0.2	1.1	0.5	0.5	1.0	0.5	0.5	0.1	0.2	0.3	0.5	0.1	1.0
37	(34)	Saudi Arabia	0.4	1.0	0.8	0.2	1.0	0.8	0.2	0.3	0.3	0.6	0.3	0.1	1.0
38	(35)	Oman	-	1.0	0.7	0.2	1.0	0.7	0.2	0.1	0.2	0.3	0.6	0.1	1.0
39	(42)	Indonesia	0.3	0.9	0.5	0.4	0.9	0.5	0.3	0.1	0.5	0.6	0.3	-	0.9
40	(43)	Ghana	0.7	0.8	0.5	0.3	0.9	0.6	0.3	0.1	0.4	0.4	0.3	0.1	0.9
41	(41)	Australia	0.5	0.9	0.4	0.4	0.8	0.4	0.4	0.2	0.3	0.5	0.2	0.1	0.8
42	(45)	Brazil	0.5	0.7	0.4	0.3	0.8	0.4	0.4	0.2	0.4	0.6	0.2	-	0.8
43	(39)	Israel	0.2	0.9	0.6	0.3	0.8	0.5	0.3	0.1	0.2	0.4	0.4	-	0.8
44	(36)	Brunei	1.0	1.0	0.5	0.5	0.7	0.4	0.4	-	0.1	0.1	0.6	0.1	0.7
45	(44)	Botswana	0.1	0.7	0.5	0.3	0.7	0.4	0.2	-	0.1	0.2	0.4	0.1	0.7
46	(46)	South Africa	0.4	0.7	0.4	0.3	0.7	0.4	0.3	0.1	0.3	0.4	0.2	0.1	0.7
47	(47)	Jordan	1.2	0.6	0.4	0.2	0.6	0.4	0.2	0.1	0.2	0.4	0.2	-	0.6
48	(48)	United Arab Emirates	0.1	0.6	0.4	0.2	0.6	0.4	0.2	-	0.1	0.2	0.4	-	0.6
49	(49)	Luxembourg	-	0.6	0.3	0.3	0.6	0.3	0.3	-	0.1	0.1	0.5	-	0.6
50	(50)	Iran	6.6	0.5	0.4	0.1	0.6	0.5	0.1	0.3	0.2	0.5	0.1	-	0.6
		Other/unknown	17.5	15.1	8.7	6.4	16.1	9.2	6.9	2.5	5.7	8.2	6.4	1.9	16.1
		TOTAL	75.6	179.1	92.9	86.2	183.7	94.7	89.0	15.7	49.8	65.5	90.8	27.5	183.7

Full-time students from overseas
of which

			1980/81 All	1999/00 All	Males	Females	2000/01 All	Males	Females	PhD	Masters	Total post-graduate	First degree	Other under-graduate	Total Higher Education
		European Union[4]	6.3[5]	85.7	42.6	43.0	83.3	41.3	41.9	5.0	18.1	23.1	45.9	14.2	83.3
		Other Europe[4]	2.6[5]	13.1	6.3	6.7	13.5	6.5	7.0	1.2	3.4	4.6	8.0	0.9	13.5
		Commonwealth[4]	39.6[5]	39.1	22.5	16.6	39.9	22.7	17.2	3.1	10.5	13.6	22.0	4.2	39.9
		Other Countries[6]	27.0[5]	45.1	23.4	21.7	51.0	26.3	24.7	6.5	18.6	25.1	17.8	8.2	51.0

Sources: Department for Education and Skills; National Assembly for Wales; Scottish Executive; Northern Ireland Department for Employment and Learning

1 Provisional. Figures for higher education students in further education institutions in England relate to 1998/99, and in Wales and Scotland to 1999/00.
2 Figures for students (other than in Scotland further education institutions) are snapshots counted at a particular point in the year [December for UK HE institutions and FE institutions in Wales, November for FE institutions in England and Northern Ireland]. Students starting courses after these dates will not therefore be counted. Figures for Scotland, however, are whole year (not snapshot) enrolments (rather than headcounts) for 1999/00.
3 Data are for 1981/82.
4 Except for 19980/81 Gibraltar is included in both EC and Commonwealth figures, and Cyprus and Malta are included in Other Europe and Commonwealth figures. Numbers in grouped countries do not sum to overall student numbers due to overlaps.
5 Estimated.
6 Includes those students whose country of domicile is not known.

POST COMPULSORY EDUCATION AND TRAINING: STUDENTS AND STARTERS
Students in further education[1] by country of study, mode of study[2], gender and age[3], during 1999/00

United Kingdom   Home and Overseas Students   Thousands

	United Kingdom		England[4]		Wales		Scotland[5]		Northern Ireland	
	Full-time	Part-time	Full-time	Part-time	Full-time	Part-time	Full-time	Part-time	Full-time	Part-time
All										
Age <16	9.9	66.0	7.9	33.8	0.6	4.1	1.3	25.5	0.1	2.6
16	255.6	79.4	226.4	54.5	13.9	4.0	7.8	14.8	7.4	6.1
17	214.2	88.4	188.8	65.6	11.1	4.5	7.5	13.5	6.9	4.7
18	109.6	91.7	94.4	72.8	5.7	5.0	5.4	10.8	4.0	3.0
19	47.5	81.5	41.5	65.6	2.4	4.8	2.5	8.8	1.1	2.3
20	28.1	69.7	25.1	57.0	1.2	4.2	1.4	6.8	0.4	1.7
21	21.1	61.9	19.1	51.5	0.8	3.6	1.1	5.3	0.2	1.5
22	18.0	60.2	16.4	50.5	0.6	3.5	0.8	4.9	0.1	1.3
23	16.6	62.3	15.3	52.4	0.6	3.6	0.7	4.9	0.1	1.4
24	15.6	64.2	14.5	54.4	0.4	3.5	0.6	4.9	0.1	1.3
25	14.7	65.0	13.7	55.4	0.4	3.6	0.6	4.7	-	1.3
26	14.3	67.2	13.3	57.3	0.4	3.8	0.5	4.9	-	1.2
27	14.0	70.6	13.1	60.4	0.4	3.9	0.5	5.1	-	1.2
28	13.8	73.9	12.9	62.9	0.4	4.2	0.5	5.6	-	1.3
29	13.4	73.3	12.5	62.4	0.4	4.1	0.5	5.6	-	1.2
30+	225.2	1,885.4	212.5	1,595.5	5.9	117.7	6.7	147.5	0.2	24.8
Unknown	4.7	54.3	4.6	50.7	0.1	3.2	-	0.1	-	0.4
All ages	1,036.3	3,015.2	932.0	2,502.7	45.3	181.5	38.2	273.7	20.7	57.3
Males										
Age <16	5.5	35.0	4.4	19.0	0.4	2.2	0.7	12.3	0.1	1.6
16	127.4	41.1	111.6	29.5	7.1	2.0	4.7	6.9	4.0	2.7
17	104.6	49.0	91.9	37.4	5.3	2.7	3.9	6.8	3.4	2.1
18	57.1	50.2	49.4	39.5	2.8	2.9	2.7	6.4	2.1	1.5
19	26.4	41.6	23.1	32.9	1.3	2.7	1.4	5.0	0.7	1.0
20	15.5	32.7	13.9	26.4	0.7	2.1	0.7	3.5	0.2	0.6
21	11.1	27.1	10.1	22.4	0.3	1.6	0.6	2.5	0.1	0.6
22	9.3	25.4	8.5	21.3	0.3	1.5	0.4	2.1	-	0.5
23	8.5	25.9	7.9	21.7	0.2	1.5	0.3	2.1	-	0.5
24	8.1	26.5	7.5	22.6	0.2	1.4	0.3	2.1	-	0.4
25	7.4	26.9	6.9	23.1	0.2	1.4	0.3	2.0	-	0.4
26	6.9	27.7	6.5	23.9	0.1	1.5	0.2	1.9	-	0.3
27	6.8	29.1	6.5	25.2	0.1	1.5	0.2	2.0	-	0.3
28	6.7	30.1	6.3	25.8	0.1	1.6	0.2	2.2	-	0.4
29	6.4	30.0	6.1	25.9	0.1	1.6	0.2	2.2	-	0.4
30+	108.1	730.5	103.8	620.9	1.8	44.7	2.5	57.6	0.1	7.2
Unknown	2.5	22.4	2.5	20.8	-	1.4	-	-	-	0.1
All ages	518.2	1,251.1	466.9	1,038.2	21.1	74.3	19.5	117.8	10.8	20.7
Females										
Age <16	4.3	31.0	3.5	14.9	0.3	1.9	0.5	13.2	-	1.0
16	128.2	38.3	114.9	25.0	6.8	2.1	3.1	7.9	3.5	3.3
17	109.6	39.4	96.9	28.2	5.8	1.9	3.5	6.7	3.5	2.6
18	52.5	41.5	45.0	33.3	2.9	2.1	2.7	4.4	1.9	1.6
19	21.1	39.9	18.4	32.7	1.1	2.1	1.1	3.8	0.5	1.2
20	12.6	37.1	11.2	30.6	0.6	2.1	0.6	3.3	0.1	1.0
21	10.0	34.9	9.0	29.2	0.4	2.0	0.5	2.8	0.1	0.9
22	8.7	34.8	7.9	29.2	0.3	2.0	0.4	2.7	-	0.9
23	8.1	36.5	7.3	30.7	0.3	2.1	0.4	2.8	-	1.0
24	7.5	37.7	7.0	31.8	0.2	2.1	0.3	2.9	-	0.9
25	7.3	38.1	6.8	32.3	0.2	2.1	0.3	2.7	-	0.9
26	7.4	39.5	6.8	33.4	0.3	2.3	0.3	2.9	-	0.9
27	7.1	41.5	6.6	35.2	0.3	2.4	0.3	3.1	-	0.9
28	7.1	43.9	6.6	37.1	0.3	2.6	0.3	3.4	-	0.9
29	7.1	43.3	6.5	36.5	0.3	2.5	0.3	3.4	-	0.9
30+	117.1	1,155.0	108.7	974.6	4.0	73.0	4.2	89.9	0.2	17.5
Unknown	2.2	31.9	2.1	29.9	-	1.8	-	-	-	0.3
All ages	518.1	1,764.1	465.1	1,464.5	24.2	107.1	18.8	155.9	10.0	36.5

Sources: Department for Education and Skills; National Assembly for Wales; Scottish Executive; Northern Ireland Department for Employment and Learning

1 Further education figures are whole year counts and differ from the higher education tables which use annual snapshots. Data for Northern Ireland however, are collected on a snapshot basis.

2 Full-time includes sandwich, and for Scotland, short full-time. Part-time comprises both day and evening, including block release (except for Scotland) and open/distance learning.

3 Ages as at 31 August 1999 (1 July for Northern Ireland and 31 December for Scotland).

4 Excludes approximately 175,650 students in further education institutions in England since the information cannot be broken down in this way. External institutions and specialist designated colleges are also excluded.

5 Figures for Scotland further education institutions are enrolments rather than headcounts.

Students in higher[1] education by level, mode of study[2], gender and age[3], 2000/01[4,5]

| United Kingdom | | | | | Home and Overseas Students | | | | | | Thousands |

	PHD's & equivalent		Masters and Others		Total Postgraduate		First degree		Other Undergraduate		Total higher education students[6]	
	Full-time	Part-time	Full-time	Part-time	Full-time	Part-time	Full-time	Part-time	Full-time	Part-time	Full-time[6]	Part-time[6]
All												
Age <16	.	.	.	.	.	.	.	.	.	0.1	0.1	0.1
16	.	.	.	.	.	.	0.4	-	0.6	0.4	1.0	0.4
17	.	.	.	.	.	.	9.9	-	4.1	1.2	14.1	1.2
18	.	.	.	.	.	.	145.5	0.5	22.9	6.3	168.5	6.9
19	.	.	0.1	0.1	0.1	0.1	202.9	2.3	31.4	11.2	234.6	13.7
20	0.1	-	1.1	0.2	1.2	0.2	210.8	3.9	26.6	12.3	238.6	16.4
21	0.8	-	13.7	1.2	14.5	1.2	138.7	4.9	17.8	11.2	171.1	17.4
22	2.7	0.1	17.8	3.7	20.5	3.8	61.0	4.5	12.1	10.9	93.6	19.2
23	4.2	0.2	15.5	5.3	19.7	5.5	30.2	4.0	9.1	11.4	59.0	20.9
24	4.6	1.1	12.0	6.2	16.5	7.4	18.2	3.5	6.9	12.0	41.6	22.9
25	3.8	2.2	9.4	7.0	13.2	9.1	12.6	3.4	5.5	12.0	31.3	24.6
26	3.0	2.1	7.4	7.3	10.5	9.4	9.9	3.4	4.8	12.7	25.1	25.5
27	2.6	2.1	6.1	7.9	8.7	10.0	8.2	3.3	4.1	13.3	21.0	26.6
28	2.2	1.9	5.5	8.3	7.7	10.2	7.2	3.3	3.8	13.8	18.6	27.4
29	1.8	1.8	4.6	8.4	6.4	10.3	6.5	3.3	3.4	14.1	16.3	27.7
30+	12.1	25.5	31.1	146.8	43.2	172.3	59.5	55.1	37.7	302.2	140.5	530.2
Unknown	-	0.1	0.3	2.0	0.3	2.1	0.5	0.3	0.4	7.3	1.2	9.7
All ages	**38.1**	**37.2**	**124.5**	**204.4**	**162.6**	**241.6**	**922.0**	**95.7**	**191.2**	**452.6**	**1,276.3**	**791.0**
Males												
Age <16	.	.	.	.	.	.	.	.	.	0.1	-	0.1
16	.	.	.	.	.	.	0.2	-	0.3	0.2	0.4	0.2
17	.	.	.	.	.	.	4.4	-	1.8	0.6	6.2	0.6
18	.	.	.	.	.	.	65.9	0.3	10.6	3.9	76.6	4.3
19	.	.	0.1	0.1	0.1	0.1	93.7	1.3	15.0	6.9	108.8	8.3
20	-	-	0.5	0.1	0.5	0.1	98.0	2.2	11.9	6.8	110.4	9.2
21	0.5	-	5.7	0.5	6.1	0.5	67.8	2.8	7.5	5.8	81.5	9.0
22	1.6	-	8.0	1.5	9.6	1.5	31.9	2.5	5.2	4.9	46.6	8.9
23	2.5	0.1	7.1	2.2	9.6	2.3	16.4	2.1	3.9	4.8	29.9	9.2
24	2.6	0.6	5.7	2.6	8.3	3.2	9.7	1.6	2.9	4.9	20.9	9.8
25	2.1	1.3	4.5	2.9	6.6	4.2	6.5	1.5	2.2	4.8	15.3	10.5
26	1.7	1.2	3.6	3.0	5.3	4.2	4.9	1.4	1.9	5.2	12.1	10.8
27	1.5	1.2	3.1	3.4	4.6	4.6	4.0	1.4	1.5	5.5	10.1	11.6
28	1.3	1.1	2.8	3.7	4.0	4.8	3.5	1.4	1.4	5.9	9.0	12.1
29	1.1	1.0	2.4	4.0	3.5	5.0	3.0	1.3	1.3	6.1	7.7	12.4
30+	7.3	14.9	16.3	71.3	23.6	86.2	21.9	17.9	11.3	121.2	56.9	225.6
Unknown	-	-	0.2	1.1	0.2	1.2	0.2	0.1	0.2	2.9	0.6	4.2
All ages	**22.1**	**21.6**	**59.8**	**96.3**	**81.9**	**117.9**	**432.1**	**37.9**	**78.8**	**190.3**	**593.1**	**346.7**
Females												
Age <16	.	.	.	.	.	.	.	.	.	0.1	-	0.1
16	.	.	.	.	.	.	0.2	-	0.3	0.2	0.5	0.2
17	.	.	.	.	.	.	5.6	-	2.3	0.6	7.9	0.6
18	.	.	.	.	.	.	79.6	0.2	12.3	2.4	91.9	2.7
19	.	.	0.1	-	0.1	-	109.2	1.0	16.4	4.4	125.8	5.4
20	-	-	0.6	0.1	0.6	0.1	112.8	1.7	14.7	5.4	128.2	7.3
21	0.3	-	8.1	0.7	8.4	0.7	70.8	2.2	10.3	5.5	89.6	8.3
22	1.2	-	9.8	2.3	10.9	2.3	29.1	2.1	7.0	6.0	47.0	10.4
23	1.8	0.1	8.4	3.1	10.1	3.2	13.8	1.9	5.2	6.6	29.2	11.7
24	1.9	0.5	6.3	3.7	8.2	4.2	8.5	1.9	4.0	7.1	20.7	13.2
25	1.7	0.9	4.9	4.1	6.6	5.0	6.1	1.9	3.3	7.2	16.0	14.1
26	1.3	0.9	3.8	4.3	5.2	5.2	4.9	1.9	2.9	7.5	13.0	14.7
27	1.2	0.9	3.0	4.4	4.2	5.4	4.2	1.9	2.6	7.8	11.0	15.0
28	1.0	0.8	2.7	4.6	3.7	5.4	3.7	1.8	2.3	8.0	9.7	15.3
29	0.7	0.8	2.1	4.4	2.9	5.2	3.5	2.0	2.1	8.1	8.5	15.3
30+	4.8	10.6	14.8	75.5	19.6	86.1	37.5	37.2	26.3	181.1	83.5	304.6
Unknown	-	-	0.1	0.9	0.1	0.9	0.2	0.2	0.2	4.5	0.6	5.6
All ages	**15.9**	**15.6**	**64.8**	**108.1**	**80.7**	**123.7**	**489.9**	**57.9**	**112.3**	**262.2**	**683.2**	**444.4**

Sources: Department for Education and Skills; National Assembly for Wales; Scottish Executive; Northern Ireland Department for Employment and Learning

1 Higher education institutions include Open University students. Part-time figures include dormant modes, those writing up at home and on sabbaticals, which are not included in HESA SFR48.

2 Full-time includes sandwich, and for Scotland, short full-time. Part-time comprises both day and evening, including block release (except for Scotland) and open/distance learning.

3 Ages as at 31 August 2000 (1 July for Northern Ireland and 31 December for Scotland).

4 Figures for students (other than in Scotland further education institutions) are snapshots counted at a particular point in the year [December for UK HE institutions and FE institutions in Wales, November for FE institutions in England and Northern Ireland]. Students starting courses after these dates will not therefore be counted. Figures for Scotland, however, are whole year (not snapshot) enrolments (rather than headcounts) for 1999/00.

5 Provisional. Figures for higher education students in further education institutions (except for Northern Ireland) relate to 1999/00.

6 Includes data for FE institutions in Wales which cannot be split by level.

POST COMPULSORY EDUCATION AND TRAINING: STUDENTS AND STARTERS
Participants in TEC Delivered Government-Supported Training programmes by region – time series

England   Thousands

	March 91[1]	March 96	March 99[1]	March 00[1]	March 01
Work-Based Training for Young People[2]					
Government Office Region[3]					
North East	19.7	17.3	20.8	21.3	21.6
North West	30.6	46.4	50.0	52.0	50.7
Yorkshire and the Humber	28.8	26.3	32.0	33.5	34.5
East Midlands[4]	22.8	23.6	25.7	25.6	22.6
West Midlands	32.3	26.3	30.4	31.7	30.6
Eastern[4]	..	24.1	25.0	25.1	24.0
London	12.7	18.4	22.2	23.8	24.2
South East	25.8	31.8	33.9	33.8	32.2
South West	20.5	21.6	26.5	26.8	26.1
England[5]	193.2	235.8	266.3	273.5	266.4
Advanced Modern Apprenticeships[6]					
North East	.	2.4	9.7	9.8	9.4
North West	.	6.5	25.0	26.3	25.4
Yorkshire and the Humber	.	3.9	14.1	14.2	14.7
East Midlands	.	2.5	11.1	11.7	10.2
West Midlands	.	2.3	14.6	15.3	14.4
Eastern	.	1.6	12.2	12.3	10.7
London	.	2.0	10.5	11.1	10.4
South East	.	1.7	16.6	16.9	15.6
South West	.	1.9	12.6	14.0	13.2
England[5]	.	24.8	126.5	131.4	123.8
Foundation Modern Apprenticeships[7]					
England	.	.	27.8	69.4	89.6
Other Training[8]					
England	193.2	211.0	112.0	69.1	45.2
Life Skills/Skill Build					
England	.	.	.	3.6	7.8
Work-Based Learning for Adults[9]					
Government Office Region[3]					
North East	16.0	7.3	2.6	2.4	2.2
North West	16.3	13.1	5.6	5.9	4.7
Yorkshire and the Humber	20.0	8.5	4.9	3.7	4.4
East Midlands[4]	7.0	5.6	2.2	2.2	1.9
West Midlands	15.6	6.9	3.4	3.5	3.5
Eastern[4]	..	4.8	2.2	2.1	2.3
London	18.2	10.1	7.2	8.3	8.5
South East	11.4	5.7	2.7	3.0	2.8
South West	10.2	6.3	2.4	2.5	1.9
England[5]	114.7	68.2	33.1	33.4	32.2
All participants in TEC Delivered Government-Supported Training programmes					
England	307.9	304.0	299.4	306.9	298.6

Sources: TEC Management Information.

1 Includes revised figures.

2 Includes Advanced Modern Apprenticeships, Foundation Modern Apprenticeships, Other Training, and, from October 1999, Life Skills (LS) and Skill Build.

3 Government Office Regions in England plus country total for England.

4 For 1991, Eastern figures were included with East Midlands.

5 The England figure may not be the sum of the regional figures shown due to rounding.

6 Formerly known as Modern Apprenticeships.

7 Formerly known as National Traineeships.

8 Other Training includes Youth Credits & Youth Training.

9 The Employment Training programme ran from 1990 until 1993 when it was replaced by Training for Work (TfW). In 1997-98 this was replaced by Work-Based Training for Adults (WBTA) which became Work-Based Learning for Adults (WBLA) in March 1999. 1996-97 in-training figures for TfW included Pre-Vocational Pilots but from April 1997 onwards Pre-Vocational Training became part of mainstream Work-Based Learning for Adults.

3.11 POST COMPULSORY EDUCATION AND TRAINING: STUDENTS AND STARTERS

Further education[1] students in the first year of their course of study, by country of study, mode of study[2], gender and age[3], 1999/00[4,5]

United Kingdom · Home and Overseas Students · Thousands

		United Kingdom		England[4]		Wales[5]		Scotland[6]		Northern Ireland	
		Full-time	Part-time	Full-time	Part-time	Full-time	Part-time	Full-time	Part-time	Full-time	Part-time
All											
Age	<16	8.8	57.3	6.9	26.9	0.6	2.6	1.2	25.5	0.1	2.3
	16	240.3	80.9	213.0	57.2	12.1	3.6	7.7	14.7	7.4	5.4
	17	104.2	73.1	89.3	54.0	4.5	3.0	7.2	12.4	3.3	3.7
	18	69.8	81.5	59.9	67.0	2.7	3.1	5.3	9.1	1.9	2.3
	19	32.9	70.2	28.8	57.9	1.2	2.9	2.4	7.7	0.5	1.7
	20	22.0	58.9	19.8	49.0	0.6	2.4	1.3	6.3	0.2	1.3
	21	18.3	56.6	16.6	48.1	0.5	2.4	1.1	5.1	0.1	1.1
	22	17.2	58.9	15.8	50.7	0.4	2.6	0.8	4.7	0.1	1.0
	23	16.3	60.6	15.2	52.2	0.4	2.5	0.7	4.8	-	1.1
	24	15.5	61.8	14.5	53.4	0.3	2.7	0.6	4.8	-	0.9
	25	14.6	63.7	13.7	55.4	0.3	2.8	0.6	4.6	-	1.0
	26	14.3	66.3	13.4	57.8	0.3	2.8	0.5	4.7	-	0.9
	27	14.1	68.6	13.3	59.8	0.3	3.0	0.5	5.0	-	0.9
	28	13.6	68.1	12.8	58.7	0.3	3.1	0.4	5.4	-	0.9
	29	13.2	67.8	12.4	58.5	0.3	3.0	0.4	5.4	-	0.9
	30+	216.9	1,640.3	206.1	1,398.8	4.1	79.1	6.5	145.2	0.2	17.1
	Unknown	5.1	52.8	5.1	49.8	0.1	2.6	-	0.1	-	0.3
	All ages	837.1	2,687.3	756.7	2,255.3	29.0	124.0	37.3	265.4	14.1	42.6
Males											
Age	<16	5.0	29.6	3.9	14.6	0.3	1.4	0.7	12.3	0.1	1.5
	16	117.7	41.9	102.9	30.7	6.1	1.9	4.7	6.8	4.0	2.5
	17	55.1	37.3	47.5	28.2	2.3	1.5	3.8	5.9	1.6	1.7
	18	35.7	41.1	30.7	33.6	1.4	1.6	2.6	4.9	1.0	1.0
	19	18.0	32.9	15.8	26.7	0.6	1.5	1.3	4.0	0.3	0.7
	20	11.7	26.2	10.5	21.6	0.3	1.1	0.7	3.1	0.1	0.5
	21	9.4	23.9	8.5	20.2	0.2	1.0	0.6	2.3	0.1	0.4
	22	8.7	24.0	8.0	20.6	0.2	1.0	0.4	2.1	-	0.3
	23	8.3	24.8	7.8	21.4	0.2	1.0	0.3	2.1	-	0.4
	24	7.9	25.5	7.4	22.1	0.2	1.1	0.3	2.0	-	0.3
	25	7.1	26.2	6.7	22.9	0.1	1.0	0.3	2.0	-	0.3
	26	7.0	27.4	6.6	24.2	0.1	1.1	0.2	1.9	-	0.3
	27	6.8	28.3	6.5	24.9	0.1	1.1	0.2	2.0	-	0.3
	28	6.6	28.2	6.3	24.6	0.1	1.1	0.2	2.2	-	0.3
	29	6.3	28.0	6.1	24.5	0.1	1.1	0.2	2.1	-	0.3
	30+	104.8	646.5	100.9	554.4	1.3	30.2	2.5	56.8	-	5.1
	Unknown	2.9	22.5	2.9	21.1	-	1.3	-	-	-	0.1
	All ages	419.0	1,114.4	378.9	936.0	13.7	50.0	19.0	112.6	7.3	15.9
Females											
Age	<16	3.7	27.6	2.9	12.4	0.2	1.2	0.5	13.2	-	0.9
	16	122.5	39.0	110.0	26.5	6.0	1.7	3.1	7.9	3.4	2.9
	17	49.1	35.8	41.8	25.8	2.2	1.5	3.4	6.5	1.7	2.0
	18	34.1	40.4	29.2	33.5	1.4	1.5	2.6	4.1	0.9	1.3
	19	14.9	37.3	13.1	31.3	0.6	1.4	1.1	3.6	0.2	1.0
	20	10.3	32.7	9.3	27.4	0.3	1.3	0.6	3.2	0.1	0.8
	21	8.9	32.6	8.0	27.9	0.3	1.4	0.5	2.7	0.1	0.7
	22	8.5	34.9	7.8	30.1	0.2	1.6	0.4	2.6	-	0.6
	23	8.0	35.8	7.4	30.9	0.2	1.5	0.4	2.7	-	0.7
	24	7.6	36.3	7.1	31.4	0.2	1.6	0.3	2.8	-	0.6
	25	7.5	37.5	7.1	32.6	0.2	1.7	0.3	2.6	-	0.6
	26	7.3	38.9	6.8	33.7	0.2	1.7	0.3	2.8	-	0.7
	27	7.2	40.3	6.7	34.8	0.2	1.9	0.3	3.0	-	0.6
	28	7.0	39.9	6.6	34.1	0.2	1.9	0.3	3.3	-	0.6
	29	6.8	39.8	6.3	34.0	0.2	1.9	0.3	3.3	-	0.6
	30+	112.1	993.8	105.1	844.5	2.8	49.0	4.1	88.4	0.2	12.0
	Unknown	2.3	30.3	2.2	28.7	-	1.3	-	-	-	0.2
	All ages	418.1	1,572.9	377.7	1,319.3	15.3	74.0	18.3	152.8	6.8	26.8

Sources: Department for Education and Skills; National Assembly for Wales; Scottish Executive; Northern Ireland Department for Employment and Learning

1 Further education figures are whole year counts and differ from the higher education tables which use annual snapshots. Data for Northern Ireland however, are collected on a snapshot basis.

2 Full-time includes sandwich, and for Scotland, short full-time. Part-time comprises both day and evening, including block release (except for Scotland) and open/distance learning.

3 Ages as at 31 August 1999 (1 July for Northern Ireland and 31 December for Scotland).

4 Provisional. Includes estimated breakdowns by subjects for students in further education institutions in England but excludes approximately 175,650 aggregate return students in further education institutions in England since the information cannot be broken down in this way. External institutions and specialist designated colleges are also excluded.

5 Further education institution data for Wales refer to 1998/99.

6 Figures for Scotland further education institutions are enrolments rather than headcounts.

3.12 POST COMPULSORY EDUCATION AND TRAINING: STUDENTS AND STARTERS

New entrants to higher education[1] by level, mode of study[2], gender and age[3], 2000/01[4,5]

United Kingdom   Home and Overseas Students   Thousands

| | Postgraduate level | | | | | | First degree | | Other Undergraduate | | Total higher education students[6] | |
| | PHD's & equivalent | | Masters and Others | | Total Postgraduate | | | | | | | |
	Full-time	Part-time	Full-time	Part-time	Full-time	Part-time	Full-time	Part-time	Full-time	Part-time	Full-time[6]	Part-time[6]
All												
Age <16	-	-	-	-	-	-	-	-	-	0.1	-	0.1
16	-	-	-	-	-	-	0.3	-	0.3	0.4	0.6	0.4
17	-	-	-	-	-	-	9.6	-	3.5	1.0	13.1	1.1
18	-	-	-	-	-	-	136.4	0.4	19.4	5.5	155.9	5.9
19	-	-	0.1	0.1	0.1	0.1	74.0	0.6	17.0	7.8	91.2	8.5
20	0.1	-	1.0	0.1	1.1	0.1	29.3	1.2	13.0	8.5	43.4	9.9
21	0.8	-	13.4	1.0	14.1	1.0	18.6	1.5	9.2	7.9	41.9	10.4
22	1.8	0.1	16.1	2.1	17.8	2.1	11.4	1.3	7.0	7.9	36.2	11.4
23	1.3	0.1	12.6	2.5	13.9	2.6	7.4	1.2	5.2	8.4	26.6	12.2
24	1.0	0.1	9.4	2.9	10.4	3.0	5.1	1.2	3.8	8.7	19.2	12.9
25	0.8	0.1	7.2	3.2	8.0	3.3	3.9	1.2	2.9	8.6	14.8	13.1
26	0.7	0.1	5.8	3.3	6.5	3.4	3.2	1.2	2.4	8.8	12.1	13.4
27	0.6	0.1	4.6	3.5	5.3	3.6	2.7	1.2	2.1	9.0	10.1	13.9
28	0.5	0.1	4.1	3.6	4.6	3.7	2.4	1.2	1.9	9.0	9.0	14.0
29	0.4	0.1	3.4	3.7	3.9	3.8	2.2	1.2	1.7	9.0	7.9	14.0
30+	2.9	3.1	23.7	58.0	26.5	61.0	21.3	19.0	18.9	165.1	66.8	245.4
Unknown	-	-	0.3	0.9	0.3	0.9	0.3	0.2	0.4	5.7	1.0	6.8
All ages	**10.8**	**3.9**	**101.7**	**84.9**	**112.5**	**88.8**	**328.2**	**32.7**	**108.7**	**271.2**	**549.9**	**393.3**
Males												
Age <16	-	-	-	-	-	-	-	-	-	0.1	-	0.1
16	-	-	-	-	-	-	0.2	-	0.1	0.2	0.3	0.2
17	-	-	-	-	-	-	4.2	-	1.5	0.5	5.7	0.5
18	-	-	-	-	-	-	62.0	0.2	9.1	3.4	71.2	3.6
19	-	-	-	0.1	-	0.1	35.8	0.3	8.4	4.5	44.3	5.0
20	-	-	0.4	0.1	0.5	0.1	15.1	0.6	6.0	4.5	21.5	5.1
21	0.4	-	5.5	0.4	5.9	0.4	9.9	0.7	4.0	3.7	19.9	4.8
22	1.0	-	7.2	0.7	8.2	0.8	6.2	0.6	3.1	3.4	17.5	4.8
23	0.7	-	5.7	0.9	6.4	1.0	4.1	0.5	2.4	3.4	12.9	4.9
24	0.6	-	4.4	1.1	4.9	1.1	2.7	0.5	1.8	3.5	9.4	5.1
25	0.4	-	3.4	1.2	3.8	1.3	2.0	0.5	1.3	3.4	7.1	5.2
26	0.4	0.1	2.8	1.3	3.2	1.3	1.5	0.5	1.1	3.4	5.7	5.3
27	0.4	0.1	2.3	1.5	2.7	1.5	1.3	0.4	0.8	3.7	4.9	5.7
28	0.3	0.1	2.1	1.5	2.4	1.6	1.2	0.5	0.8	3.7	4.3	5.8
29	0.3	0.1	1.8	1.7	2.0	1.7	1.0	0.4	0.7	3.8	3.7	6.0
30+	1.7	1.7	12.3	25.8	14.0	27.5	7.5	5.9	6.0	62.4	27.6	95.9
Unknown	-	-	0.2	0.5	0.2	0.5	0.2	0.1	0.2	2.3	0.5	2.9
All ages	**6.2**	**2.1**	**48.1**	**36.7**	**54.3**	**38.8**	**154.7**	**11.6**	**47.4**	**110.0**	**256.6**	**160.8**
Females												
Age <16	-	-	-	-	-	-	-	-	-	-	-	-
16	-	-	-	-	-	-	0.2	-	0.2	0.2	0.3	0.2
17	-	-	-	-	-	-	5.4	-	2.0	0.5	7.4	0.5
18	-	-	-	-	-	-	74.4	0.2	10.3	2.1	84.7	2.3
19	-	-	-	-	-	-	38.2	0.3	8.6	3.2	46.9	3.6
20	-	-	0.6	0.1	0.6	0.1	14.2	0.6	7.1	4.1	21.9	4.8
21	0.3	-	7.9	0.6	8.2	0.6	8.7	0.8	5.1	4.1	22.0	5.5
22	0.7	-	8.9	1.3	9.6	1.4	5.2	0.7	3.8	4.5	18.7	6.6
23	0.5	-	7.0	1.6	7.5	1.6	3.3	0.7	2.8	5.0	13.6	7.3
24	0.4	-	5.0	1.8	5.4	1.9	2.4	0.8	2.0	5.1	9.8	7.8
25	0.4	0.1	3.8	1.9	4.2	2.0	1.9	0.8	1.6	5.2	7.7	7.9
26	0.3	0.1	3.0	2.0	3.3	2.0	1.6	0.8	1.4	5.3	6.4	8.1
27	0.3	0.1	2.3	2.0	2.6	2.1	1.4	0.7	1.3	5.4	5.2	8.2
28	0.2	0.1	2.1	2.0	2.3	2.1	1.3	0.7	1.1	5.3	4.7	8.1
29	0.2	0.1	1.7	2.0	1.9	2.1	1.3	0.7	1.0	5.2	4.2	8.0
30+	1.2	1.4	11.3	32.2	12.5	33.6	13.8	13.1	12.8	102.6	39.2	149.5
Unknown	-	-	0.1	0.4	0.1	0.5	0.2	0.1	0.2	3.3	0.5	3.9
All ages	**4.6**	**1.8**	**53.6**	**48.2**	**58.2**	**50.0**	**173.5**	**21.0**	**61.3**	**161.2**	**293.3**	**232.5**

Sources: Department for Education and Skills; National Assembly for Wales; Scottish Executive; Northern Ireland Department for Employment and Learning

1 Figures reflect those on a first year of study, i.e. not necessarily brand new entrants to higher education. Higher Education Institution figures include Open University students.

2 Full-time includes sandwich, and for Scotland, short full-time. Part-time comprises both day and evening, including block release (except for Scotland) and open/distance learning.

3 Ages as at 31 August 2000 (1 July for Northern Ireland and 31 December for Scotland).

4 Figures for students (other than in Scotland further education institutions) are snapshots counted at a particular point in the year [December for UK HE institutions and FE institutions in Wales, November for FE institutions in England and Northern Ireland]. Students starting courses after these dates will not therefore be counted. Figures for Scotland, however, are whole year (not snapshot) enrolments (rather than headcounts) for 1999/00.

5 Provisional. Figures for higher education students in further education institutions (except for Northern Ireland) relate to 1999/00.

6 Includes students in FEIs in Wales who cannot be identified by level of study.

3.13 POST COMPULSORY EDUCATION AND TRAINING: STUDENTS AND STARTERS

Starts in TEC Delivered Government-Supported Training programmes by region – time series

England   Thousands

	1990-91	1995-96	1998-99	1999-00[1]	2000-01
Work-Based Training for Young People[2,3]					
Government Office Region[4]					
North East	23.9	20.5	18.5	19.7	20.3
North West	46.5	52.2	43.4	45.9	47.2
Yorkshire and the Humber	30.7	31.3	27.9	30.1	31.7
East Midlands[5]	30.9	25.2	20.5	21.8	21.8
West Midlands	33.9	28.0	25.8	28.3	29.2
Eastern[5]	..	23.3	19.1	19.9	21.7
London	13.6	23.9	20.7	24.5	26.1
South East	24.8	32.8	26.0	26.8	28.4
South West	21.5	22.7	20.5	20.7	21.2
England[6]	225.9	259.8	222.6	237.7	247.6
Advanced Modern Apprenticeships[7]					
North East	.	2.5	6.1	6.2	6.2
North West	.	6.8	15.6	15.7	16.0
Yorkshire and the Humber	.	4.3	8.8	8.5	9.4
East Midlands	.	2.7	7.1	7.4	7.3
West Midlands	.	2.4	10.2	10.5	10.3
Eastern	.	1.5	8.1	7.7	7.3
London	.	1.9	8.2	9.0	9.4
South East	.	1.9	10.4	10.7	10.6
South West	.	1.8	7.8	8.4	8.1
England[6]	.	25.8	82.3	84.1	84.6
Foundation Modern Apprenticeships[8]					
England	.	.	36.8	86.6	103.7
Other Training[9]					
England	225.9	250.7	119.1	78.8	57.0
Life Skills/Skill Build					
England	.	.	.	6.0	23.8
Work-Based Learning for Adults[10]					
Government Office Region[4]					
North East	35.8	19.7	8.3	8.1	7.9
North West	52.7	39.8	16.6	16.9	16.7
Yorkshire and the Humber	44.9	26.6	11.2	10.7	12.0
East Midlands[5]	26.7	16.6	6.8	6.7	7.5
West Midlands	36.4	25.0	10.9	12.1	13.3
Eastern[5]	..	15.8	6.4	6.5	7.1
London	38.7	31.7	22.3	25.2	26.9
South East	25.4	18.5	8.3	8.9	9.3
South West	19.5	18.8	7.2	7.7	7.6
England[6]	280.2	212.4	98.1	102.7	108.3
All starts in TEC delivered Government-Supported Training programmes					
England	506.1	488.8	320.0	340.4	355.9

Sources: TEC Management Information.

1 Includes revised figures.

2 Includes Advanced Modern Apprenticeships, Foundation Modern Apprenticeships, Other Training, and, from October 1999, Life Skills (LS) and Skill Build.

3 From 1995-96, figures for Work-Based Training do not equate the sum of the starts on Modern Apprenticeships, National Traineeships and Other Training because they exclude conversions between programmes whereas the figures for individual programmes include conversions from other programmes.

4 Government Office Regions in England plus country total for England.

5 For 1991, Eastern figures were included with East Midlands.

6 The England figure may not be the sum of the regional figures shown due to rounding.

7 Formerly known as Modern Apprenticeships.

8 Formerly known as National Traineeships.

9 Other Training includes Youth Credits & Youth Training.

10 The Employment Training programme ran from 1990 until 1993 when it was replaced by Training for Work (TfW). In 1997-98 this was replaced by Work-based Training for Adults (WBTA) which became Work-Based Learning for Adults (WBLA) in March 1999. 1996-97 in-training figures for TfW included Pre-Vocational Pilots but from April 1997 onwards Pre-Vocational Training became part of mainstream Work-Based Learning for Adults.

POST COMPULSORY EDUCATION AND TRAINING: STUDENTS AND STARTERS
Work-Based Training for Young People: characteristics of starts – time series

England   Percentages

	1997-98	1998-99	1999-00	2000-01	Apr 00-Jun 00	Jul 00-Sep 00	Oct 00-Dec 00	Jan 01-Mar 01
ADVANCED MODERN APPRENTICESHIPS[1]								
As a percentage of all starters								
gender								
Males	53	53	52	51	42	59	51	45
Females	47	47	48	49	58	41	49	55
ethnic origin								
White	96	95	95	95	95	95	95	95
Black/African/Caribbean	1	2	2	2	2	2	2	2
Asian	2	2	2	2	2	2	2	2
Other	1	1	1	1	1	1	1	1
special needs								
People with disabilities[2]	3	2	2	2	2	2	2	2
Literacy/numeracy needs	..	..	..	..	..	..	..	..
English/Welsh/Gaelic for speakers of other languages	..	..	..	..	..	..	..	..
FOUNDATION MODERN APPRENTICESHIPS[3]								
As a percentage of all starters								
gender								
Males	51	44	47	46	43	50	46	45
Females	49	56	53	54	57	50	54	55
ethnic origin								
White	93	95	94	94	92	95	94	94
Black/African/Caribbean	2	2	2	2	3	2	2	2
Asian	2	2	3	3	3	2	3	3
Other	3	1	1	1	2	1	1	1
special needs								
People with disabilities[2]	7	4	3	3	3	3	3	2
Literacy/numeracy needs	..	..	..	..	..	..	..	..
English/Welsh/Gaelic for speakers of other languages	..	..	..	..	..	..	..	..
OTHER TRAINING[4]								
As a percentage of all starters								
gender								
Males	52	54	59	59	57	60	61	58
Females	48	46	41	41	43	40	39	42
ethnic origin								
White	93	92	89	87	89	89	87	87
Black/African/Caribbean	3	3	4	5	4	4	5	5
Asian	3	4	5	6	5	5	6	6
Other	1	1	2	2	2	2	2	2
special needs								
People with disabilities[2]	6	7	7	6	5	7	5	6
Literacy/numeracy needs	8	13	19	18	15	20	17	16
English/Welsh/Gaelic for speakers of other languages	1	-	1	-	1	-	-	1

Source: Department for Education and Skills

1 Formerly known as Modern Apprenticeships.
2 Based on trainee's self-assessment.
3 Formerly known as National Traineeships.
4 Other Training includes Youth Credits & Youth Training.

3.15 POST COMPULSORY EDUCATION AND TRAINING: STUDENTS AND STARTERS
Work-Based Learning for Adults[1,2] : characteristics of starts – time series

England   Percentages

	1997-98	1998-99	1999-00	2000-01	Apr 00- Jun 00	Jul 00- Sep 00	Oct 00- Dec 00	Jan 01- Mar 01
As a percentage of all starters								
gender								
Males	68	68	69	69	69	69	68	69
Females	32	32	31	31	31	31	32	31
age								
18-24[3]	24	.	.	.	.	.	.	.
25-49	65	84	82	81	82	81	81	81
50-59	11	16	17	18	18	18	19	19
unemployment duration before entry								
0-5 months	19	22	22	24	23	23	25	27
6-12 months	29	28	28	28	28	29	27	27
13-23 months	21	18	18	17	18	17	16	17
24-35 months	11	11	12	12	12	12	11	12
36+ months	19	21	21	19	19	19	20	18
ethnic origin								
White	85	82	81	79	80	78	79	81
Black/African/Caribbean	7	9	9	9	9	10	9	9
Indian/Pakistani/Bangladeshi/Sri Lankan	5	5	5	6	6	6	6	6
Other	3	4	5	6	5	6	6	5
special needs group								
People with disabilities[4]	19	21	21	21	21	20	21	22
Literacy/numeracy needs[4]	9	12	13	15	15	16	16	15
English/Welsh/Gaelic for speakers of other languages	3	4	6	7	6	7	7	8

Source: Department for Education and Skills

1 Starts up to and including March 1993 were on Employment Training. Starts after that were on Training for Work (TfW), which superseded Employment Training and Employment
   Action. Differences in the coverage of the programme and its eligibility rules account for much of the change since March 1993.
2 Prior to April 1993 Training for Work was Employment Training/Employment Action. 1996-97 starts figures for TfW include Pre-Vocational Pilots. From April 1997
   onwards Pre-Vocational Training became part of mainstream work-based learning for adults (WBLA).
3 There is no provision for 18-24 year olds on WBLA from April 1998.
4 Based on trainee's self-assessment.

THIS PAGE HAS BEEN LEFT BLANK

POST COMPULSORY EDUCATION AND TRAINING: JOB-RELATED TRAINING

3.16 Participation in job-related training[1] in the last four weeks by economic activity and region[2], 2001

United Kingdom: People of working age[3]

Thousands and percentages[4]

	Thousands			Percentages[4]		
	All	Males	Females	All	Males	Females
All people						
United Kingdom	5,327	2,539	2,788	14.6	13.3	16.0
North East	222	111	111	14.1	13.5	14.7
North West	636	304	333	15.2	13.8	16.8
Yorkshire and the Humber	467	223	244	15.1	13.7	16.8
East Midlands	347	162	185	13.4	11.9	15.1
West Midlands	455	202	253	14.0	11.8	16.5
Eastern	474	236	238	14.3	13.5	15.1
London	767	374	393	16.3	15.2	17.5
South East	728	344	384	14.7	13.3	16.3
South West	447	221	226	15.2	14.3	16.2
England	4,543	2,175	2,367	14.8	13.5	16.3
Wales	232	112	121	13.2	12.1	14.5
Scotland	435	196	239	13.7	12.0	15.7
Northern Ireland	117	56	61	11.5	10.6	12.4
Employees[5,6]						
United Kingdom	3,934	1,855	2,079	16.4	14.4	18.5
North East	152	76	77	15.6	14.3	17.1
North West	471	226	244	17.2	15.7	18.9
Yorkshire and the Humber	340	156	184	16.7	14.4	19.4
East Midlands	249	118	132	14.4	12.6	16.4
West Midlands	360	158	201	16.5	13.4	20.3
Eastern	373	183	190	16.1	14.7	17.6
London	504	245	259	17.6	15.8	19.8
South East	581	272	308	16.6	14.5	19.1
South West	341	168	173	17.1	16.0	18.3
England	3,370	1,602	1,768	16.6	14.7	18.7
Wales	168	76	92	16.1	13.7	18.8
Scotland	319	141	179	15.3	13.0	17.7
Northern Ireland	77	37	40	13.0	11.8	14.3
Self-employed[6,7]						
United Kingdom	237	146	91	8.0	6.6	12.3
North East	*	*	*	*	*	*
North West	26	16	10	9.2	7.3	15.6
Yorkshire and the Humber	19	11	*	9.2	7.0	*
East Midlands	13	*	*	6.4	*	*
West Midlands	17	10	*	7.9	6.1	*
Eastern	26	18	*	8.2	7.6	*
London	40	23	17	8.8	6.9	14.0
South East	31	21	10	6.6	6.3	7.5
South West	26	14	12	8.6	6.4	14.3
England	206	125	81	8.1	6.6	12.3
Wales	*	*	*	*	*	*
Scotland	19	12	*	9.0	7.5	*
Northern Ireland	*	*	*	*	*	*

Source: Labour Force Survey, Spring 2001[10]

1 Job-related training includes both on and off-the-job training.
2 Government Office Regions in England and each UK country.
3 Working age is defined as males aged 16-64 and females 16-59.
4 Expressed as a percentage of the total number of people in each group.
5 Employees are those in employment excluding the self-employed, unpaid family workers and those on government employment and training programmes.
6 The split into employees and self-employed is based on respondents' own assessment of their employment status.
7 Self-employed are those in employment excluding employees, unpaid family workers and those on government employment and training programmes.
8 Unemployed according to the International Labour Office (ILO) definition.
9 Economically inactive are those who are neither in employment nor ILO unemployed.
10 Users of these data should read the LFS entry in Annex A, as it contains important information about the LFS and the concepts and definitions used.

3.16

POST COMPULSORY EDUCATION AND TRAINING: JOB-RELATED TRAINING

Participation in job-related training[1] in the last four weeks by economic activity and region[2], 2001

United Kingdom: People of working age[3]   Thousands and percentages[4]

	Thousands			Percentages[4]		
	All	Males	Females	All	Males	Females
ILO unemployed[8]						
United Kingdom	153	80	72	11.0	9.4	13.5
North East	*	*	*	*	*	*
North West	18	*	10	10.7	*	18.4
Yorkshire and the Humber	12	*	*	9.8	*	*
East Midlands	13	*	*	13.1	*	*
West Midlands	17	*	*	13.1	*	*
Eastern	11	*	*	10.7	*	*
London	28	16	12	13.1	12.3	14.3
South East	17	10	*	14.1	14.5	*
South West	*	*	*	*	*	*
England	133	69	64	11.8	10.2	14.2
Wales	*	*	*	*	*	*
Scotland	*	*	*	*	*	*
Northern Ireland	*	*	*	*	*	*
Economically inactive[9]						
United Kingdom	889	387	502	11.2	12.4	10.5
North East	42	20	22	10.3	11.8	9.2
North West	106	44	62	10.9	10.8	11.0
Yorkshire and the Humber	83	41	42	11.8	13.7	10.3
East Midlands	66	26	40	12.4	12.7	12.2
West Midlands	54	21	33	7.6	7.5	7.7
Eastern	57	25	33	10.0	12.0	8.8
London	182	83	99	15.9	19.5	13.8
South East	89	35	54	10.4	11.6	9.8
South West	66	31	35	12.3	14.2	11.0
England	746	326	420	11.6	13.0	10.7
Wales	43	23	20	8.8	10.9	7.2
Scotland	79	31	48	11.3	10.8	11.6
Northern Ireland	21	*	14	7.4	*	7.8

Source: Labour Force Survey, Spring 2001[10]

See previous page for footnotes.

POST COMPULSORY EDUCATION AND TRAINING: JOB-RELATED TRAINING

3.17 Participation by employees[1] in job-related training[2] in the last four weeks by type of training and a range of personal characteristics, 2001

United Kingdom: Employees[1] of working age[3]   Thousands and percentages[4]

	Total number of employees (thousands)	of which: receiving off-the-job training only (%)	receiving on-the-job training only (%)	receiving both on and off-the-job training (%)	receiving any training (%)
All employees	24,056	8.1	5.1	3.2	16.4
By gender					
Males	12,841	6.8	4.7	2.9	14.4
Females	11,214	9.5	5.5	3.6	18.5
By age					
16-19	1,407	11.5	5.7	6.7	23.8
20-24	2,322	10.2	7.8	5.4	23.5
25-29	2,941	9.0	5.3	3.6	17.9
30-39	6,783	8.6	5.0	3.2	16.8
40-49	5,663	7.8	5.0	2.7	15.4
50-64	4,939	5.1	3.7	1.6	10.4
By ethnic origin					
White	21,279	8.0	5.0	3.2	16.2
Non-white	1,197	9.3	5.3	3.4	18.0
of which:					
Mixed	119	*	*	*	17.7
Asian or Asian British	562	8.7	4.1	2.7	15.4
Black or Black British	336	10.7	5.7	4.4	21.2
Chinese	48	*	*	*	20.0
Other ethnic group	131	10.4	*	*	21.0
DNA/Imputed	1,576	8.3	5.4	3.3	17.1
By highest qualification held[5]					
Degree or equivalent	4,329	12.8	6.1	4.7	23.7
Higher Education qualification (below degree level)	2,358	12.1	6.3	5.5	23.9
GCE A level or equivalent	5,867	8.9	5.2	3.1	17.1
GCSE grades A* to C or equivalent	5,590	6.7	5.4	3.3	15.5
Other	3,184	4.8	4.1	1.7	10.6
None	2,566	1.6	2.5	0.7	4.7
By region					
United Kingdom	24,056	8.1	5.1	3.2	16.4
North East	976	7.1	5.1	3.4	15.6
North West	2,738	8.3	5.2	3.7	17.2
Yorkshire and the Humber	2,030	7.6	5.8	3.3	16.7
East Midlands	1,736	6.1	5.4	2.8	14.4
West Midlands	2,178	7.9	5.2	3.4	16.5
Eastern	2,320	7.5	5.4	3.2	16.1
London	2,863	9.5	5.1	2.9	17.6
South East	3,491	8.4	5.1	3.0	16.6
South West	1,996	9.2	4.5	3.4	17.1
England	20,327	8.1	5.2	3.2	16.6
Wales	1,046	8.1	4.3	3.7	16.1
Scotland	2,093	7.6	4.6	3.1	15.3
Northern Ireland	590	7.4	3.6	2.0	13.0
Time series (Spring of each year)[6]					
1991	21,920	8.3	4.3	2.3	14.9
1996	22,092	8.5	3.9	2.4	14.8
1999	23,392	8.7	4.4	2.9	15.9
2000	23,802	8.3	4.6	3.2	16.1
2001	24,056	8.1	5.1	3.2	16.4

Source: Labour Force Survey, Spring 2001[7]

1 Employees are those in employment excluding the self-employed, unpaid family workers and those on government employment and training programmes.
2 Job-related training includes both on and off-the-job training.
3 Working age is defined as males aged 16-64 and females aged 16-59.
4 Expressed as a percentage of the total number of people in each group.
5 Apart from rounding, figures may not sum to grand totals because of questions in the LFS which were unanswered or did not apply.
6 Due to a change in the LFS questionnaire, data from Summer 1994 onwards are not comparable with earlier figures.
7 Users of these data should read the LFS entry in Annex A, as it contains important information about the LFS and the concepts.

POST COMPULSORY EDUCATION AND TRAINING: JOB-RELATED TRAINING

Participation by employees[1] in job-related training[2] in the last four weeks by a range of economic characteristics, 2001

United Kingdom: Employees[1] of working age[3]

Thousands and percentages[4]

	Thousands			Percentages[4]		
	All	Males	Females	All	Males	Females
All employees	3,934	1,855	2,079	16.4	14.4	18.5
By industry						
Agriculture, forestry & fishing	12	*	*	6.5	*	*
Energy and water supply	50	39	11	16.2	15.9	17.2
Manufacturing	468	354	114	10.9	11.0	10.7
Construction	162	145	17	12.0	12.3	10.4
Distribution, hotels & restaurants	614	275	340	13.2	12.7	13.7
Transport	204	145	60	11.7	11.3	13.1
Banking, finance & insurance	619	323	296	16.7	16.3	17.2
Public administration, education & health	1,625	495	1,129	24.6	24.2	24.7
Other services	177	70	107	14.9	12.7	16.8
By occupation						
Managers & administrators	473	300	173	14.7	13.2	18.3
Professional	755	369	386	26.6	22.3	32.7
Associate professional & technical	772	361	411	24.1	21.1	27.5
Clerical & secretarial	527	122	405	15.2	16.2	14.9
Craft & related	287	267	20	12.3	12.5	9.8
Personal & protective services	371	55	316	21.1	19.9	21.3
Sales	307	96	211	15.1	15.4	15.0
Plant & machine operatives	154	131	23	7.3	7.6	6.0
Other	286	152	134	9.3	9.0	9.6
By full-time/part-time work[5]						
Full-time	3,003	1,672	1,331	16.4	14.1	20.7
Part-time	931	183	748	16.1	18.3	15.7
of which[6]:						
students	332	132	199	30.7	28.2	32.7
could not find full-time job	69	19	49	12.8	9.9	14.4
did not want full-time job	518	26	492	12.8	8.8	13.1
By employment status[6]						
Permanent job	3,593	1,711	1,882	16.1	14.3	18.2
Temporary job	327	138	189	20.7	18.5	22.7
of which:						
seasonal / casual work	61	26	35	17.7	16.5	18.7
contract for fixed term or task	188	78	110	24.6	21.7	27.2
agency temping	34	13	21	12.1	9.1	15.4
other	44	21	24	23.8	26.2	22.1

Source: Labour Force Survey, Spring 2001[7]

1 Employees are those in employment excluding the self-employed, unpaid family workers and those on government employment and training programmes.

2 Job-related training includes both on and off-the-job training.

3 Working age is defined as males aged 16-64 and females aged 16-59.

4 Expressed as a percentage of the total number of people in each group.

5 The split between employees working full-time and part-time is based on respondents' own assessment.

6 Apart from rounding, figures may not sum to grand totals because of questions in the LFS which were unanswered or did not apply.

7 Users of these data should read the LFS entry in Annex A, as it contains important information about the LFS and the concepts and definitions used.

3.19 POST COMPULSORY EDUCATION AND TRAINING: JOB-RELATED TRAINING

Participation by employees[1] in job-related training[2] in the last four weeks by type of training and a range of economic characteristics, 2001

United Kingdom: Employees[1] of working age[3]

Thousands and percentages[4]

	Total number of employees (thousands)	of which: receiving off-the-job training only (%)	receiving on-the-job training only (%)	receiving both on and off-the-job training (%)	receiving any training (%)
All employees	24,056	8.1	5.1	3.2	16.4
By industry[5]					
Agriculture, forestry & fishing	186	3.5	*	*	6.5
Energy & water supply	307	7.2	5.8	3.2	16.2
Manufacturing	4,304	4.8	3.8	2.3	10.9
Construction	1,345	5.3	3.3	3.4	12.0
Distribution, hotels & restaurants	4,651	7.4	4.1	1.8	13.2
Transport	1,740	5.5	4.5	1.7	11.7
Banking, finance & insurance	3,700	8.1	5.2	3.4	16.7
Public administration, education & health	6,615	11.9	7.4	5.2	24.6
Other services	1,184	8.7	3.6	2.6	14.9
By occupation[5]					
Managers & administrators	3,212	8.1	3.8	2.8	14.7
Professional	2,834	13.5	7.0	6.0	26.6
Associate professional & technical	3,203	11.6	7.2	5.3	24.1
Clerical & secretarial	3,478	7.8	5.2	2.1	15.2
Craft & related	2,339	4.5	3.6	4.1	12.3
Personal & protective services	1,762	8.9	6.8	5.3	21.1
Sales	2,030	8.1	5.6	1.4	15.1
Plant & machine operatives	2,109	2.7	3.5	1.0	7.3
Other	3,076	5.4	2.9	0.9	9.3
By full-time/part-time work[5,6]					
Full-time	18,274	7.5	5.4	3.5	16.4
Part-time	5,777	9.9	3.9	2.3	16.1
of which:					
students	1,079	24.5	2.5	3.6	30.7
could not find full-time job	536	5.9	4.8	2.2	12.8
did not want full-time job	4,046	6.7	4.1	2.0	12.8
By employment status[5]					
Permanent	22,302	7.9	5.1	3.2	16.1
Temporary	1,577	10.9	5.6	4.2	20.7
of which:					
seasonal / casual work	345	11.0	*	*	17.7
contract for fixed term or task	766	11.4	7.6	5.6	24.6
agency temping	281	5.9	3.3	2.8	12.1
other	185	11.5	7.1	5.2	23.8

Source: Labour Force Survey, Spring 2001[7]

1 Employees are those in employment excluding the self-employed, unpaid family workers and those on government employment and training programmes.
2 Job-related training includes both on and off-the-job training.
3 Working age is defined as males aged 16-64 and females aged 16-59.
4 Expressed as a percentage of the total number of people in each group.
5 Apart from rounding, figures may not sum to grand totals because of questions in the LFS which were unanswered or did not apply.
6 The split between employees working full-time and part-time is based on respondents' own assessment.
7 Users of these data should read the LFS entry in Annex A, as it contains important information about the LFS and the concepts and definitions used.

THIS PAGE HAS BEEN LEFT BLANK

3.20 POST COMPULSORY EDUCATION AND TRAINING: JOB-RELATED TRAINING

Participation by employees[1] in job-related training[2] in the last four weeks by region[3] and a range of personal and economic characteristics, 2001

United Kingdom: Employees[1] of working age[4]

Thousands and percentages[5]

	Region[3]						
	United Kingdom	North East	North West	Yorkshire and the Humber	East Midlands	West Midlands	Eastern
All employees	3,934	152	471	340	249	360	373
By gender							
Males	1,855	76	226	156	118	158	183
Females	2,079	77	244	184	132	201	190
By age							
16-19	335	14	48	29	28	29	32
20-24	546	27	53	48	35	49	54
25-29	526	14	61	39	28	47	51
30-39	1,140	41	140	105	67	103	101
40-49	872	34	108	74	59	81	80
50-64	515	21	60	45	34	51	55
By highest qualification held[6]							
Degree or equivalent	1,025	28	124	78	64	93	91
Higher Education qualification (below degree level)	565	26	73	51	37	57	44
GCE A level or equivalent	1,006	40	114	88	56	81	112
GCSE grades A* to C or equivalent	864	36	117	75	61	83	81
Other	338	14	28	35	23	32	31
None	121	*	14	11	*	13	12
By industry							
Agriculture & fishing	12	*	*	*	*	*	*
Energy & water	50	*	*	*	*	*	*
Manufacturing	468	23	68	45	38	55	50
Construction	162	10	17	14	13	10	16
Distribution, hotels & restaurants	614	20	76	55	39	54	53
Transport & communication	204	*	17	17	*	15	20
Banking, finance & insurance etc	619	13	69	44	30	44	59
Public admin, education & health	1,625	68	195	146	107	163	149
Other services	177	*	24	12	11	12	19
By occupation							
Managers & administrators	473	13	57	31	31	38	44
Professional	755	24	86	57	50	84	67
Associate professional & technical	772	28	91	69	42	62	77
Clerical & secretarial	527	18	73	39	35	45	51
Craft & related	287	14	41	30	15	26	32
Personal & protective services	371	16	38	36	24	38	37
Sales	307	15	36	34	18	25	24
Plant & machine operatives	154	12	15	12	16	17	18
Other	286	11	34	30	19	25	23

Percentages[5]

	United Kingdom	North East	North West	Yorkshire and the Humber	East Midlands	West Midlands	Eastern
All employees	16.4	15.6	17.2	16.7	14.4	16.5	16.1
By gender							
Males	14.4	14.3	15.7	14.4	12.6	13.4	14.7
Females	18.5	17.1	18.9	19.4	16.4	20.3	17.6
By age							
16-19	23.8	23.0	29.3	25.9	26.2	20.8	22.9
20-24	23.5	27.8	22.4	23.6	21.7	23.3	26.2
25-29	17.9	13.7	17.9	16.9	14.4	19.0	17.7
30-39	16.8	15.6	17.8	18.4	13.7	17.3	15.6
40-49	15.4	13.9	16.2	15.2	14.3	15.7	14.8
50-64	10.4	10.5	11.1	10.6	8.9	10.8	10.9
By highest qualification held							
Degree or equivalent	23.7	22.5	28.7	26.4	24.4	29.4	23.8
Higher Education qualification (below degree level)	23.9	26.3	25.6	25.5	24.7	25.9	22.5
GCE A level or equivalent	17.1	15.9	15.9	16.8	13.3	16.0	19.3
GCSE grades A* to C or equivalent	15.5	14.6	17.0	16.3	14.4	15.5	13.6
Other	10.6	11.3	9.4	12.1	10.0	10.4	9.3
None	4.7	*	4.7	4.6	*	4.8	5.2
By industry							
Agriculture & fishing	6.5	*	*	*	*	*	*
Energy & water	16.2	*	*	*	*	*	*
Manufacturing	10.9	11.5	12.3	10.8	9.1	9.8	12.0
Construction	12.0	16.8	11.9	11.0	14.3	9.2	11.9
Distribution, hotels & restaurants	13.2	11.4	13.8	13.4	12.0	12.8	12.0
Transport & communication	11.7	*	9.1	12.9	*	10.2	11.0
Banking, finance & insurance etc	16.7	13.2	19.4	17.5	14.1	17.6	14.7
Public admin, education & health	24.6	22.9	24.8	25.9	24.4	29.0	25.5
Other services	14.9	*	20.5	13.9	13.9	15.0	17.0
By occupation							
Managers & administrators	14.7	14.3	17.0	14.0	14.6	14.5	13.1
Professional	26.6	25.1	27.8	29.1	28.4	34.4	25.5
Associate professional & technical	24.1	23.1	25.2	27.2	20.5	24.9	24.3
Clerical & secretarial	15.2	14.0	17.1	15.5	15.2	16.2	14.2
Craft & related	12.3	14.0	15.6	12.9	7.6	9.7	14.4
Personal & protective services	21.1	22.5	19.3	21.9	19.0	25.6	21.0
Sales	15.1	14.3	15.3	17.8	13.8	13.4	13.4
Plant & machine operatives	7.3	10.2	5.7	5.9	7.4	7.1	9.0
Other	9.3	8.1	9.6	9.8	7.7	8.4	8.5

Source: Labour Force Survey, Spring 2001[7]

1 Employees are those in employment excluding the self-employed, unpaid family workers and those on government employment and training programmes.
2 Job-related training includes both on and off-the-job training.
3 Government Office Regions in England and each UK country.
4 Working age is defined as males aged 16-64 and females aged 16-59.
5 Expressed as a percentage of the total number of people in each group.
6 Apart from rounding, figures may not sum to grand totals because of questions in the LFS which were unanswered or did not apply.
7 Users of these data should read the LFS entry in Annex A, as it contains important information about the LFS and the concepts and definitions used.

3.20 POST COMPULSORY EDUCATION AND TRAINING: JOB-RELATED TRAINING

Participation by employees[1] in job-related training[2] in the last four weeks by region[3] and a range of personal and economic characteristics, 2001

United Kingdom: Employees[1] of working age[4]

Thousands and percentages[5]

	London	South East	South West	England	Wales	Scotland	Northern Ireland
				Region[3]			
All employees	504	581	341	3,370	168	319	77
By gender							
Males	245	272	168	1,602	76	141	37
Females	259	308	173	1,768	92	179	40
By age							
16-19	26	45	30	280	15	33	*
20-24	80	74	43	463	23	48	11
25-29	92	78	44	455	18	42	11
30-39	166	165	88	976	49	92	22
40-49	87	138	85	746	43	67	16
50-64	53	81	51	450	21	36	*
By highest qualification held[6]							
Degree or equivalent	182	152	79	891	41	72	21
Higher Education qualification (below degree level)	49	71	49	457	27	70	11
GCE A level or equivalent	113	146	92	844	39	104	19
GCSE grades A* to C or equivalent	75	146	83	756	42	48	18
Other	65	51	26	306	13	16	*
None	17	11	10	102	*	*	*
By industry							
Agriculture & fishing	*	*	*	10	*	*	*
Energy & water	*	*	*	37	*	*	*
Manufacturing	30	62	36	407	23	29	*
Construction	22	26	13	141	*	12	*
Distribution, hotels & restaurants	78	85	60	519	22	61	13
Transport & communication	33	41	17	176	*	18	*
Banking, finance & insurance etc	128	102	56	546	17	47	*
Public admin, education & health	180	229	141	1,378	82	129	35
Other services	29	26	12	154	*	13	*
By occupation							
Managers & administrators	71	84	45	414	20	31	*
Professional	117	107	68	659	31	51	14
Associate professional & technical	99	127	55	650	36	73	13
Clerical & secretarial	72	78	41	451	19	43	13
Craft & related	21	33	26	240	16	24	*
Personal & protective services	42	57	38	325	13	25	*
Sales	37	40	29	258	10	35	*
Plant & machine operatives	*	21	11	129	11	11	*
Other	36	34	28	241	12	28	*

Percentages[5]

	London	South East	South West	England	Wales	Scotland	Northern Ireland
All employees	17.6	16.6	17.1	16.6	16.1	15.3	13.0
By gender							
Males	15.8	14.5	16.0	14.7	13.7	13.0	11.8
Females	19.8	19.1	18.3	18.7	18.8	17.7	14.3
By age							
16-19	24.1	19.2	22.6	23.5	22.8	27.2	*
20-24	23.2	24.3	24.3	23.9	22.7	23.0	16.3
25-29	21.7	18.3	19.3	18.3	15.2	16.7	12.6
30-39	18.6	17.5	16.3	17.0	16.8	15.6	12.8
40-49	14.2	16.8	17.8	15.6	17.1	13.4	11.8
50-64	10.9	10.6	11.6	10.7	9.4	8.6	*
By highest qualification held							
Degree or equivalent	20.9	21.9	23.6	24.0	24.9	20.6	21.4
Higher Education qualification (below degree level)	24.3	23.3	23.7	24.5	21.7	22.1	19.5
GCE A level or equivalent	20.7	17.9	19.7	17.4	16.8	15.9	13.2
GCSE grades A* to C or equivalent	14.6	16.9	15.3	15.5	16.3	14.5	12.7
Other	14.0	10.7	9.7	10.9	9.7	7.8	*
None	7.0	3.6	6.1	4.9	*	*	*
By industry							
Agriculture & fishing	*	*	*	6.6	*	*	*
Energy & water	*	*	*	17.0	*	*	*
Manufacturing	11.9	11.8	11.1	11.1	10.9	8.8	*
Construction	17.6	13.1	12.4	12.9	*	8.8	*
Distribution, hotels & restaurants	15.0	12.6	13.7	13.1	10.9	15.3	12.0
Transport & communication	13.2	14.4	15.2	11.6	*	12.4	*
Banking, finance & insurance etc	16.5	15.9	18.6	16.6	17.1	18.3	*
Public admin, education & health	24.9	25.2	24.5	25.4	24.0	20.7	16.5
Other services	14.6	14.7	13.2	15.4	*	12.7	*
By occupation							
Managers & administrators	14.4	14.3	16.4	14.7	17.9	13.4	*
Professional	26.5	23.7	29.1	27.4	24.3	21.7	21.4
Associate professional & technical	21.0	26.5	21.4	23.9	25.8	25.8	20.1
Clerical & secretarial	14.8	14.7	15.0	15.2	14.0	14.8	14.9
Craft & related	13.2	11.4	13.7	12.4	14.4	10.5	*
Personal & protective services	22.4	22.1	23.8	21.9	17.9	16.3	*
Sales	18.2	14.3	15.8	15.2	11.2	17.0	*
Plant & machine operatives	*	10.0	6.6	7.5	9.9	5.2	*
Other	12.3	8.4	10.7	9.3	8.3	10.5	*

Source: Labour Force Survey, Spring 2001[7]

See previous page for footnotes.

POST COMPULSORY EDUCATION AND TRAINING: JOB-RELATED TRAINING
Length of job-related training[1], 2001

United Kingdom: People of working age[2]

Thousands and percentages[3]

	Total receiving training[5] (thousands)	Length of training[4,11]							
		Under 1 week	1 week < 1 month	1 month < 6 months	6 months < 1 year	1 year < 2 years	2 years < 3 years	3 years or more	Ongoing or no definite limit
All people[2]	5,327	26.5	3.3	6.8	7.1	8.5	8.7	14.6	17.2
Economic activity									
Employees[6,7]	3,934	33.3	3.9	6.8	5.9	6.9	6.9	9.7	19.2
Self-employed[7,8]	237	34.5	*	6.8	7.7	5.8	4.6	5.2	26.6
ILO unemployed[9]	153	*	*	14.9	14.2	14.9	11.1	15.1	15.0
Economically inactive[10]	889	1.1	*	4.8	9.9	13.5	16.3	38.8	6.9
All employees	3,934	33.3	3.9	6.8	5.9	6.9	6.9	9.7	19.2
By gender									
Males	1,855	34.7	4.9	5.5	4.4	4.9	7.0	11.0	20.2
Females	2,079	32.1	2.9	8.0	7.3	8.7	6.8	8.5	18.2
By age									
16-19	335	5.1	*	*	5.4	11.9	22.8	27.4	13.5
20-24	546	15.9	3.4	5.3	6.2	7.0	9.5	21.9	20.8
25-29	526	31.0	3.6	6.8	5.6	5.5	7.1	9.8	19.0
30-39	1,140	38.0	5.0	7.1	5.5	7.7	5.1	6.3	18.9
40-49	872	41.9	3.9	8.3	7.0	6.4	4.7	3.9	19.0
50-64	515	47.9	3.6	8.0	5.3	4.3	*	2.4	22.5
By highest qualification held[11]									
Degree or equivalent	1,025	42.0	2.7	5.3	5.2	6.5	5.8	5.8	19.0
Higher Education qualification (below degree level)	565	39.7	3.6	8.0	6.3	5.5	6.4	7.6	17.6
GCE A level or equivalent	1,006	28.6	4.7	6.7	5.0	6.3	7.1	16.6	17.9
GCSE grades A* to C or equivalent	864	27.3	3.9	7.2	6.7	9.2	9.7	9.1	20.0
Other qualification	338	29.3	5.2	8.7	7.8	6.1	4.7	7.5	21.9
No qualification	121	25.7	*	*	8.2	9.2	*	*	23.7
By industry									
Agriculture, forestry & fishing	12	*	*	*	*	*	*	*	*
Energy & water supply	50	51.1	*	*	*	*	*	*	*
Manufacturing	468	32.6	5.5	6.2	5.3	5.9	6.7	11.7	20.3
Construction	162	33.7	*	*	*	*	9.9	18.4	15.0
Distribution, hotels & restaurants	614	20.3	2.7	5.3	6.3	9.6	10.8	17.1	18.2
Transport	204	36.7	9.1	8.7	3.8	5.3	*	*	20.3
Banking, finance & insurance	619	32.6	3.7	6.6	5.2	4.3	4.9	8.2	25.1
Public administration, education & health	1,625	38.7	3.4	7.6	6.4	7.5	5.6	6.8	18.1
Other services	177	25.4	*	8.5	8.8	9.8	13.1	8.2	14.0
By occupation									
Managers & administrators	473	44.5	3.6	6.4	3.9	5.8	4.7	4.0	19.2
Professional	755	41.5	3.2	5.9	4.2	5.4	4.9	8.7	19.5
Associate professional & technical	772	36.3	4.8	7.4	6.4	5.6	6.6	7.5	19.1
Clerical & secretarial	527	32.7	3.5	7.6	8.1	6.2	5.1	7.8	21.8
Craft & related	287	26.6	4.5	4.5	4.6	4.5	10.2	22.2	14.9
Personal & protective services	371	25.8	*	9.2	7.7	11.6	8.3	7.7	19.7
Sales	307	20.0	3.3	5.9	6.2	10.3	11.1	15.8	18.3
Plant & machine operatives	154	35.7	6.5	7.7	7.1	6.8	*	*	22.7
Other occupations	286	16.6	4.7	6.6	6.8	10.7	12.1	17.2	16.2
By region[12]									
United Kingdom	3,934	33.3	3.9	6.8	5.9	6.9	6.9	9.7	19.2
North East	152	35.3	*	7.1	6.6	6.8	*	12.7	14.8
North West	471	30.7	4.3	8.5	5.7	6.9	8.9	9.3	19.1
Yorkshire and the Humber	340	33.2	4.0	6.8	5.5	6.6	5.1	9.2	22.9
East Midlands	249	35.7	*	5.5	5.4	6.1	9.0	8.2	21.5
West Midlands	360	33.1	4.2	6.7	6.9	8.6	6.3	8.7	17.6
Eastern	373	35.1	4.6	6.0	5.7	7.1	5.3	8.3	21.7
London	504	32.4	4.6	5.7	5.7	5.9	6.6	9.9	17.9
South East	581	36.4	3.0	7.4	5.3	7.4	6.4	7.7	18.4
South West	341	33.3	4.0	8.5	5.8	7.5	6.2	10.9	16.9
England	3,370	33.8	3.9	7.0	5.8	7.0	6.7	9.2	19.1
Wales	168	33.6	*	*	8.2	8.4	8.7	11.4	17.5
Scotland	319	31.4	4.0	6.2	6.0	5.6	7.1	13.5	19.9
Northern Ireland	77	22.8	*	*	*	*	12.6	13.2	25.0

Source: Labour Force Survey, Spring 2001[13]

1 Job-related training includes both on and off-the-job training.
2 Working age is defined as males aged 16-64 and females 16-59. These figures include unpaid family workers, those on government employment and training programmes, or those who did not answer, who are excluded from the Economic activity analyses below.
3 Expressed as a percentage of those in the group who received training in the last four weeks.
4 The total length of the course was recorded not just the part completed. For people engaged on day or block release, the total length of training is given. For people who dropped out of a course the time spent on the course, not the total length is recorded.
5 People of working age who received on or off-the-job training in the last four weeks.
6 Employees are those in employment excluding the self-employed, unpaid family workers and those on government employment and training programmes.
7 The split into employees and self-employed is based on respondents' own assessment of their employment status.
8 Self-employed are those in employment excluding employees, unpaid family workers and those on government employment and training programmes.
9 Unemployed according to the International Labour Office (ILO) definition.
10 Economically inactive are those who are neither in employment nor ILO unemployed.
11 Apart from rounding, figures may not sum to grand totals because of questions in the LFS which were unanswered or did not apply.
12 Government Office Regions in England and each UK country.
13 Users of these data should read the LFS entry in Annex A, as it contains important information about the LFS and the concepts and definitions used.

3.22

POST COMPULSORY EDUCATION AND TRAINING: JOB-RELATED TRAINING

Location of off-the-job training[1], 2001

United Kingdom: People of working age[2]

Thousands and percentages[3]

	Total receiving training[1] (thousands)	Main place of training (percentages)[4]						
		Employer's premises	Another employer's premises	Private training centre	At home[5]	Further Education college or University	Other educational institution	Others
All people[2]	4,045	21.1	3.8	6.7	6.4	41.8	4.0	9.4
Economic activity								
Employees[6,7]	2,712	29.9	4.6	7.9	6.7	30.7	3.7	9.7
Self-employed[7,8]	201	7.0	7.6	11.9	11.9	27.9	6.0	21.4
ILO unemployed[9]	153	*	*	*	7.8	60.1	*	11.1
Economically inactive[10]	889	*	*	1.8	3.9	76.2	4.3	4.4
All employees	2,712	29.9	4.6	7.9	6.7	30.7	3.7	9.7
By gender								
Males	1,249	30.7	5.0	9.4	7.7	28.4	2.5	9.4
Females	1,463	29.1	4.2	6.6	6.0	32.7	4.6	9.9
By age								
16-19	255	14.9	*	*	*	64.3	5.9	*
20-24	364	22.0	*	4.9	4.9	50.3	2.7	4.7
25-29	370	28.9	5.4	8.6	8.9	26.8	*	7.8
30-39	800	32.3	4.3	9.6	9.1	23.9	3.4	11.4
40-49	591	35.4	5.9	8.6	6.4	23.2	4.6	11.7
50-64	331	36.0	7.9	9.7	4.8	17.8	3.6	14.8
By highest qualification held[4]								
Degree or equivalent	760	33.6	5.7	11.4	8.7	22.9	3.8	12.4
Higher Education qualification (below degree level)	415	34.9	5.5	7.0	6.7	28.0	2.4	11.1
GCE A level or equivalent	702	26.8	4.0	6.6	7.0	38.0	3.1	7.4
GCSE grades A* to C or equivalent	559	27.4	4.5	6.8	5.2	37.9	3.8	7.5
Other qualification	207	30.0	*	6.8	5.8	34.3	6.3	10.1
No qualification	57	33.3	*	*	*	27.1	*	*
By industry[4]								
Agriculture, forestry & fishing	10	*	*	*	*	*	*	*
Energy & water supply	32	37.5	*	*	*	*	*	*
Manufacturing	306	28.1	4.6	10.8	9.5	29.4	3.3	10.1
Construction	117	20.5	*	12.8	*	40.2	*	8.5
Distribution, hotels & restaurants	426	19.5	*	4.0	4.7	49.8	5.4	5.9
Transport	126	37.3	*	11.9	*	20.6	*	7.9
Banking, finance & insurance	427	30.0	4.4	10.1	11.2	22.2	3.0	10.5
Public administration, education & health	1,132	35.4	6.1	6.8	5.7	26.1	3.4	10.8
Other services	133	19.5	*	7.5	*	40.6	*	9.8
By occupation								
Managers & administrators	351	32.8	5.7	12.5	7.1	16.5	3.1	13.7
Professional	554	32.5	6.0	10.8	7.6	21.1	3.2	12.6
Associate professional & technical	540	36.9	5.9	8.5	8.1	24.4	2.4	8.0
Clerical & secretarial	344	28.5	*	6.4	9.0	33.7	4.1	9.9
Craft & related	202	31.2	*	6.9	5.0	37.6	*	5.9
Personal & protective services	251	28.3	5.2	4.4	4.0	37.1	4.0	9.2
Sales	193	18.7	*	*	*	53.4	5.2	6.2
Plant & machine operatives	80	35.0	*	*	*	25.0	*	*
Other occupations	196	9.7	*	*	5.1	59.2	7.1	5.1
By region[11]								
United Kingdom	2,712	29.9	4.6	7.9	6.7	30.7	3.6	9.7
North East	103	30.1	*	*	*	33.0	*	11.7
North West	328	26.2	4.9	6.1	5.8	35.1	3.7	11.6
Yorkshire and the Humber	221	32.6	4.5	5.9	5.9	31.7	*	10.4
East Midlands	156	32.7	*	9.0	7.7	32.1	*	9.0
West Midlands	248	32.3	4.0	7.7	5.6	30.6	*	9.3
Eastern	248	33.1	4.0	10.1	8.5	27.0	*	8.1
London	355	25.9	5.4	9.6	5.9	28.7	5.1	7.9
South East	400	30.0	5.0	10.5	7.3	26.8	3.0	9.8
South West	252	28.6	6.3	8.3	7.9	28.6	*	11.1
England	2,310	29.7	4.7	8.4	6.6	30.0	3.5	9.7
Wales	124	33.9	*	*	*	26.6	*	10.5
Scotland	223	30.0	4.5	*	7.2	35.4	*	9.4
Northern Ireland	55	27.3	*	*	*	49.1	*	*

Source: Labour Force Survey, Spring 2001[12]

1 Excludes those receiving on-the-job training only.
2 Working age is defined as males aged 16-64 and females 16-59. These figures include unpaid family workers, those on government employment and training programmes, or those who did not answer, who are excluded from the Economic activity analyses below.
3 Expressed as a percentage of those in the group who received training in the last four weeks.
4 Apart from rounding, figures may not sum to grand totals because of questions in the LFS which were unanswered or did not apply.
5 Includes open university, open tech, correspondence course and college.
6 Employees are those in employment excluding the self-employed, unpaid family workers and those on government employment and training programmes.
7 The split into employees and self-employed is based on respondents' own assessment of their employment status.
8 Self-employed are those in employment excluding employees, unpaid family workers and those on government employment and training programmes.
9 Unemployed according to the International Labour Office (ILO) definition.
10 Economically inactive are those who are neither in employment nor ILO unemployed.
11 Government Office Regions in England and each UK country.
12 Users of these data should read the LFS entry in Annex A, as it contains important information about the LFS and the concepts and definitions used.

POST COMPULSORY EDUCATION AND TRAINING: JOB-RELATED TRAINING

Hours spent on job-related training[1] in the last week, 2001

United Kingdom: People of working age[2]

Thousands and percentages[3]

	Total receiving training[4] (thousands)	Hours spent on training[10]						
		Less than 7.5 hours	7.5 to <15 hours	15 to < 22.5 hours	22.5 to < 30 hours	30 to < 37.5 hours	37.5 hours or more	Average number of hours per week
All people[2]	2,807	37.2	19.7	13.0	5.9	11.1	12.9	17.1
Economic activity								
Employees[5,6]	1,869	45.9	23.3	12.1	4.4	6.2	7.9	13.1
Self-employed[6,7]	113	64.7	17.8	12.7	*	*		8.0
ILO unemployed[8]	102	24.3	22.1	21.3	9.6	10.5	12.1	18.8
Economically inactive[9]	639	11.4	9.4	14.4	9.9	25.5	28.6	29.4
All employees	1,869	45.9	23.3	12.1	4.4	6.2	7.9	13.1
By gender								
Males	848	39.4	25.7	12.9	4.6	7.4	9.8	14.6
Females	1,021	51.3	21.3	11.4	4.3	5.3	6.3	11.9
By age								
16-19	209	21.9	15.4	17.0	10.6	17.0	18.0	21.4
20-24	300	33.5	22.7	12.7	5.6	11.5	13.8	17.2
25-29	241	44.0	23.7	13.6	4.1	5.0	9.6	13.8
30-39	516	49.8	26.1	12.5	3.1	3.6	4.8	11.2
40-49	394	54.0	26.0	9.9	3.4	3.0	3.5	10.0
50-64	210	64.7	19.6	7.9	*	*	*	8.7
By highest qualification held[10]								
Degree or equivalent	441	51.0	23.8	11.9	2.9	4.5	5.8	11.5
Higher Education qualification (below degree level)	268	47.0	28.3	11.1	4.5	*	5.3	11.5
GCE A level or equivalent	499	40.0	22.9	13.4	5.3	7.8	10.5	15.1
GCSE grades A* to C or equivalent	431	44.1	22.0	11.2	5.7	7.5	9.4	14.0
Other qualification	168	50.0	21.1	12.7	*	5.9	6.8	12.4
No qualification	55	54.2	*	*	*	*	*	12.0
By industry[10]								
Agriculture, forestry & fishing	*	*	*	*	*	*	*	8.8
Energy & water supply	16	*	*	*		*	*	11.1
Manufacturing	238	43.9	26.3	14.1	*	4.4	8.5	12.6
Construction	76	34.3	34.8	*	*	*	*	14.3
Distribution, hotels & restaurants	334	36.6	16.0	14.0	10.9	11.5	10.9	17.0
Transport	95	46.0	18.8	11.6	*	*	*	15.3
Banking, finance & insurance	272	49.8	22.2	13.3	*	5.6	6.5	12.1
Public administration, education & health	742	51.2	25.0	10.8	3.1	3.7	6.2	11.4
Other services	90	38.8	26.4	*	*	11.3	*	14.8
By occupation								
Managers & administrators	190	49.0	27.3	12.0	*	*	*	11.0
Professional	326	50.9	23.0	14.0	2.9	3.1	5.9	11.5
Associate professional & technical	367	44.7	28.2	11.0	4.0	4.9	7.0	12.5
Clerical & secretarial	241	57.8	22.3	9.8	*	5.1	*	9.7
Craft & related	152	32.8	30.7	11.6	*	*	15.8	16.1
Personal & protective services	193	54.0	21.3	8.8	*	5.3	8.7	12.1
Sales	174	36.4	11.6	14.6	9.1	14.4	13.5	18.3
Plant & machine operatives	74	39.5	32.1	12.8	*	*	*	12.8
Other occupations	151	31.9	12.9	16.0	11.9	15.5	11.9	18.5
By region[11]								
United Kingdom	1,869	45.9	23.3	12.1	4.4	6.2	7.9	13.1
North East	79	45.8	23.7	12.9	*	*	*	12.9
North West	225	45.9	23.1	12.4	4.3	8.1	6.4	12.9
Yorkshire and the Humber	158	46.7	22.9	13.3	*	*	6.5	12.6
East Midlands	121	53.9	22.9	9.8	*	*	*	10.9
West Midlands	161	51.3	20.3	10.9	*	*	7.8	12.3
Eastern	161	45.0	25.4	11.3	*	7.4	7.9	13.3
London	235	41.2	23.5	15.6	*	6.7	9.3	14.2
South East	278	47.6	23.5	12.0	*	6.1	7.5	12.7
South West	170	43.7	23.4	11.4	6.2	5.9	9.3	13.9
England	1,588	46.4	23.2	12.3	4.0	6.2	7.7	13.0
Wales	83	47.6	27.0	*	*	5.4	7.6	12.0
Scotland	157	39.6	22.7	11.4	9.1	7.0	9.8	15.1
Northern Ireland	41	46.9	*	*	*	*	*	13.0

Source: Labour Force Survey, Spring 2001[12]

1　Job-related training includes both on and off-the-job training.
2　Working age is defined as males aged 16-64 and females 16-59. These figures include unpaid family workers, those on government employment and training programmes,
　or those who did not answer, who are excluded from the Economic activity analyses below.
3　Expressed as a percentage of those in the group who received training in the last week, who specified a valid length of training.
4　Those who specified a valid length of training.
5　Employees are those in employment excluding the self-employed, unpaid family workers and those on government employment and training programmes.
6　The split into employees and self-employed is based on respondents' own assessment of their employment status.
7　Self-employed are those in employment excluding employees, unpaid family workers and those on government employment and training programmes.
8　Unemployed according to the International Labour Office (ILO) definition.
9　Economically inactive are those who are neither in employment nor ILO unemployed.
10　Apart from rounding, figures may not sum to grand totals because of questions in the LFS which were unanswered or did not apply.
11　Government Office Regions in England and each UK country.
12　Users of these data should read the LFS entry in Annex A, as it contains important information about the LFS and the concepts and definitions used.

THIS PAGE HAS BEEN LEFT BLANK

3.24 POST COMPULSORY EDUCATION AND TRAINING: JOB-RELATED TRAINING

Participation by employees[1] in job-related training[2] in the last thirteen weeks by a range of personal and economic characteristics
— time series

United Kingdom: Employees[1] of working age[3]

Thousands

	1995			1998			2001		
	All	Males	Females	All	Males	Females	All	Males	Females
All employees[1]	5,559	2,856	2,703	6,454	3,292	3,162	7,349	3,597	3,752
By age									
16-19	288	151	137	438	228	209	460	239	221
20-24	694	348	346	751	384	367	868	431	437
25-29	925	492	433	1,010	538	472	1,007	518	489
30-39	1,619	861	759	1,899	1,017	881	2,143	1,083	1,060
40-49	1,382	663	719	1,495	709	786	1,742	786	956
50-64	651	342	309	861	416	445	1,130	541	589
By highest qualification held[4,5]									
Degree or equivalent	1,297	752	545	1,538	841	697	1,895	968	927
Higher Education qualification (below degree level)	900	378	523	1,003	418	585	1,053	415	638
GCE A level or equivalent	1,314	853	461	1,525	961	564	1,807	1,074	733
GCSE grades A* to C or equivalent	1,162	471	691	1,476	541	836	1,593	674	919
Other	595	279	316	626	305	321	681	329	353
None	282	119	164	256	112	145	287	122	166
By industry[4]									
Agriculture, forestry & fishing	30	19	10	33	23	10	27	16	11
Energy & water supply	111	88	23	100	79	21	101	79	22
Manufacturing	839	636	204	971	744	227	938	726	213
Construction	193	164	29	254	220	33	305	269	36
Distribution, hotels & restaurants	784	376	408	966	460	506	1,073	504	570
Transport	313	221	92	336	232	104	436	313	123
Banking, finance & insurance	900	517	383	1,065	591	474	1,201	648	553
Public administration, education & health	2,145	719	1,426	2,436	803	1,634	2,946	893	2,053
Other services	236	111	125	289	137	152	316	145	171
By occupation[4]									
Managers & administrators	978	624	354	1,087	700	387	1,025	677	348
Professional	1,030	544	486	1,104	579	525	1,337	678	659
Associate professional & technical	832	363	469	992	418	574	1,414	677	737
Clerical & secretarial	884	242	642	1,009	269	740	1,001	232	769
Craft & related	387	362	24	468	442	26	517	484	34
Personal & protective services	636	253	383	795	310	486	665	98	567
Sales	366	149	217	461	177	284	517	166	351
Plant & machine operatives	258	221	37	309	265	45	341	289	51
Other	178	92	85	227	132	95	527	293	234
By full-time/part-time work[6]									
Full-time	4,529	2,693	1,836	5,169	3,056	2,113	5,815	3,343	2,472
Part-time	1,030	163	867	1,284	236	1,048	1,534	254	1,280
of which:									
students	247	106	141	355	152	204	393	155	238
could not find full-time job	127	35	91	130	41	89	125	34	91
did not want full-time job	643	19	624	780	39	741	991	57	933
By employment status[4]									
Permanent	5,132	2,670	2,462	5,945	3,074	2,872	6,798	3,363	3,435
Temporary	401	172	230	487	206	281	524	218	306
of which:									
seasonal/casual work	60	26	33	90	37	51	83	35	49
contract for fixed term or task	275	117	157	292	126	167	313	129	185
agency temping	27	11	16	48	19	28	61	28	34
other	40	17	23	58	24	34	66	27	39

Source: Labour Force Survey, Spring 1995, 1998, 2001[7]

1 Employees are those in employment excluding the self-employed, unpaid family workers and those on government employment and training programmes.
2 Job-related training includes both on and off-the-job training.
3 Working age is defined as males aged 16-64 and females aged 16-59.
4 Apart from rounding, figures may not sum to grand totals because of questions in the LFS which were unanswered or did not apply.
5 Highest qualifications held figures for 1995 are not directly comparable with later years due to changes in the level of detail collected for qualifications from the 1996 LFS onwards.
6 The split between employees working full-time and part-time is based on respondents' own assessment.
7 Users of these data should read the LFS entry in Annex A, as it contains important information about the LFS and the concepts and definitions used.
8 Expressed as a percentage of the total number of people in each group.

3.24 CONTINUED
POST COMPULSORY EDUCATION AND TRAINING: JOB-RELATED TRAINING
Participation by employees[1] in job-related training[2] in the last thirteen weeks by a range of personal and economic characteristics
— time series
United Kingdom: Employees[1] of working age[3]

Percentages[8]

	1995			1998			2001		
	All	Males	Females	All	Males	Females	All	Males	Females
All employees[1]	25.6	24.9	26.5	28.1	26.8	29.5	30.6	28.0	33.5
By age									
16-19	25.6	27.5	23.8	32.0	33.1	30.9	32.7	33.9	31.5
20-24	28.8	27.8	29.9	33.3	32.1	34.7	37.4	35.0	40.0
25-29	29.7	29.6	29.8	32.1	31.5	32.9	34.2	32.2	36.7
30-39	27.6	27.1	28.2	29.2	28.8	29.8	31.6	29.5	34.1
40-49	26.2	24.9	27.4	28.0	26.3	29.6	30.8	27.4	34.2
50-64	16.8	15.7	18.1	19.6	16.8	23.1	22.9	19.6	27.0
By highest qualification held[5]									
Degree or equivalent	42.6	39.7	47.5	43.4	40.1	48.0	43.8	39.0	50.2
Higher Education qualification (below degree level)	42.7	38.5	46.5	43.7	38.7	48.0	44.7	37.4	51.2
GCE A level or equivalent	25.7	24.2	29.1	28.3	26.1	32.9	30.8	27.9	36.4
GCSE grades A* to C or equivalent	24.8	25.0	24.7	27.1	28.0	26.3	28.5	28.4	28.6
Other	17.9	16.6	19.3	18.8	17.2	20.6	21.4	19.5	23.6
None	8.4	8.1	8.7	9.2	8.8	9.6	11.2	9..8	12.5
By industry									
Agriculture, forestry & fishing	14.0	12.6	17.5	15.9	14.9	18.5	14.7	12.0	22.7
Energy & water supply	33.8	33.4	35.7	37.3	36.5	40.3	32.9	32.0	36.3
Manufacturing	18.4	19.3	16.2	20.8	21.6	18.6	21.8	22.5	19.8
Construction	19.7	19.5	20.8	21.1	20.8	23.0	22.7	22.8	21.9
Distribution, hotels & restaurants	18.2	19.5	17.2	21.2	21.8	20.7	23.1	23.3	22.9
Transport	22.1	20.4	27.6	22.0	20.5	26.1	25.1	24.4	27.1
Banking, finance & insurance	30.3	34.0	26.4	32.2	34.2	30.1	32.5	32.7	32.2
Public administration, education & health	37.5	39.4	36.7	40.1	42.0	39.2	44.5	43.6	45.0
Other services	20.4	20.9	19.9	24.6	25.3	23.9	26.7	26.4	26.9
By occupation									
Managers & administrators	30.1	28.6	33.2	31.2	29.8	34.1	31.9	29.8	36.9
Professional	46.2	42.8	50.8	46.4	42.0	52.4	47.2	41.0	55.9
Associate professional & technical	41.4	36.7	46.0	44.6	39.1	49.7	44.1	39.6	49.4
Clerical & secretarial	24.6	26.4	24.0	26.6	27.4	26.4	28.8	30.9	28.2
Craft & related	17.2	18.5	8.7	19.8	20.8	10.8	22.1	22.6	16.6
Personal & protective services	25.9	28.9	24.2	29.4	33.4	27.3	37.7	35.1	38.2
Sales	20.2	24.1	18.2	24.1	26.8	22.6	25.5	26.6	25.0
Plant & machine operatives	11.7	12.7	8.2	13.5	14.4	10.0	16.1	16.8	13.4
Other	9.6	10.4	8.9	12.3	13.7	10.8	17.1	17.4	16.8
By full-time/part-time work									
Full-time	27.2	25.0	31.2	29.5	26.8	34.5	31.8	28.2	38.4
Part-time	20.5	23.2	20.0	23.4	26.0	22.9	26.6	25.4	26.8
of which:									
students	33.2	31.6	34.5	36.6	35.3	37.7	36.4	33.1	39.0
could not find full-time job	17.9	16.5	18.6	20.1	18.1	21.2	23.2	17.6	26.4
did not want full-time job	18.4	14.4	18.5	20.6	17.6	20.8	24.5	19.1	24.9
By employment status									
Permanent	25.7	25.1	26.4	28.0	26.8	29.4	30.5	28.1	33.3
Temporary	26.8	24.6	28.8	30.4	28.5	32.0	33.2	29.4	36.7
of which:									
seasonal/casual work	16.9	16.7	16.5	25.5	31.1	25.4	24.1	22.6	27.7
contract for fixed term or task	33.6	30.1	36.8	35.4	32.8	37.6	40.9	35.5	45.7
agency temping	17.1	14.3	19.7	19.1	15.9	22.1	21.8	19.2	24.7
other	24.4	22.1	26.4	34.0	35.2	33.2	24.6	21.5	27.2

Source: Labour Force Survey, Spring 1995, 1998, 2001[7]

See previous page for footnotes.

POST COMPULSORY EDUCATION AND TRAINING: JOB-RELATED TRAINING

Employees[1] of working age[2] in the UK — summary of job-related training[3] received, 2001

United Kingdom: Employees[1] of working age[2]

Thousands and percentages

	Total number of employees (thousands)	Number who received training in the last			Never offered training by current employer (thousands)	Percentage who received training in the last			Never offered training by current employer (percentage)
		13 weeks	4 weeks	1 week		13 weeks	4 weeks	1 week	
All employees[1]	24,056	7,349	3,934	2,113	7,202	30.6	16.4	8.8	29.9
By gender									
Males	12,841	3,597	1,855	964	3,985	28.0	14.4	7.5	31.0
Females	11,214	3,752	2,079	1,149	3,217	33.5	18.5	10.2	28.7
By age									
16-19	1,407	460	335	252	425	32.7	23.8	17.9	30.2
20-24	2,322	868	546	353	779	37.4	23.5	15.2	33.5
25-29	2,941	1,007	526	289	811	34.2	17.9	9.8	27.6
30-39	6,783	2,143	1,140	566	1,860	31.6	16.8	8.3	27.4
40-49	5,663	1,742	872	428	1,612	30.8	15.4	7.6	28.5
50-64	4,939	1,130	515	225	1,715	22.9	10.4	4.6	34.7
By ethnic origin									
White	21,279	6,457	3,449	1,838	6,310	30.3	16.2	8.6	29.7
Non-white	1,197	378	216	135	389	31.5	18.1	11.3	32.5
Mixed	119	40	21	12	34	33.8	17.7	10.5	28.8
Asian or Asian British	562	159	87	52	202	28.2	15.4	9.3	35.9
Black or Black British	336	121	71	47	85	36.0	21.2	13.9	25.4
Chinese	48	17	10	*	18	34.7	20.0	*	37.4
Other Ethnic Group	131	41	27	17	49	31.2	21.0	13.2	37.4
DNA/Imputed	1,576	512	269	139	502	32.5	17.1	8.8	31.9
By highest qualification held[4]									
Degree or equivalent	4,329	1,895	1,025	497	718	43.8	23.7	11.5	16.6
Higher Education qualification (below degree level)	2,358	1,053	565	290	387	44.7	23.9	12.3	16.4
GCE A level or equivalent	5,867	1,807	1,006	562	1,747	30.8	17.1	9.6	29.8
GCSE grades A* to C or equivalent	5,590	1,593	864	492	1,706	28.5	15.5	8.8	30.5
Other qualification	3,184	681	338	192	1,192	21.4	10.6	6.0	37.4
No qualification	2,566	287	121	69	1,395	11.2	4.7	2.7	54.4
By industry[4]									
Agriculture, forestry & fishing	186	27	12	*	91	14.7	6.5	*	49.1
Energy & water supply	307	101	50	18	58	32.9	16.2	5.8	18.8
Manufacturing	4,304	938	468	266	1,603	21.8	10.9	6.2	37.2
Construction	1,345	305	162	88	540	22.7	12.0	6.6	40.1
Distribution, hotels & restaurants	4,651	1,073	614	394	1,884	23.1	13.2	8.5	40.5
Transport	1,740	436	204	106	570	25.1	11.7	6.1	32.8
Banking, finance & insurance	3,700	1,201	619	313	1,004	32.5	16.7	8.4	27.1
Public administration, education & health	6,615	2,946	1,625	819	1,024	44.5	24.6	12.4	15.5
Other services	1,184	316	177	101	419	26.7	14.9	8.5	35.4
By occupation[4]									
Managers & administrators	3,212	1,025	473	210	731	31.9	14.7	6.5	22.7
Professional	2,834	1,337	755	362	384	47.2	26.6	12.8	13.5
Associate professional & technical	3,203	1,414	772	406	505	44.1	24.1	12.7	15.8
Clerical & secretarial	3,478	1,001	527	274	983	28.8	15.2	7.9	28.3
Craft & related	2,339	517	287	175	920	22.1	12.3	7.5	39.4
Personal & protective services	1,762	665	371	217	374	37.7	21.1	12.3	21.2
Sales	2,030	517	307	203	766	25.5	15.1	10.0	37.7
Plant & machine operatives	2,109	341	154	81	992	16.1	7.3	3.9	47.0
Other occupations	3,076	527	286	182	1,544	17.1	9.3	5.9	50.2
By region[5]									
United Kingdom	24,056	7,349	3,934	2,113	7,202	30.6	16.4	8.8	29.9
North East	976	300	152	88	290	30.7	15.6	9.1	29.7
North West	2,738	877	471	253	838	32.0	17.2	9.2	30.6
Yorkshire and the Humber	2,030	629	340	179	663	31.0	16.7	8.8	32.7
East Midlands	1,736	484	249	135	560	27.9	14.4	7.8	32.3
West Midlands	2,178	647	360	188	698	29.7	16.5	8.6	32.1
Eastern	2,320	710	373	180	636	30.6	16.1	7.8	27.4
London	2,863	924	504	271	783	32.3	17.6	9.5	27.4
South East	3,491	1,102	581	312	940	31.6	16.6	8.9	26.9
South West	1,996	622	341	190	574	31.2	17.1	9.5	28.8
England	20,327	6,294	3,370	1,797	5,984	31.0	16.6	8.8	29.4
Wales	1,046	304	168	95	347	29.0	16.1	9.1	33.1
Scotland	2,093	605	319	172	675	28.9	15.3	8.2	32.2
Northern Ireland	590	146	77	48	197	24.7	13.0	8.2	33.3

Source: Labour Force Survey, Spring 2001[6]

1 Employees are those in employment excluding the self-employed, unpaid family workers and those on government employment and training programmes.
2 Working age is defined as males aged 16-64 and females aged 16-59.
3 Job-related training includes both on and off-the-job training.
4 Apart from rounding, figures may not sum to grand totals because of questions in the LFS which were unanswered or did not apply.
5 Government Office Regions in England and each UK country.
6 Users of these data should read the LFS entry in Annex A, as it contains important information about the LFS and the concepts and definitions used.

POST COMPULSORY EDUCATION AND TRAINING: JOB-RELATED TRAINING

3.26

Participation by employees in job-related training[1] in the last thirteen weeks by disability status and a range of personal characteristics, 2001

United Kingdom: Employees[2] of working age[3]

Thousands and percentages[4]

	Total number of employees by disability status (thousands)					Percentage receiving job-related training in the last thirteen weeks				
	Total number of employees (thousands)	Both DDA disabled and work-limiting disabled	DDA disabled only	Work-limiting disabled only	Not disabled	All employees	Both DDA disabled and work-limiting disabled	DDA disabled only	Work-limiting disabled only	Not disabled
All employees	24,056	1,088	941	714	21,313	30.6	24.4	29.9	30.7	30.9
By gender										
Males	12,841	560	457	416	11,409	28.0	20.7	25.2	26.4	28.5
Females	11,214	528	484	298	9,904	33.5	28.2	34.3	36.6	33.6
By age										
16-19	1,407	36	24	33	1,314	32.7	27.8	*	33.3	32.8
20-24	2,322	54	52	62	2,154	37.4	37.0	48.1	33.9	37.2
25-29	2,941	85	64	76	2,715	34.2	29.4	31.3	34.2	34.5
30-39	6,783	257	191	178	6,158	31.6	25.3	33.0	32.6	31.8
40-49	5,663	272	259	170	4,962	30.8	27.6	31.7	32.9	30.8
50-64	4,939	383	351	196	4,009	22.9	18.3	24.2	23.5	23.1
By highest qualification held[5]										
Degree or equivalent	4,329	112	125	93	3,998	43.8	38.4	44.0	49.5	43.8
Higher Education qualification (below degree level)	2,358	102	101	62	2,093	44.7	40.2	48.5	38.7	44.9
GCE A level or equivalent	5,867	270	223	185	5,190	30.8	28.5	31.4	31.9	30.8
GCSE grades A* to C or equivalent	5,590	239	196	162	4,993	28.5	22.6	31.6	33.3	28.5
Other qualification	3,184	177	152	106	2,750	21.4	16.4	19.1	20.8	21.9
No qualification	2,566	184	138	102	2,141	11.2	10.3	10.9	12.7	11.3
By industry[5]										
Agriculture, forestry & fishing	186	*	*	*	169	14.7	*	*	*	15.4
Energy & water supply	307	12	10	*	275	32.9	*	*	*	32.4
Manufacturing	4,304	188	171	136	3,809	21.8	12.8	20.5	22.8	22.3
Construction	1,345	56	46	42	1,202	22.7	*	*	*	23.5
Distribution, hotels & restaurants	4,651	215	171	130	4,135	23.1	20.9	21.1	22.3	23.3
Transport	1,740	82	62	59	1,537	25.1	20.7	25.8	20.3	25.4
Banking, finance & insurance	3,700	141	132	101	3,325	32.5	26.2	31.1	30.7	32.8
Public administration, education & health	6,615	323	301	189	5,802	44.5	36.5	44.2	49.2	44.8
Other services	1,184	61	38	45	1,041	26.7	16.4	*	*	27.7
By occupation[5]										
Managers & administrators	3,212	108	120	64	2,920	31.9	30.6	30.8	35.9	31.9
Professional	2,834	88	99	73	2,574	47.2	40.9	46.5	50.7	47.3
Associate professional & technical	3,203	119	120	78	2,886	44.1	40.3	43.3	44.9	44.3
Clerical & secretarial	3,478	171	145	105	3,057	28.8	26.3	26.9	32.4	28.9
Craft & related	2,339	101	90	80	2,067	22.1	10.9	17.8	23.8	22.8
Personal & protective services	1,762	86	80	55	1,541	37.7	31.4	43.8	47.3	37.5
Sales	2,030	102	81	65	1,782	25.5	24.5	24.7	18.5	25.8
Plant & machine operatives	2,109	119	86	77	1,828	16.1	10.9	17.4	16.9	16.4
Other	3,076	194	119	118	2,646	17.1	13.4	17.6	17.8	17.3
By full-time/part-time work[5]										
Full-time	18,274	741	715	521	16,297	31.8	26.0	31.0	31.9	32.1
Part-time	5,777	346	226	194	5,012	26.6	20.8	26.1	27.3	26.9
of which:										
Males										
Full-time	11,838	491	430	370	10,546	28.2	22.2	25.6	27.3	28.7
Part-time	1,000	69	27	46	859	25.4	11.6	22.2	19.6	26.9
Females										
Full-time	6,436	250	285	151	5,751	38.4	33.6	39.6	43.0	38.4
Part-time	4,777	277	199	148	4,153	26.8	23.1	26.6	29.1	26.9

Source: Labour Force Survey, Spring 2001[6]

1 Job-related training includes both on and off-the-job training.
2 Employees are those in employment excluding the self-employed, unpaid family workers and those on government employment and training programmes.
3 Working age is defined as males aged 16-64 and females aged 16-59.
4 Expressed as a percentage of those in the group who received training in the last thirteen weeks.
5 Apart from rounding, figures may not sum to grand totals because of questions in the LFS which were unanswered or did not apply.
6 Users of these data should read the LFS entry in Annex A, as it contains important information about the LFS and the concepts and definitions used.

Chapter 4
Qualifications

CHAPTER 4: QUALIFICATIONS

Key Facts

GCE, GCSE, SCE and GNVQ/GSVQ qualifications

- In 1999/00, 34.5 per cent of young people in the United Kingdom achieved 2 or more GCE A level passes or equivalent in schools and FE colleges. At GCSE / Standard Grade level, of pupils in their last year of compulsory schooling:

  - 50.4 per cent gained 5 or more passes at grades A*-C / 1-3

  - 24.5 per cent gained 1-4 passes at grades A*-C / 1-3

  - 19.7 per cent gained no passes at grades A*-C / 1-3 but gained at least one grade D-G

  - 5.5 per cent had no graded results (**Table 4.1**)

- Nearly 5.7 million entries were made for GCSE / Standard Grade examinations by pupils in their last year of compulsory education in schools in the United Kingdom in 1999/00. 57% of all entries achieved passes at grade A* -C. (**Table 4.2**)

- A total of 890,700 entries were made by pupils aged 16-18 for GCE A level / Higher Grade examinations in the United Kingdom in 1999/00. 62% of all entries achieved grades A - C. (**Table 4.3**)

- Of the 18,100 Intermediate and Foundation GNVQ entries in England, Wales and Northern Ireland in 1999/00, 73% achieved GNVQ Part One, and 18% achieved a Full GNVQ. (**Table 4.4**)

Subject Choice

- Most frequently studied subjects at GCE A level / Higher Grade were English (English 47,200, English Literature 63,900), General Studies (88,600), Mathematics (84,500), Social Studies (63,300) and Biological Sciences (61,100). (**Table 4.3**)

- Of the 43,500 Advanced GNVQ entries in England, Wales and Northern Ireland in 1999/00, the largest subject area was Business with over 15,000 entrants. 27% of female Advanced GNVQ entries achieved a distinction compared with 17% of male entries. (**Table 4.4**)

Vocational Awards

- There were 454,000 NVQs awarded in the United Kingdom in 1999/00. Over half (58%) were awarded at level 2. 117,000 GNVQs and 502,000 "other" vocational qualifications were awarded in 1999/00. Over half (53%) of "other" vocational qualifications were awarded at level 1. (**Table 4.5**)

National Learning Targets for England, 2002

- In Spring/Summer 2001, progress towards the targets was:

  - 75% of 11-year-olds reaching the expected standard for their age in literacy (target 80%)

  - 71% of 11-year-olds reaching the expected standard in numeracy (target 75%)

  - 50% of 16-year-olds gaining at least five "good GCSE passes" (target 50%)

  - 94.5% of 16-year-olds gaining at least one exam pass (target 95%)

  - 75.9% of 19-year-olds with a "level 2" qualification (target 85%)

  - 54.5% of 21-year-olds with a "level 3" qualification (target 60%)

  - 47.2% of adults with a "level 3" qualification (target 50%)

  - 27.5% of adults with a "level 4" qualification (target 28%) (**Table 4.7**)

Higher Education Qualifications

- A total of 460,300 higher education qualifications were awarded in higher education institutions in the United Kingdom in 1999/00. Of these, 72,500 were sub-degree qualifications, 265,300 were first degrees, 11,500 were PhD or equivalents and 110,900 were at Masters / other postgraduate level. 55% of these qualifications were awarded to women. (**Table 4.8**)

Highest Qualification Held

- 42% of people of working age were qualified to NVQ level 3 equivalent or above in Spring 2001, with 24% of people of working age qualified to NVQ level 4 equivalent or above, and 16% having no qualification. (**Table 4.9**)

- Attainment levels vary by Government Office region, with London having a higher proportion of highly qualified people (i.e. qualified to NVQ level 4 and 5 or equivalent) than any other UK region in Spring 2001. (**Table 4.9**)

- Attainment levels varied greatly by economic activity with 33% of the economically inactive and 23% of the unemployed having no qualifications, compared to 11% of employees. (**Table 4.9**)

- 90% of employees in professional occupations held two or more A levels, or a higher level qualification, compared with 63% of managers and administrators and only 21% of plant and machine operatives. (**Table 4.9**)

People Working Towards a Qualification

- 67% of leavers from Advanced Modern Apprenticeships in England in 1999-00 gained a qualification, 10 percentage points higher than the previous 12 months. The proportion of "Other Training" leavers who gained a full qualification was 45%, compared to 46% in 1998-99. **(Table 4.6)**

- 40% of leavers from Work-based Learning for Adults in England in 1999-00 gained a qualification – the same as in 1998-99. **(Table 4.6)**

- 17% of all people of working age were studying towards a qualification in Spring 2001. Young people aged 16-24 were far more likely to be working towards a qualification than people in any other age group. **(Table 4.10)**

- People of non-white ethnic origin were far more likely to be studying towards a qualification than people of white ethnic origin; 27.7% compared to 16.5%. **(Table 4.10)**

CHAPTER 4: QUALIFICATIONS – LIST OF TABLES

4.1 GCE, GCSE and SCE qualifications obtained by pupils and students at a typical age, and GCE, GCSE, SCE and GNVQ/GSVQ qualifications obtained by students of all ages – time series

4.2 GCSE/SCE Standard Grade entries and achievements for pupils in their last year of compulsory education in all schools by subject and gender by the end of 1999/00

4.3 GCE A level/SCE Higher Grade entries and achievements for pupils aged 16-18 in all Schools and Further Education Sector Colleges by subject and gender, 1999/00

4.4 Intermediate, Foundation and Advanced GNVQ entries and results, by subject and gender, 1999/00

4.5 Full vocational awards by type of qualification, equivalent level and gender – time series

4.6 Work-Based Training for Young People and Work-Based Learning for Adults: qualifications of leavers – time series

4.7 National Learning Targets for England, 2002 – time series

4.8 Students obtaining higher education qualifications by type of course, gender and subject group, 1999/00

4.9 Highest qualification held by people of working age by gender, age, region and economic activity and, for employees of working age, by occupation, 2001

4.10 People currently working towards a qualification, 2001

4.1

QUALIFICATIONS

GCE, GCSE and SCE[1] qualifications obtained by pupils and students at a typical age[2,3], and GCE, GCSE, SCE[1] and GNVQ/GSVQ qualifications obtained by students of all ages — time series

United Kingdom   (i) Students at a typical age   Percentages and thousands

| | Pupils in their last year of compulsory education[2] | | | | | Pupils/students in education[3] | | | |
| | | | | | | % Achieving GCE A Levels and equivalent | | | |
	5 or more grades A*-C[4] (%)	1-4 grades A*-C[4] (%)	Grades D-G[5] only (%)	No graded results (%)	Total (=100%) (thousands)	2 or more passes[6,7]	1 pass[8]	1 or more passes	population aged 17 (thousands)
1995/96[9]									
All	45.2	25.9	21.3	7.5	696.4	29.5	8.0	37.5	648.3
Males	40.4	25.4	25.4	8.7	355.7	26.7	7.3	34.0	333.6
Females	50.2	26.4	17.0	6.3	340.7	32.5	8.8	41.3	314.6
1997/98									
All	47.5	25.2[9]	21.1[9]	6.5	698.4	33.5	6.5	40.1	751.0
Males	42.3	25.4[9]	24.9[9]	7.5	356.1	29.9	6.0	35.9	384.9
Females	52.8	25.0[9]	17.1[9]	5.3	342.3	37.4	7.2	44.5	366.1
1998/99									
All	49.1	24.8	20.3	5.9	703.6	33.7	6.7	40.3	744.2
Males	43.8	25.2	24.1	6.9	359.6	30.1	6.1	36.2	381.4
Females	54.6	24.3	16.3	4.8	344.0	37.4	7.3	44.7	362.8
1999/00[1]									
All	50.4	24.5	19.7	5.5	703.7	34.5	6.5	41.0	732.2
Males	45.0	25.0	23.6	6.4	357.7	30.5	6.0	36.6	376.0
Females	55.9	23.9	15.7	4.5	346.0	38.6	7.1	45.6	356.3

United Kingdom   (ii) Students of any age achieving   Thousands

| | GCSE and SCE S Grade/Standard Grade (SG) | | | | GCE A Level and SCE/NQ Higher Grade | | |
	5 or more grades A*-C[4,10]	1-4 grades A*-C[4,10]	Grades D-G[5,11] only	No graded results[12]	2 or more passes[6,7]	1 pass[8]	Total 1 or more passes
1995/96							
All	331.4	371.7	236.5	40.0	204.5	78.2	282.6
Males	151.3	175.3	130.9	20.0	95.2	33.8	129.0
Females	180.1	196.4	105.6	20.0	109.3	44.3	153.6
1997/98							
All	335.3	336.4	233.9	37.4	260.4	70.3	330.6
Males	152.8	162.3	129.5	18.3	119.2	30.5	149.7
Females	182.5	174.1	104.5	19.2	141.2	39.8	181.0
1998/99							
All	341.0	323.7	229.8	31.2	257.9	69.9	327.8
Males	162.3	150.6	128.1	15.6	118.4	30.6	149.0
Females	178.7	173.2	101.7	15.6	139.5	39.3	178.8
1999/00[1]							
All	357.7	311.6	224.4	30.3	258.8	65.6	324.4
Males	162.8	150.9	125.3	15.2	118.0	28.7	146.6
Females	194.9	160.7	99.1	15.1	140.9	36.9	177.7

Source: Department for Education and Skills; National Assembly for Wales; Scottish Executive; Northern Ireland Department of Education

1 From 1999/00 National Qualifications (NQ) were introduced in Scotland. NQs include Standard Grades, Intermediate 1 & 2 and Higher Grades. The figures for Higher Grades combine the new NQ Higher and the old SCE Higher.

2 Pupils aged 15 at the start of the academic year, pupils in Year S4 in Scotland.

3 Pupils in schools and students in further education institutions aged 16-18 at the start of the academic year in England, Wales and Northern Ireland as a percentage of the 17 year old population. Pupils in Scotland generally sit Highers one year earlier and the figures tend to relate to the results of pupils in Year S5/S6.

4 Standard Grades 1-3 in Scotland.

5 Grades D-G at GCSE and Scottish Standard Grades 4-7.

6 3 or more SCE/NQ Higher Grades in Scotland.

7 Includes Advanced level GNVQ/GSVQ which is equivalent to 2 GCE A levels or AS equivalents/3 SCE/NQ Higher grades.

8 2 AS levels or 2 Highers, in Scotland, count as 1 A level pass. Includes those with 1.5 A level passes.

9 Great Britain only.

10 Includes GNVQ/GSVQ Intermediate Part 1, Full and Language unit which are equivalent to 2, 4 and 0.5 GCSE grades A*-C/SCE Standard grades 1-3 respectively. Figures include those with 4.5 GCSEs.

11 Includes GNVQ/GSVQ Foundation Part 1, Full and Language unit which are equivalent to 2, 4 and 0.5 GCSE grades D-G/SCE Standard grades 4-7 respectively.

12 Figures for Scotland include students in Year S4 only. Time series has been revised.

QUALIFICATIONS

4.2 GCSE/SCE Standard grade entries and achievements[1] for pupils in their last year of compulsory education[2], in all schools by subject and gender by the end of 1999/00

United Kingdom

Thousands and percentages

Subject group	Number of entries (000s)			Percentage achieving grade A*-C			Percentage achieving grade D-G		
	All	Males	Females	All	Males	Females	All	Males	Females
Biological Science	67.5	32.4	35.1	85	86	85	14	13	14
Chemistry	66.5	36.8	29.7	88	87	89	11	12	11
Physics	62.3	39.2	23.1	88	88	89	11	11	11
Science Single Award[3]	77.2	39.8	37.4	21	19	23	72	73	70
Science Double Award[4]	493.8	244.0	249.8	52	50	54	46	48	44
Other Science[4]	5.4	3.7	1.7	44	43	45	51	51	52
Mathematics[5]	671.4	338.5	332.9	51	50	52	46	46	45
Computer Studies[6]	118.9	71.9	47.0	58	55	62	39	41	35
Design and Technology[7]	454.0	243.9	210.1	52	45	60	45	51	38
Business Studies	123.3	60.9	62.4	57	53	60	39	42	36
Home Economics	54.1	5.3	48.8	48	31	50	46	59	45
Art and Design	216.2	97.7	118.6	67	56	76	31	41	22
Geography	264.0	148.8	115.2	59	56	62	39	41	36
History	232.4	113.6	118.8	62	59	65	35	38	33
Economics	6.4	4.5	1.9	66	67	65	31	30	33
Humanities[4]	19.7	9.5	10.2	43	37	49	52	58	48
Religious Studies	115.9	47.3	68.7	58	49	65	37	45	32
Social Studies	15.9	4.6	11.3	52	41	56	43	52	40
English	647.3	322.8	324.5	60	52	68	39	46	31
Welsh[8]	4.1	1.9	2.2	70	59	79	30	41	21
English Literature[4]	505.6	242.2	263.4	64	56	70	35	42	28
Drama	94.1	35.2	58.9	70	60	76	29	38	23
Communication Studies[4]	34.4	14.9	19.5	56	47	63	41	50	35
Modern Languages									
French	375.9	179.3	196.6	53	44	60	46	53	38
German	147.8	70.2	77.5	57	49	64	41	48	35
Spanish	47.7	20.4	27.3	57	49	63	41	49	35
Other languages[9]	32.5	14.5	18.0	70	63	76	28	34	23
Classical Studies	15.8	8.1	7.7	87	85	89	11	12	9
Physical Education	123.1	80.2	42.9	56	55	57	43	43	42
Vocational Studies	21.4	9.4	12.0	50	43	55	44	49	40
Modern Studies[10]	13.1	5.3	7.8	67	62	71	33	38	29
Music	55.6	22.7	32.8	72	66	75	25	29	22
Other subjects	**6.6**	**3.2**	**3.4**	**58**	**50**	**66**	**40**	**47**	**32**
All entries[11]	5,683.5	2,816.5	2,867.1	57	53	62	40	45	36
English and Mathematics[12,13,14]	638.4	318.4	320.0	46	43	50	51	54	48
English, Maths and a Science[12,13,14]	627.7	312.9	314.8	43	40	45	54	57	52
English, Maths, Science and Modern Languages[14,15]	519.3	249.5	269.8	40	35	44	57	62	53
Mathematics and Science[14,15]	607.6	304.9	302.7	45	44	46	52	53	51
Any Subject	671.7	338.7	333.1	76	72	81	22	27	18

Source: Department for Education and Skills; National Assembly for Wales; Scottish Executive; Northern Ireland Department of Education

1 Where a candidate attempted an examination in the same subject more than once, only the highest value pass has been counted. However, some double counting may occur if a student enters for more than one subject within a subject category.
2 Those in all schools who were 15 at the start of the academic year, i.e. 31 August 1999. Pupils in Year S4 in Scotland.
3 Standard Grade in General Science in Scotland.
4 England and Wales only.
5 Includes related subjects such as Statistics.
6 Includes Information Systems in England and Wales.
7 Craft and Design, Graphic Communications and Technological Studies in Scotland.
8 Welsh as a first language.
9 Includes Welsh as a second language.
10 Scotland only.
11 Science Double Award are counted twice in this row.
12 English or Welsh as a first language in Wales.
13 Only includes *successful* entries (grade A* to G) in Wales so the number of entries is an underestimate.
14 Percentages are those achieving grades A*-C or D-G respectively in all these subjects.
15 England and Scotland only.

4.3 QUALIFICATIONS

GCE A level/SCE Higher grade[1] entries and achievements for pupils aged 16-18[2] in all Schools and Further Education Sector Colleges by subject and gender, 1999/00

United Kingdom   Thousands and percentages

Subject group	Number of entries(000s)			Percentage achieved grades A-C			Percentage achieved grades D-E[3]			Percentage with no graded results		
	All	Males	Females	All	Males	Females	All	Males	Females	All	Males	Females
Biological Sciences	61.1	22.8	38.3	59	56	61	28	30	27	13	14	12
Chemistry	48.9	24.9	24.1	68	66	70	22	23	20	10	11	9
Physics	41.0	31.0	10.0	66	64	71	22	23	19	13	13	10
Other Science	9.8	4.1	5.7	55	50	58	31	35	28	15	15	14
Mathematics	84.5	50.8	33.7	67	66	70	20	21	19	12	13	11
Computer Studies[4]	23.8	18.3	5.4	49	48	50	34	34	34	17	18	15
Design and Technology[5]	21.6	15.8	5.8	60	58	64	27	28	26	13	14	10
Business Studies[6]	46.5	22.6	23.9	62	59	65	26	30	23	11	11	11
Home Economics	2.0	0.1	1.9	53	33	54	34	43	34	13	24	12
Art and Design	41.9	14.9	27.0	71	65	74	22	26	21	7	9	5
Geography	45.5	24.6	20.9	66	63	70	25	27	22	9	10	8
History	45.0	20.0	24.9	64	63	64	25	26	25	11	11	11
Economics	20.4	13.1	7.3	60	60	61	29	29	28	11	11	11
Religious Studies	10.5	2.6	8.0	64	64	64	26	24	26	10	12	10
Social Studies[7]	63.3	18.7	44.6	54	50	56	31	32	31	15	18	14
English	47.2	18.2	29.1	63	62	64	20	18	21	17	20	15
Welsh[8,9]	0.6	0.1	0.4	58	52	60	37	41	36	5	7	4
Gaelic	0.1	-	0.1	95	100	94	3	-	4	2	-	2
English Literature[7]	63.9	18.6	45.3	63	62	63	32	31	32	5	6	5
Welsh Literature[8]	0.3	0.1	0.3	61	51	63	33	41	31	6	8	6
Drama	4.7	1.3	3.4	77	72	78	18	21	17	5	6	4
Communication studies[7]	29.0	10.2	18.8	55	49	59	36	39	34	9	12	7
Modern Languages	41.4	12.4	29.0	71	72	71	22	21	22	7	8	7
of which												
French	21.3	5.9	15.4	69	71	69	23	22	24	8	7	8
German	10.1	3.1	7.1	71	73	71	22	20	23	7	7	6
Spanish	5.7	1.6	4.1	72	74	71	21	21	22	7	6	7
Other Languages	4.3	1.8	2.5	78	73	82	15	17	13	7	10	4
Classical Studies[10]	6.3	2.6	3.6	74	72	76	18	20	17	7	8	7
Creative Arts[11]	9.7	4.0	5.8	73	70	75	20	22	19	7	8	6
Physical Education	20.8	13.0	7.8	52	48	58	37	39	33	11	13	9
Vocational Studies[7]	3.1	1.6	1.5	45	43	47	30	29	32	25	28	22
General Studies[7]	88.6	42.1	46.5	48	49	48	36	36	37	15	15	16
Modern Studies[12]	7.4	2.9	4.5	81	79	83	7	8	7	11	13	10
Other subjects	1.5	0.3	1.2	79	73	80	9	10	9	12	17	11
All entries	**890.7**	**411.8**	**478.9**	**62**	**60**	**63**	**27**	**28**	**26**	**12**	**13**	**10**

Sources: Department for Education and Skills; National Assembly for Wales; Scottish Executive; Northern Ireland Department of Education

1 Includes the new Scottish qualification framework which contains different subject categories to those previously used. The new Intermediate 1 and 2 qualifications (which overlap with Standard Grades and Highers) are not included in the table. Data for 1999/00 are not therefore directly comparable with earlier years shown.

2 Pupils in schools and students in further education institutions aged 16-18 at the start of the academic year in England, Wales and Northern Ireland. Pupils in Scotland generally sit Highers one year earlier and the figures tend to relate to the result of pupils in Year S5/S6.

3 Compensatory Award in Scotland.

4 Includes Information Systems.

5 Craft and Design, Graphic Communication and Technological Studies in Scotland and Northern Ireland.

6 Includes Accounting, Management and Information Studies and Secretarial Studies in Scotland. Accounting only in Northern Ireland.

7 England and Wales only.

8 Wales only.

9 Welsh as a second language.

10 Includes Classical Greek and Latin.

11 Includes music.

12 Scotland only.

| | Intermediate and Foundation GNVQ Pupils aged 15 in all schools[2,3] | | | | | | | | Advanced GNVQ Students aged 16-18 years old in schools and colleges[4] | | | |
| | Total Entries | | GNVQ Part One | | Full GNVQ[3] | | GNVQ Language Unit[5] | | Total Entries | Grade obtained | | |
	Interm-ediate	Found-ation	Interm-ediate	Found-ation	Interm-ediate	Found-ation	Interm-ediate	Found-ation	Advanced	Distin-ction	Merit	Pass
All												
Art & Design	894	156	620	67	193	89	-	-	4,509	1,166	1,745	824
Business	4,088	1,110	3,112	839	645	241	-	-	15,076	3,728	6,092	2,668
Health & Social Care	2,640	986	2,143	706	313	257	-	-	5,891	1,477	2,361	900
Leisure and Tourism	1,539	813	1,029	444	310	248	-	-	7,577	1,536	2,949	1,657
Manufacturing	920	495	793	401	75	80	-	-	117	26	42	28
Construction	49	87	-	1	12	86	-	-	730	147	288	142
Hospitality and Catering	45	67	-	-	41	67	-	-	755	98	237	235
Science	32	-	-	-	16	-	-	-	1,423	254	564	251
Engineering	559	220	473	159	51	61	-	-	1,159	184	392	296
Information Technology	2,629	381	2,132	315	378	51	-	-	4,506	706	1,538	1,050
Media: Communication and Production	54	-	-	-	40	-	-	-	1,279	353	522	178
Retail and Distribution	-	-	-	-	-	-	-	-	113	24	41	35
Performing Arts	33	7	1	-	32	7	-	-	274	89	98	27
Total[6]	**13,550**	**4,553**	**10,320**	**2,961**	**2,107**	**1,187**	**50**	**202**	**43,494**	**9,794**	**16,916**	**8,316**
Males												
Art & Design	419	87	271	33	92	54	-	-	2,038	436	750	471
Business	2,007	651	1,567	510	286	124	-	-	7,582	1,435	3,078	1,733
Health & Social Care	141	102	109	88	24	10	-	-	283	35	93	82
Leisure and Tourism	650	403	444	234	125	144	-	-	2,769	329	1,083	811
Manufacturing	642	419	534	331	62	74	-	-	97	21	33	27
Construction	47	67	-	1	12	66	-	-	711	139	281	141
Hospitality and Catering	15	22	-	-	14	22	-	-	299	23	81	112
Science	24	-	-	-	14	-	-	-	808	104	319	181
Engineering	508	205	426	146	49	59	-	-	1,110	169	379	289
Information Technology	1,707	255	1,351	205	258	35	-	-	3,764	553	1,336	967
Media: Communication and Production	33	-	-	-	25	-	-	-	664	165	272	120
Retail and Distribution	-	-	-	-	-	-	-	-	63	12	20	25
Performing Arts	5	3	-	-	5	3	-	-	85	13	36	13
Total[6]	**6,231**	**2,327**	**4,710**	**1,569**	**966**	**591**	**25**	**92**	**20,316**	**3,437**	**7,784**	**4,987**
Females												
Art & Design	475	69	349	34	101	35	-	-	2,471	730	995	353
Business	2,081	459	1,545	329	359	117	-	-	7,494	2,293	3,014	935
Health & Social Care	2,499	884	2,034	618	289	247	-	-	5,608	1,442	2,268	818
Leisure and Tourism	889	410	585	210	185	104	-	-	4,808	1,207	1,866	846
Manufacturing	278	76	259	70	13	6	-	-	20	5	9	1
Construction	2	20	-	-	-	20	-	-	19	8	7	1
Hospitality and Catering	30	45	-	-	27	45	-	-	456	75	156	123
Science	8	-	-	-	2	-	-	-	615	150	245	70
Engineering	51	15	75	13	2	2	-	-	49	15	13	7
Information Technology	922	126	753	110	120	16	-	-	742	153	202	83
Media: Communication and Production	21	-	-	-	15	-	-	-	615	188	250	58
Retail and Distribution	-	-	-	-	-	-	-	-	50	12	21	10
Performing Arts	28	4	1	-	27	4	-	-	189	76	62	14
Total[6]	**7,319**	**2,226**	**5,610**	**1,392**	**1,141**	**596**	**25**	**110**	**23,178**	**6,357**	**9,132**	**3,329**

Source: Department for Education and Skills; National Assembly for Wales; Northern Ireland Department of Education

1 Including attempts and achievements by these students in previous years.

2 Those in all schools who were 15 at the start of the academic year, i.e. 31 August 1999.

3 In Northern Ireland, Full Intermediate and Foundation GNVQ figures relate to pupils aged 16 and 17 in schools and FE colleges at the start of the academic year.

4 Pupils in schools and students in further education institutions aged 16-18 at the start of the academic year i.e. 31 August 1999.

5 England and Wales only. In England, GNVQ Language Units include French, German and Spanish, but the composition is not known for Wales.

6 Includes subjects in England and Wales which are not specified in the table.

United Kingdom   Thousands and percentages

	Year[2]				
	1995/96	1996/97	1997/98	1998/99	1999/00[3]
All (thousands)[4]					
Full vocational awards:					
By qualification & level					
NVQs/SVQs					
Level 1	62	79	72	62	65
Level 2	218	277	271	261	262
Level 3	65	93	102	104	113
Level 4 and 5	9	10	12	15	15
Total	**354**	**459**	**458**	**442**	**454**
GNVQs/GSVQs					
Level 1	6	9	9	12	13
Level 2	44	48	49	54	55
Level 3	34	36	44	47	49
Total	**84**	**93**	**103**	**113**	**117**
Other Vocational Qualifications[5,7]					
Level 1	188	235	252	279	266
Level 2	89	75	82	96	114
Level 3	94	75	66	74	83
Level 4 and 5	53	54	48	52	39
Total	**423**	**439**	**449**	**501**	**502**
Males (percentages)[4]					
Full vocational awards:					
By qualification					
NVQs/SVQs[6]	41	43	47	47	48
GNVQs/GSVQs	47	48	49	50	50
Other vocational qualifications[7,8]	57	49	47	47	46
Females (percentages)[4]					
Full vocational awards:					
By qualification					
NVQs/SVQs[6]	59	57	53	53	52
GNVQs/GSVQs	53	52	51	50	50
Other vocational qualifications[7,8]	43	51	53	53	54

Source: National Information System for Vocational Qualifications/Qualifications & Curriculum Authority (QCA)

1   Based on all awards where the gender of the candidate is identified.
2   Academic years from October to September.
3   In 1999/00 SQA were unable to provide information on their numbers of Other Vocational Qualification awards, therefore data for 1999/00 only relates to awards made by City and Guilds, Edexcel and OCR
4   Awards are excluded if the centre or qualification was not identified.
5   Numbers may not add to column totals due to rounding.
6   Prior to 1997/98 data available on gender for NVQs/SVQs was limited therefore this table may not be representative of the gender split for all NVQs/SVQs awarded nationally for these years.
7   Other Vocational Qualifications made by City & Guilds, RSA, Edexcel and Scottish Qualifications Agency (SQA) only, not UK estimates. For other vocational qualifications, notional NVQ levels are allocated by QCA for analytical purposes as part of the NISVQ project.
8   Due to limited data available, awards for other non regulated vocational qualifications in this table may not be representative of the gender split for all other vocational qualifications awarded nationally.

4.6

QUALIFICATIONS
Work-Based Training for Young People[1,2] and Work-Based Learning for Adults[3]: qualifications of leavers — time series

England   Percentages

| | Work-Based Training for Young People | | | | | | | WBLA |
| | Advanced Modern Apprenticeships[1] survey respondents who: | | Other Training[1,2] survey respondents who: | | Total[4] survey respondents who: | | | survey respondents who: |
	Gained any full qualification	Gained any full qualification at Level 3 or above[5]	Gained any full qualification	Gained any full qualification at Level 2 or above[5]	Gained any full qualification	Gained any full qualification at Level 2 or above[5]	Gained any full qualification at Level 3 or above[5]	Gained any full qualification [5]
Period of leaving[6]								
1990-91	.	.	39	..	39	..	..	28
1991-92	.	.	34	23	34	15	7	29
1992-93	.	.	35	27	35	18	8	34
1993-94	.	.	38	31	38	20	10	36
1994-95	.	.	40	34	40	22	12	39
1995-96	28	9	43	38	43	25	13	42
1996-97	43	22	44	40	44	26	14	38
1997-98	47	27	45	40	45	27	14	37
1998-99[7]	57	36	46	40	48	27	16	40
1999-00	67	48	45	38	51	25	22	40
April to June 2000	65	43	42	34	51	27	20	39
July to Sept 2000	72	55	43	36	55	25	26	41
Oct to Dec 2000	65	48	35	28	49	24	21	40

Sources: WBTYP and WBLA trainee databases

1 Other Training (shown as Youth Training (YT) in the 1997 Volume and which includes Youth Credits) forms part of Work-Based Training for Young People (WBTYP) along with Modern Apprenticeships (MA).

2 From April 1995 the definition of Other Training leavers changed, no longer counting those making planned transfers from one training provider to another as leavers. Many of these transferring trainees will not have gained a job or qualification or completed their training. Therefore the change in definition will increase slightly the proportions with jobs and qualifications and those completing their training. The way that data on qualifications gained are collected was changed from August 1991 on. The effect appears to have been to decrease the proportion recorded as gaining full qualifications, but to increase by a similar amount the proportion gaining part qualifications. Data for 1990-91 are therefore not strictly comparable with those for later years.

3 Work-Based Learning for Adults (WBLA) superseded Work-Based Training for Adults (WBTA) in April 1999. Figures for 1990-91 are for Employment Training.

4 Includes Foundation Modern Apprenticeships (formerly known as National Traineeships) from November 1999 onwards.

5 Information on levels of qualifications is not available for 1990-91 leavers and is not published for WBLA leavers.

6 Leavers to September 1990 surveyed three months after leaving. Leavers in October and November 1990 surveyed in June 1991. Leavers from December 1990 surveyed six months after leaving.

7 Includes revised data.

4.7 QUALIFICATIONS
National Learning Targets[1] for England, 2002 — time series

England   Percentages

	1991[2]			1999			2000			2001[3]		
	All	Males	Females	All	Males	Females	All	Males	Females[4]	All	Males	Females
Targets for 11-year-olds												
By 2002												
80% of 11-year olds reaching the expected standard[5] for their age in literacy	..	..	..	71	65	76	75	70	79	75	70	80
75% of 11-year olds reaching the expected standard[5] for their age in numeracy	..	..	..	69	69	69	72	72	71	71	71	70
Targets for 16-year-olds												
By 2002												
50% of 16-year olds should gain at least five good GCSE passes[6]	..	..	..	47.9	42.8	53.4	49.2	44.0	54.6	50.0	44.8	55.4
95% of 16-year olds should gain at least one exam pass[7]	..	..	..	94.0	93.0	95.0	94.4	93.5	95.4	94.5	93.5	95.6
Targets for Young people												
By 2002												
85% of 19-year-olds with a "level 2" qualification[8]	54	54	53	74.6	73.9	75.3	74.8	72.3	77.5	75.9	73.6	78.3
60% of 21-year-olds with a "level 3" qualification[9]	30	31	28	53.8	55.3	52.2	54.0	56.5	51.5	54.5	53.8	55.2
Targets for Adults[1,10]												
By 2002												
28% of adults with a "level 4" qualification[11]	..	..	..	26.3	26.5	26.0	27.1	27.3	26.7	27.5	27.4	27.6
50% of adults with a "level 3" qualification[9]	..	..	..	45.3	49.5	39.9	46.6	50.8	41.1	47.2	50.8	42.5

Source: Department for Education and Skills; Labour Force Survey, Spring Quarter of each year[12]

1 There is a further 'learning participation' target for adults, and targets for organisations which are not included in this table. These targets are
   – a 7% reduction in non-learners – the learning participation target
   – 45% of medium sized or large organisations recognised as Investors in People
   – 10,000 small organisations recognised as Investors in People
2 Due to changes in the coverage of the Labour Force Survey, 1991 figures are not directly comparable to later years.
3 2001 figures for the targets for 11-year-olds and 16-year-olds are provisional and subject to change of up to one percentage point.
4 Includes revised data.
5 The expected standard is level 4 or above in the national tests set for 11-year-olds in English and mathematics.
6 5 "good GCSEs" is 5 GCSEs at grades A*-C, or equivalent.
7 1 GCSE is any GCSE grade A*-G, or equivalent.
8 "level 2" is 5 GCSEs at grades A*-C, an NVQ level 2, an Intermediate GNVQ or equivalent.
9 "level 3" is 2 A levels, an NVQ level 3, an Advanced GNVQ or equivalent.
10 Adults consist of males aged 18-64 and females aged 18-59, who are in employment or actively seeking employment.
11 "level 4" is a degree, NVQ level 4 or a vocational equivalent.
12 More up-to-date information may be available through the DfES Statistics Website 'www.dfes.gov.uk/statistics'.

QUALIFICATIONS

Students[1] obtaining higher education qualifications[2,3] by type of course, gender and subject group, 1999/00

United Kingdom   Thousands

| | Sub-degree[4] | First Degree | Postgraduate | | | Total Higher Education |
			PHD's & equivalent	Masters and Others	Total	
All						
Medicine & Dentistry	-	6.0	1.0	2.0	3.0	9.0
Subjects Allied to Medicine	21.5	17.8	0.6	4.5	5.1	44.4
Biological Sciences	1.1	18.4	1.8	3.0	4.7	24.3
Vet. Science, Agriculture & related	1.1	2.9	0.3	0.9	1.2	5.3
Physical Sciences	0.8	13.2	1.8	2.5	4.3	18.3
Mathematical and Computer Sciences	5.0	15.3	0.7	5.5	6.2	26.5
Engineering & Technology	4.6	20.6	1.7	6.3	8.0	33.2
Architecture, Building & Planning	1.5	6.6	0.1	3.2	3.3	11.4
Social Sciences	5.7	32.9	1.1	16.3	17.4	56.0
Business & Financial Studies	10.1	31.9	0.4	21.4	21.8	63.8
Librarianship & Info Science	0.4	4.6	0.1	2.4	2.4	7.4
Languages	1.5	16.6	0.7	2.9	3.5	21.6
Humanities	1.1	10.4	0.6	2.8	3.5	14.9
Creative Arts & Design	2.7	21.3	0.1	3.8	4.0	28.0
Education[5]	4.5	11.9	0.4	26.6	27.0	43.4
Combined, general	10.7	34.9	0.1	6.8	7.0	52.6
All subjects	**72.5**	**265.3**	**11.5**	**110.9**	**122.5**	**460.3**
Males						
Medicine & Dentistry	-	2.9	0.5	0.9	1.4	4.3
Subjects Allied to Medicine	2.3	3.6	0.3	1.2	1.4	7.3
Biological Sciences	0.5	6.9	0.8	1.1	1.9	9.3
Vet. Science, Agriculture & related	0.6	1.3	0.2	0.5	0.7	2.6
Physical Sciences	0.6	8.0	1.3	1.4	2.7	11.3
Mathematical and Computer Sciences	3.6	11.3	0.5	3.8	4.3	19.2
Engineering & Technology	4.2	17.3	1.4	5.1	6.5	28.0
Architecture, Building & Planning	1.1	5.0	0.1	2.1	2.1	8.2
Social Sciences	1.7	13.2	0.6	7.3	7.9	22.8
Business & Financial Studies	4.4	14.8	0.3	11.8	12.1	31.3
Librarianship & Info Science	0.2	1.7	-	0.8	0.8	2.7
Languages	0.5	4.6	0.3	0.9	1.2	6.3
Humanities	0.4	4.6	0.4	1.3	1.7	6.8
Creative Arts & Design	1.3	8.5	0.1	1.6	1.7	11.5
Education[5]	1.4	2.7	0.2	7.6	7.8	11.9
Combined, general	4.1	14.8	0.1	4.0	4.1	22.9
All subjects	**26.7**	**121.2**	**7.1**	**51.3**	**58.4**	**206.4**
Females						
Medicine & Dentistry	-	3.1	0.5	1.1	1.6	4.7
Subjects Allied to Medicine	19.3	14.2	0.3	3.4	3.7	37.1
Biological Sciences	0.6	11.6	0.9	1.9	2.9	15.0
Vet. Science, Agriculture & related	0.5	1.6	0.1	0.4	0.5	2.7
Physical Sciences	0.3	5.1	0.5	1.1	1.6	7.0
Mathematical and Computer Sciences	1.5	4.0	0.1	1.7	1.8	7.3
Engineering & Technology	0.5	3.2	0.3	1.2	1.5	5.2
Architecture, Building & Planning	0.4	1.6	0.1	1.1	1.2	3.2
Social Sciences	4.0	19.7	0.5	9.0	9.5	33.2
Business & Financial Studies	5.7	17.1	0.1	9.6	9.7	32.5
Librarianship & Info Science	0.2	2.9	-	1.6	1.6	4.7
Languages	1.0	12.1	0.4	1.9	2.3	15.4
Humanities	0.7	5.7	0.2	1.5	1.8	8.2
Creative Arts & Design	1.4	12.8	0.1	2.2	2.3	16.5
Education[5]	3.1	9.2	0.2	19.0	19.2	31.5
Combined, general	6.7	20.2	-	2.8	2.9	29.7
All subjects	**45.8**	**144.1**	**4.4**	**59.6**	**64.1**	**253.9**

Sources: Department for Education and Skills; Higher Education Statistics Agency (HESA)

1 Includes students on Open University courses.
2 Excludes qualifications from the private sector.
3 Includes higher education in higher education institutions in the United Kingdom only. Higher education qualifications in further education institutions
   (approximately 6% of the total number of students) are excluded.
4 Excludes students who successfully completed courses for which formal qualifications are not awarded.
5 Including ITT and INSET.

4.9 QUALIFICATIONS

Highest qualification held by people of working age[1], by gender, age, region and economic activity and, for employees of working age[1], by occupation, 2001[2]

United Kingdom

Thousands & percentages

	All people of working age[1] (000s)	Percentage of people of working age					
		NVQ level 5[3]	NVQ level 4[4]	NVQ level 3[5]	NVQ level 2[6]	Below NVQ level 2[7]	No qualifications
Personal and economic characteristics							
By gender							
Males	19,155	5	20	23	21	17	15
Females	17,399	4	19	14	22	23	18
By age							
16-19	2,910	*	1	17	41	20	21
20-24	3,537	2	19	35	21	16	8
25-29	3,913	5	27	18	20	21	9
30-39	9,447	5	22	17	21	24	11
40-49	7,991	5	22	17	19	19	17
50-64	8,756	4	17	16	19	16	27
By Government Office region[8]							
United Kingdom	36,554	4	19	19	22	20	16
North East	1,573	3	15	19	23	20	19
North West	4,185	4	18	20	22	19	17
Yorkshire & the Humber	3,087	3	17	20	21	21	19
East Midlands	2,587	3	17	19	21	21	19
West Midlands	3,246	3	17	18	22	20	20
Eastern	3,324	4	18	19	23	22	14
London	4,707	7	24	16	19	19	15
South East	4,956	5	21	19	22	21	12
South West	2,945	4	21	19	23	21	12
England	30,609	4	19	19	22	20	16
Wales	1,758	4	18	17	22	19	21
Scotland	3,164	4	23	21	20	15	17
Northern Ireland	1,023	4	15	17	23	15	26
By economic activity							
Employees[9,10,11]	24,056	5	23	19	22	20	11
of which:							
Managers & administrators	3,212	8	35	21	19	14	5
Professional	2,834	25	56	9	6	4	1
Associate professional & technical	3,203	5	45	19	17	11	2
Clerical & secretarial	3,478	2	16	20	29	27	6
Craft & related	2,339	*	7	37	27	17	11
Personal & protective services	1,762	1	13	19	29	25	12
Sales	2,030	1	8	19	31	26	15
Plant & machine operatives	2,109	*	4	17	24	31	23
Other	3,076	*	4	15	24	29	28
Self-employed[10,12]	2,963	5	22	23	21	15	14
ILO unemployed[13]	1,390	2	11	14	22	27	23
Inactive[14]	7,911	2	10	17	20	19	33
Time series							
1999	36,177	4	19	18	22	20	17
2000	36,312	4	19	19	22	20	16
2001	36,554	4	19	19	22	20	16

Labour Force Survey, Spring Quarters[15,16]

1 Working age is defined as males aged 16-64 and females 16-59. These figures include unpaid family workers, those on government employment and training programmes, or those who did not answer, who are excluded from the economic activity analyses below.
2 Data on Ethnic origin, previously recorded in the table, are not included due to changes in classifications in the Spring 2001 LFS resulting in a discontinuity and also missing data.
3 Includes Higher degrees and other qualifications at Level 5.
4 Includes First degree, Other degree and sub-degree higher education qualifications such as teaching and nursing certificates, HNC/HNDs, other HE diplomas and other qualifications at Level 4.
5 Vocational qualifications include those with RSA Advanced Diploma, BTEC Nationals, ONC/ONDs, City and Guilds Advanced Craft or trade apprenticeships and other professional or vocational qualifications at Level 3. Academic qualifications include those with more than one GCE A level or SCE Highers/Scottish Certificates of Sixth Year Studies (CSYS) at Level 3.
6 Vocational qualifications include those with RSA Diplomas, City and Guilds Craft, BTEC Firsts or trade apprenticeships and other professional or vocational qualifications at Level 2. Academic qualifications include those with one GCE A level, five or more GCSE grades A*-C or equivalent or AS examinations/SCE Highers/CSYS at Level 2.
7 Vocational qualifications include those with BTEC general certificates, YT certificates, other RSA qualifications, other City and Guilds or other professional or vocational qualifications at Level 1. Academic qualifications include those with one or more GCSE grade G or equivalent (but less than five at grades A*-C) or AS examinations at Level 1.
8 Usual region of residence - Government Office Regions in England and each UK country.
9 Employees are those in employment excluding the self-employed, unpaid family workers and those on government employment and training programmes.
10 The split into employees and self-employed is based on respondents' own assessment of their employment status.
11 Apart from rounding, figures may not sum to grand totals because of questions in the LFS which were unanswered or did not apply.
12 Self-employed are those in employment excluding employees, unpaid family workers and those on government employment and training programmes.
13 Unemployed according to the International Labour Office (ILO) definition.
14 People who are neither in employment nor ILO unemployed.
15 Users of these data should read the LFS entry Annex A, as it contains important information about the LFS and the concepts and definitions used.
16 More up-to-date information may be available through the DfES Statistics Website 'www.dfes.gov.uk/statistics'.

United Kingdom

Thousands & percentages

	Total working towards a qualification		Of which, percentage working towards[3,10]				
	Number (thousands)	Percentage (%)[4]	Degree or equivalent	Higher Education qualification (below degree level)	GCE A level or equivalent	GCSE grades A* to C or equivalent	Other qualification
All people[1]	6,373	17.4	27.9	8.8	20.0	13.9	28.6
Economic activity							
Employees[5,6]	3,780	15.7	23.7	10.9	20.2	10.1	34.4
Self-employed[6,7]	187	6.3	19.8	6.8	8.5	5.6	58.6
ILO unemployed[8]	237	17.1	17.8	7.6	16.4	20.4	36.2
Economically inactive[9]	2,036	25.7	39.0	5.4	19.6	20.6	14.7
All aged							
All	6,373	17.4	27.9	8.8	20.0	13.9	28.7
16-19	2,044	70.2	13.2	4.5	43.7	28.6	9.4
20-24	1,284	36.3	59.7	9.9	8.9	4.6	16.4
25-29	674	17.2	30.6	12.1	8.6	6.8	40.7
30-39	1,204	12.7	25.8	11.3	8.3	8.6	45.1
40-49	780	9.8	21.0	12.4	9.4	8.1	48.6
50-64	386	4.4	15.5	7.9	8.6	8.6	58.6
Males aged							
All	2,960	15.5	28.8	7.4	20.9	13.6	28.5
16-19	1,014	68.1	11.7	4.5	45.1	28.8	9.2
20-24	635	35.3	60.2	8.4	11.0	4.9	15.1
25-29	313	15.6	31.5	10.6	5.9	4.8	45.7
30-39	536	11.2	28.6	9.2	6.6	6.8	48.0
40-49	296	7.4	23.6	9.6	7.9	5.8	52.1
50-64	166	3.3	18.3	5.7	8.5	7.2	60.0
Females aged							
All	3,413	19.6	27.1	10.1	19.2	14.2	28.8
16-19	1,030	72.5	14.7	4.5	42.3	28.4	9.6
20-24	649	37.4	59.2	11.4	6.8	4.4	17.8
25-29	362	18.9	29.8	13.4	10.9	8.5	36.3
30-39	668	14.4	23.5	13.0	9.8	10.0	42.8
40-49	484	12.2	19.3	14.2	10.3	9.4	46.4
50-59	220	5.9	13.3	9.6	8.6	9.6	57.5
By highest qualification held[10]							
Degree or equivalent	920	16.6	47.6	9.9	2.3	2.6	37.0
Higher Education qualification (below degree level)	553	18.3	37.2	19.1	6.3	4.3	32.5
GCE A level or equivalent	1,882	21.6	50.4	12.1	10.9	4.0	22.2
GCSE grades A* to C or equivalent	1,839	22.7	4.0	5.0	50.0	14.1	26.3
Other qualification	572	11.5	17.7	7.1	10.1	17.1	46.8
No qualification	586	9.9	*	*	5.5	69.6	22.2
By ethnic origin							
White	5,221	16.5	26.3	9.0	20.7	14.2	29.1
Non-white	676	27.7	36.8	7.5	16.4	13.8	24.8
Mixed	58	27.8	25.6	*	*	26.9	27.1
Asian or British Asian	304	24.5	35.9	6.0	20.2	14.9	22.4
Black or Black British	190	32.3	32.7	10.9	15.1	10.6	29.6
Chinese	41	34.0	68.3	*	*	*	*
Other ethnic group	82	29.6	41.7	*	*	11.6	28.4
DNA/Imputed	476	19.6	32.5	9.1	16.7	11.2	29.4
Employees							
Full-time & part-time							
All	3,780	15.7	23.7	10.9	20.2	10.1	34.4
Males	1,718	13.4	24.8	9.1	20.7	9.1	35.5
Females	2,062	18.4	22.8	12.3	19.8	10.9	33.4
Full-time							
All	2,278	12.5	22.3	11.8	14.5	7.3	43.3
Males	1,239	10.5	22.7	9.2	15.4	6.4	45.6
Females	1,039	16.1	21.8	15.0	13.4	8.4	40.7
Part-time							
All	1,502	26.0	26.0	9.4	28.8	14.2	20.7
Males	478	47.8	30.4	8.9	34.5	16.0	9.6
Females	1,024	21.4	23.9	9.6	26.2	13.4	25.9

Source: Labour Force Survey, Spring 2001[11]

1 Only those of working age; males aged 16-64 and females aged 16-59. These figures include unpaid family workers, those on government employment and training programmes, or those who did not answer, who are excluded from the Economic activity analyses below.
2 For those who are working towards more than one qualification the highest is recorded.
3 Expressed as a percentage of those in the group working towards a qualification.
4 Expressed as a percentage of the total number of people in the group.
5 Employees are those in employment excluding the self-employed, unpaid family workers and those on government employment and training programmes.
6 The split into employee and self-employed is based on respondents' own assessment of their employment status
7 Self-employed are those in employment excluding employees, unpaid family workers and those on government employment and training programmes.
8 Unemployment according to the International Labour Office (ILO) definition.
9 People who are neither in employment nor ILO unemployed.
10 Apart from rounding, figures may not sum to grand totals because of questions in the LFS which were unanswered or did not apply.
11 Users of these data should read the LFS entry in Annex A, as it contains important information about the LFS and the concepts and definitions used.

Chapter 5
Destinations

CHAPTER 5: DESTINATIONS

Key Facts

• The number of school leavers in England increased by 6,400 between 1999 and 2000, to 570,000. The proportion of pupils at the end of compulsory education continuing their education remained at 71% - 10 percentage points higher than in 1991. In Northern Ireland, the proportion fell slightly from 68% in 1999 to 67% in 2000. This was still 9 percentage points higher than in 1991. **(Table 5.1)**

• 70% of leavers from *Work-Based Training for Young People* in 1999-00 were in a job 6 months after leaving the programme, compared to 69% in 1998-99. The proportion who were unemployed 6 months after leaving remained at 12%. **(Table 5.2)**

• 40% of leavers from *Work-Based Learning for Adults* in 1999-00 were in a job 6 months after leaving the programme, one percentage point less than in 1998-99. The proportion who were unemployed increased by one percentage point. **(Table 5.2)**

• 119,500 first-degree graduates from the academic year 1999/00 were known to go into employment, 9,500 graduates were believed to be unemployed and 36,300 graduates continued their education/training. **(Table 5.3)**

• Of those with a known destination, 67.4% were in employment, 20.4% continued their education/training and 5.4% were believed unemployed. **(Table 5.3)**

CHAPTER 5: DESTINATIONS – LIST OF TABLES

5.1 Destination of school leavers by country – time series

5.2 Work-based Training for Young People and Work-based Learning for Adults: destinations of leavers – time series

5.3 Destinations of full-time first-degree home and EU graduates by gender and subject group, 1999/00

5.1 DESTINATIONS

Destinations of school leavers by country – time series

United Kingdom   Thousands and percentages[1]

	1991	1996	1998[2]	1999[2]	2000[2]
United Kingdom					
Number of school leavers	638.3	683.3	638.7	647.3	651.3
Destination at end of compulsory schooling					
England					
Number of school leavers	522.8	562.1	553.7	563.9	570.3
of which(%):					
Education	61	68	68	71	71
Government supported training[3]	15	10	9	8	8
Employment	10	8	9	9	9
Unemployed or not available for work	9	7	7	5	6
Unknown or left area	6	8	6	5	5
Wales					
Number of school leavers	34.9	36.9	..	..	..
of which(%):					
Education	62	70	..	..	..
Government supported training[3]	16	8	..	..	..
Employment	8	9	..	..	..
Unemployed or not available for work	8	7	..	..	..
Unknown or left area	6	6	..	..	..
Northern Ireland					
Number of school leavers	25.4	26.9	25.7	26.3	25.6
of which(%):					
Education	58	67	67	68	67
Training	27	22	21	20	21
Employment	5	5	6	6	6
Unemployed or not available for work	4	4	3	3	3
Unknown or left area	6	3	3	3	3
Destination of all school leavers					
Scotland[4]					
Number of school leavers	55.2	57.4	59.3	57.2	55.5
of which(%):					
Education	32	45	49	49	50
Training	25	14	10	8	7
Employment	24	23	26	26	26
Unemployed	9	..	..	..	..
Miscellaneous/other known destinations	11	14	13	14	13
Destinations not known	..	4	3	3	3

Sources: School Leavers Destinations Surveys; Careers Service Activity Survey

1 Figures may not sum to 100% due to rounding.
2 Data for Wales are no longer collected and are therefore excluded from the UK aggregate.
3 Including those who have employed status under Work-based training for young people schemes.
4 These figures cannot be directly compared with those for England and Wales as they cover the destinations of pupils from classes S4, S5 and S6 who left Education Authority schools during or at the end of the years academic session. England and Wales figures relate to destinations of year 11 pupils leaving secondary school.

DESTINATIONS
Work-Based Training for Young People[1,2] and Work-Based Learning for Adults[3]: destinations of leavers – time series

England   Percentages

	Advanced Modern Apprenticeships[1] survey respondents who were:			Other Training[1,2] survey respondents who were:		
	In a job	In a positive outcome[4]	Unemployed	In a job	In a positive outcome[4]	Unemployed
Period of leaving[5]						
1990-91	.	.	.	58	74	20
1991-92	.	.	.	51	67	25
1992-93	.	.	.	50	67	28
1993-94	.	.	.	54	70	25
1994-95	.	.	.	58	72	22
1995-96[7]	67	86	12	63	76	18
1996-97[7]	75	89	9	66	79	15
1997-98[7]	80	90	7	65	79	14
1998-99[7]	82	92	6	64	77	15
1999-00	84	93	5	62	76	16
April to June 2000	84	94	5	62	75	17
July to Sept 2000	85	93	4	59	76	16
Oct to Dec 2000	88	94	4	60	72	19

	Work-Based Training for Young People[1,6] survey respondents who were:			Work-Based Learning for Adults[3] survey respondents who were:		
	In a job	In a positive outcome[4]	Unemployed	In a job	In a positive outcome[4]	Unemployed
Period of leaving[5]						
1990-91	58	74	20	33	36	53
1991-92	51	67	25	31	36	55
1992-93	50	67	28	34	40	52
1993-94	54	70	25	36	43	48
1994-95	58	72	22	38	42	48
1995-96	63	76	18	39	44	47
1996-97	67	80	15	44	49	42
1997-98	68	81	13	44	48	45
1998-99[7]	69	82	12	41	45	47
1999-00	70	84	12	40	46	48
April to June 2000	71	85	11	42	46	47
July to Sept 2000	69	86	10	42	47	47
Oct to Dec 2000	73	86	11	43	46	47

Sources: WBTYP and WBLA trainee databases

1 Other Training (shown as Youth Training (YT) in the 1997 Volume and which includes Youth Credits) forms part of Work-Based Training for Young People (WBTYP) along with Modern Apprenticeships (MA).

2 From April 1995 the definition of Other Training leavers changed, no longer counting those making planned transfers from one training provider to another as leavers. Many of these transferring trainees will not have gained a job or qualification or completed their training. Therefore the change in definition will increase slightly the proportions with jobs and qualifications and those completing their training. The way that data on qualifications gained are collected was changed from August 1991 on. The effect appears to have been to decrease the proportion recorded as gaining full qualifications, but to increase by a similar amount the proportion gaining part qualifications. Data for 1990-91 are therefore not strictly comparable with those for later years.

3 Work-Based Learning for Adults (WBLA) superseded Work-Based Training for Adults (WBTA) in April 1999. Figures for 1990-91 are for Employment Training.

4 In a positive outcome = in a job, full-time education or other TEC-Delivered Government Supported Training.

5 Leavers to September 1990 surveyed three months after leaving. Leavers in October and November 1990 surveyed in June 1991. Leavers from December 1990 surveyed sixth months after leaving.

6 Includes Foundation Modern Apprenticeships (formerly known as National Traineeships) from Nov 1999 onwards.

7 Includes revised data.

THIS PAGE HAS BEEN LEFT BLANK

DESTINATIONS

Destinations of full-time first degree home and EU graduates[1] by gender and subject group, 1999/00[2]

United Kingdom   (i) Numbers of first degree graduates – by destination   Thousands

	UK Employment		Overseas employment[4]	Total Employment	Continuing education/ training[5]	Believed unemployed	Other known destinations[6]	Unknown destinations[7]	All First Degree Graduates[8]
	Permanent[3]	Temporary							
All									
Medicine & Dentistry	1.0	3.2	-	4.2	0.3	-	-	0.6	5.3
Subjects Allied to Medicine	6.0	2.0	0.2	8.2	1.3	0.3	0.4	2.2	12.5
Biological Sciences	5.1	2.4	0.4	8.0	4.1	0.7	1.1	3.5	17.3
Vet. Science, Agriculture & related	1.1	0.3	0.1	1.6	0.3	0.1	0.2	0.5	2.7
Physical Sciences	3.7	1.6	0.3	5.6	3.2	0.6	0.8	2.2	12.5
Mathematical Sciences	5.9	1.5	0.3	7.7	1.5	0.7	0.6	3.0	13.5
Engineering & Technology	6.1	1.4	0.5	8.1	2.3	0.7	0.7	4.0	15.7
Architecture, Building & Planning	1.8	0.9	0.2	2.8	0.7	0.1	0.2	0.9	4.7
Social Sciences	8.5	3.8	0.6	13.0	7.0	1.2	1.7	6.5	29.2
Business & Financial Studies	11.1	3.6	0.9	15.5	2.0	1.1	1.5	6.2	26.3
Librarianship & Info Science	1.7	0.7	0.1	2.5	0.3	0.3	0.2	1.0	4.3
Languages	4.4	2.1	1.0	7.6	3.4	0.7	1.0	3.2	15.9
Humanities	2.7	1.4	0.3	4.4	2.4	0.5	0.6	1.9	9.8
Creative Arts & Design	6.4	2.9	0.4	9.7	2.4	1.2	1.4	5.1	19.8
Education	4.9	3.3	0.1	8.3	0.5	0.2	0.3	1.7	11.0
Combined, general	8.2	3.4	0.7	12.3	4.4	1.1	1.5	5.4	24.7
All subjects	**78.7**	**34.8**	**6.0**	**119.5**	**36.3**	**9.5**	**12.1**	**48.0**	**225.4**
Males									
Medicine & Dentistry	0.4	1.5	-	2.0	0.2	-	-	0.3	2.5
Subjects Allied to Medicine	1.0	0.5	-	1.5	0.5	0.1	0.1	0.6	2.7
Biological Sciences	1.8	0.9	0.1	2.9	1.5	0.4	0.4	1.4	6.5
Vet. Science, Agriculture & related	0.5	0.1	0.1	0.7	0.1	0.1	0.1	0.2	1.2
Physical Sciences	2.3	1.0	0.1	3.4	1.9	0.4	0.5	1.4	7.7
Mathematical Sciences	4.5	1.1	0.2	5.8	1.0	0.6	0.4	2.3	10.0
Engineering & Technology	5.1	1.1	0.4	6.7	1.9	0.6	0.5	3.4	13.1
Architecture, Building & Planning	1.4	0.7	0.1	2.2	0.4	0.1	0.1	0.7	3.5
Social Sciences	3.3	1.4	0.3	5.0	2.8	0.5	0.7	2.7	11.6
Business & Financial Studies	5.0	1.6	0.4	7.0	1.0	0.6	0.7	3.1	12.4
Librarianship & Info Science	0.6	0.3	-	0.9	0.1	0.1	0.1	0.4	1.6
Languages	1.2	0.6	0.3	2.0	0.9	0.2	0.3	1.0	4.4
Humanities	1.2	0.6	0.1	1.8	1.1	0.3	0.3	0.9	4.4
Creative Arts & Design	2.6	1.2	0.1	3.9	0.8	0.6	0.5	2.2	8.0
Education	1.1	0.6	-	1.7	0.1	0.1	0.1	0.5	2.5
Combined, general	3.4	1.3	0.3	5.0	1.6	0.6	0.6	2.4	10.3
All subjects	**35.5**	**14.3**	**2.7**	**52.5**	**15.9**	**5.3**	**5.4**	**23.4**	**102.4**
Females									
Medicine & Dentistry	0.5	1.7	-	2.2	0.2	-	-	0.3	2.7
Subjects Allied to Medicine	5.0	1.6	0.1	6.7	0.9	0.2	0.3	1.7	9.7
Biological Sciences	3.3	1.5	0.3	5.1	2.7	0.4	0.7	2.1	10.9
Vet. Science, Agriculture & related	0.6	0.2	0.1	0.9	0.2	0.1	0.1	0.3	1.5
Physical Sciences	1.4	0.7	0.1	2.2	1.3	0.2	0.3	0.8	4.9
Mathematical Sciences	1.4	0.4	0.1	1.9	0.5	0.2	0.2	0.7	3.5
Engineering & Technology	1.0	0.3	0.1	1.4	0.4	0.1	0.1	0.6	2.7
Architecture, Building & Planning	0.4	0.2	0.1	0.6	0.2	-	0.1	0.3	1.2
Social Sciences	5.3	2.4	0.4	8.0	4.2	0.6	1.0	3.8	17.6
Business & Financial Studies	6.1	2.0	0.5	8.5	1.1	0.5	0.8	3.1	14.0
Librarianship & Info Science	1.1	0.5	0.1	1.6	0.2	0.1	0.1	0.6	2.7
Languages	3.3	1.6	0.8	5.6	2.6	0.4	0.7	2.3	11.5
Humanities	1.5	0.9	0.1	2.5	1.3	0.2	0.3	1.0	5.4
Creative Arts & Design	3.8	1.8	0.2	5.8	1.6	0.6	0.9	2.9	11.8
Education	3.8	2.7	0.1	6.6	0.3	0.1	0.2	1.3	8.6
Combined, general	4.8	2.1	0.4	7.3	2.8	0.5	0.9	3.0	14.4
All subjects	**43.2**	**20.4**	**3.3**	**67.0**	**20.4**	**4.2**	**6.7**	**24.7**	**123.0**

Source: Department for Education and Skills; Higher Education Statistics Agency (HESA)

1 Home and EU students graduating from higher education institutions in 2000. As from 1999/00 the target population excludes non-EU overseas domiciled students, consequently direct comparisons with earlier years cannot be made.
2 Destinations from the academic year 1999/00.
3 Includes the self-employed.
4 Home and overseas students.
5 Continuing education/training in the United Kingdom or overseas.
6 Including students not available for employment.
7 Includes those overseas graduates reported as returning overseas (no other information available).
8 Includes known and unknown destinations.
9 As a percentage of known destinations.

DESTINATIONS

Destinations of full-time first degree home and EU graduates[1] by gender and subject group, 1999/00[2]

United Kingdom   (ii) Percentage of known destinations   Percentages[9] and thousands

| | UK Employment | | Overseas | Total | Continuing education/ | Believed | Other known | Total of known | All First Degree |
	Permanent[3]	Temporary	employment[4]	Employment	training[5]	unemployed	destinations[6]	destinations (000s) (=100%)	Graduates[8] (000s)
All									
Medicine & Dentistry	21.4	70.2	0.3	91.8	7.6	0.2	0.4	4.6	5.3
Subjects Allied to Medicine	58.7	19.8	1.7	80.3	13.1	2.6	4.0	10.2	12.5
Biological Sciences	37.0	17.5	2.9	57.4	29.6	5.4	7.7	13.9	17.3
Vet. Science, Agriculture & related	49.8	15.9	5.2	70.9	14.5	5.7	8.9	2.2	2.7
Physical Sciences	36.3	15.7	2.5	54.5	31.3	6.1	8.0	10.3	12.5
Mathematical Sciences	56.5	14.3	2.5	73.2	14.5	6.9	5.4	10.5	13.5
Engineering & Technology	52.3	12.0	4.3	68.6	19.6	6.2	5.6	11.7	15.7
Architecture, Building & Planning	45.9	23.6	4.8	74.3	17.1	3.6	5.1	3.8	4.7
Social Sciences	37.5	16.7	2.8	57.0	30.7	5.1	7.3	22.8	29.2
Business & Financial Studies	55.2	17.8	4.2	77.2	10.1	5.4	7.2	20.1	26.3
Librarianship & Info Science	51.4	22.2	2.6	76.3	9.7	7.7	6.2	3.3	4.3
Languages	35.0	16.9	8.1	60.0	27.0	5.1	7.8	12.7	15.9
Humanities	34.2	17.9	3.2	55.3	30.7	6.1	8.0	7.9	9.8
Creative Arts & Design	43.3	20.0	2.6	65.9	16.4	8.3	9.3	14.7	19.8
Education	52.7	35.3	1.6	89.6	5.0	1.8	3.6	9.3	11.0
Combined, general	42.4	17.5	3.7	63.7	22.7	5.8	7.9	19.3	24.7
All subjects	**44.4**	**19.6**	**3.4**	**67.4**	**20.4**	**5.4**	**6.8**	**177.3**	**225.4**
Males									
Medicine & Dentistry	20.5	70.7	0.2	91.4	8.1	0.2	0.3	2.2	2.5
Subjects Allied to Medicine	46.8	20.8	1.6	69.2	22.2	4.1	4.5	2.2	2.7
Biological Sciences	36.1	17.7	2.9	56.7	28.6	6.9	7.8	5.1	6.5
Vet. Science, Agriculture & related	48.7	14.4	6.4	69.5	12.5	6.3	11.8	0.9	1.2
Physical Sciences	37.0	15.3	2.2	54.5	30.7	7.1	7.7	6.3	7.7
Mathematical Sciences	58.2	14.1	2.6	74.9	13.1	7.3	4.7	7.7	10.0
Engineering & Technology	52.6	11.7	4.5	68.8	19.3	6.4	5.5	9.7	13.1
Architecture, Building & Planning	48.6	23.4	4.3	76.3	15.0	3.9	4.9	2.9	3.5
Social Sciences	36.4	15.7	3.0	55.1	31.3	6.0	7.6	9.0	11.6
Business & Financial Studies	54.3	17.3	4.2	75.8	10.6	6.2	7.4	9.3	12.4
Librarianship & Info Science	50.6	21.5	2.0	74.1	9.4	11.0	5.5	1.3	1.6
Languages	34.5	16.4	8.0	58.9	25.4	7.0	8.7	3.4	4.4
Humanities	34.1	15.8	3.1	53.0	31.1	7.6	8.3	3.5	4.4
Creative Arts & Design	43.9	20.0	2.4	66.4	14.0	10.8	8.8	5.8	8.0
Education	55.1	28.2	1.9	85.3	7.2	3.2	4.4	2.0	2.5
Combined, general	43.5	16.9	3.9	64.3	20.5	7.5	7.7	7.8	10.3
All subjects	**44.9**	**18.1**	**3.4**	**66.4**	**20.1**	**6.7**	**6.8**	**79.0**	**102.4**
Females									
Medicine & Dentistry	22.1	69.7	0.3	92.1	7.1	0.2	0.5	2.4	2.7
Subjects Allied to Medicine	62.0	19.5	1.8	83.2	10.6	2.2	3.9	8.1	9.7
Biological Sciences	37.6	17.3	2.9	57.8	30.1	4.5	7.6	8.8	10.9
Vet. Science, Agriculture & related	50.6	17.0	4.4	72.0	16.0	5.3	6.7	1.2	1.5
Physical Sciences	35.2	16.5	2.9	54.6	32.3	4.6	8.5	4.0	4.9
Mathematical Sciences	51.7	14.8	2.2	68.8	18.2	5.8	7.3	2.8	3.5
Engineering & Technology	50.4	13.5	3.6	67.6	21.1	5.0	6.3	2.0	2.7
Architecture, Building & Planning	37.6	24.2	6.4	68.2	23.4	2.7	5.7	1.0	1.2
Social Sciences	38.2	17.4	2.6	58.2	30.3	4.5	7.0	13.8	17.6
Business & Financial Studies	55.9	18.3	4.3	78.4	9.7	4.7	7.1	10.8	14.0
Librarianship & Info Science	52.0	22.7	3.0	77.7	9.9	5.8	6.7	2.1	2.7
Languages	35.1	17.1	8.1	60.4	27.7	4.5	7.5	9.3	11.5
Humanities	34.3	19.5	3.2	57.1	30.4	4.9	7.7	4.4	5.4
Creative Arts & Design	42.9	20.1	2.7	65.7	18.0	6.7	9.6	8.9	11.8
Education	52.1	37.3	1.5	90.8	4.4	1.5	3.3	7.3	8.6
Combined, general	41.7	17.9	3.6	63.2	24.2	4.6	8.0	11.5	14.4
All subjects	**44.0**	**20.8**	**3.4**	**68.1**	**20.7**	**4.3**	**6.9**	**98.3**	**123.0**

Source: Department for Education and Skills; Higher Education Statistics Agency (HESA)

See previous page for footnotes

Chapter 6
Population

CHAPTER 6: POPULATION

Key Facts

- UK population aged 2 and over at January 2001 was 58.4 million (28.8 million males and 29.6 million females). **(Table 6.1)**

- UK working age population at Spring 2001 was 36.6 million, of which 24.1 million were Employees, 3.0 million were Self employed, 1.4 million were ILO unemployed and 7.9 million were Economically inactive. **(Table 6.1)**

- UK population aged 2 and over increased by 5.0 per cent between 1991 (55.6 million) and 2001 (58.4 million). Over the same period the working age population increased by 4.1 per cent, from 35.1 million to 36.6 million. **(Table 6.2)**

- Of people of working age, between 1991 and 2001, Employees increased by 10 per cent (21.9 million to 24.1 million), Self employed decreased by 9 per cent (3.0 million from 3.3 million), Economically inactive increased by 13 per cent (7.0 million to 7.9 million), while ILO unemployed decreased by 44 per cent from 2.5 million to 1.4 million. **(Table 6.2)**

CHAPTER 6: POPULATION – LIST OF TABLES

POPULATION

6.1

Population[1] at 1 January by age[2] and gender at the beginning of the academic year, 2001

United Kingdom

Thousands

| | 2001[2] | | | | | | | | | | | | | | |
| | All[3] | | | | | Males | | | | | Females | | | | |
	UK	England	Wales	Scotland	NI	UK	England	Wales	Scotland	NI	UK	England	Wales	Scotland	NI
Ages															
Under 5	2,173	1,821	104	176	73	1,114	933	53	90	37	1,059	888	50	86	35
5-10	4,634	3,871	226	383	154	2,376	1,985	116	196	79	2,258	1,886	110	187	75
11-15	3,867	3,209	198	325	135	1,984	1,647	101	167	69	1,883	1,562	96	159	66
16-19	2,977	2,460	153	262	102	1,525	1,261	78	134	53	1,452	1,199	75	129	50
20-24	3,619	3,018	169	318	114	1,855	1,545	88	163	59	1,764	1,474	80	156	55
25-29	4,097	3,450	182	341	124	2,105	1,772	95	173	65	1,992	1,678	87	167	60
30-39	9,547	8,047	426	814	260	4,875	4,124	217	407	128	4,671	3,923	210	407	131
40-49	7,960	6,653	385	709	214	3,996	3,347	192	351	105	3,964	3,306	193	358	108
50-59	7,324	6,141	378	622	184	3,640	3,057	188	304	90	3,685	3,084	190	317	94
60-64	2,877	2,393	152	258	73	1,409	1,177	75	122	35	1,467	1,216	77	136	38
65+	9,316	7,797	509	788	222	3,882	3,261	212	318	90	5,435	4,537	297	470	132
Total aged 2 +	**58,391**	**48,860**	**2,881**	**4,997**	**1,654**	**28,760**	**24,109**	**1,414**	**2,426**	**811**	**29,632**	**24,751**	**1,467**	**2,571**	**843**
of which working age[4]	36,554	30,609	1,758	3,164	1,023	19,155	16,066	925	1,637	527	17,399	14,544	833	1,527	496
of which															
Employees[5,6]	24,056	20,327	1,046	2,093	590	12,841	10,895	556	1,080	311	11,214	9,432	490	1,013	279
Self employed[6,7]	2,963	2,538	137	210	79	2,221	1,883	107	164	67	742	655	30	45	12
ILO unemployed[8]	1,390	1,124	75	145	47	851	677	46	96	32	539	447	29	48	15
Economically inactive[9]	7,911	6,439	485	697	290	3,110	2,511	208	284	106	4,801	3,928	277	412	184

Sources: Department for Education and Skills; Labour Force Survey[10]; Office for National Statistics; Government Actuary's Department

1 Estimated and projected numbers based on demographic data provided by the Office for National Statistics and the Government Actuary's Department.

2 Age at 31 August 2000. For the Labour Force Survey economic data only, age is based on the age of respondents at the time of the survey.

3 Males and Females may not sum to All totals due to rounding.

4 Working age is defined as males aged 16-64 and females 16-59. These figures include unpaid family workers, those on government employment and training programmes, or those who did not answer, who are excluded from the separate analyses below.

5 Employees are those in employment excluding the self-employed, unpaid family workers and those on government employment and training programmes.

6 The split into employees and self-employed is based on respondents' own assessment of their employment status.

7 Self-employed are those in employment excluding employees, unpaid family workers and those on government employment and training programmes.

8 Unemployed according to the International Labour Office (ILO) definition.

9 Economically inactive are those who are neither in employment nor ILO unemployed.

10 Users of these data should read the LFS entry in Annex A, as it contains important information about the LFS and the concepts and definitions used.

POPULATION

6.2

Population[1] at 1 January by age[2] at the beginning of the academic year – time series

United Kingdom

Thousands

Ages	1991	1996	1999	2000	2001
Under 5	2,300	2,337	2,226	2,196	2,173
5-10	4,399	4,625	4,696	4,677	4,634
11-15	3,407	3,665	3,743	3,816	3,867
16-19	3,204	2,730	2,967	2,976	2,977
20-24	4,569	3,968	3,509	3,545	3,619
25-29	4,759	4,624	4,345	4,246	4,097
30-39	8,251	8,971	9,405	9,519	9,547
40-49	6,823	7,896	7,781	7,850	7,960
50-59	6,070	6,358	7,011	7,180	7,324
60-64	3,040	2,782	2,825	2,864	2,877
65+	8,774	9,229	9,268	9,296	9,316
Total aged 2 +	**55,596**	**57,185**	**57,775**	**58,164**	**58,391**
of which working age[3] of which	35,103	35,663	36,177	36,312	36,554
Employees[4,5]	21,920	22,092	23,392	23,802	24,056
Self employed[5,6]	3,250	3,109	2,999	2,930	2,963
ILO unemployed[7]	2,501	2,321	1,732	1,602	1,390
Economically inactive[8]	6,980	7,790	7,818	7,744	7,911

Sources: Department for Education and Skills; Labour Force Survey[9]; Office for National Statistics; Government Actuary's Department

1 Estimated and projected numbers based on demographic data provided by the Office for National Statistics and the Government Actuary's Department.

2 Age at 31 August of the previous year. For the Labour Force Survey economic data only, age is based on the age of respondents at the time of the survey.

3 Working age is defined as males aged 16-64 and females 16-59. These figures include unpaid family workers, those on government employment and training programmes, or those who did not answer, who are excluded from the separate analyses below.

4 Employees are those in employment excluding the self-employed, unpaid family workers and those on government employment and training programmes.

5 The split into employees and self-employed is based on respondents' own assessment of their employment status.

6 Self-employed are those in employment excluding employees, unpaid family workers and those on government employment and training programmes.

7 Unemployed according to the International Labour Office (ILO) definition.

8 Economically inactive are those who are neither in employment nor ILO unemployed.

9 Users of these data should read the LFS entry in Annex A, as it contains important information about the LFS and the concepts and definitions used.

Chapter 7
International Comparisons

Introduction

International comparisons of the functioning of education and training systems can help countries to identify their strengths and weaknesses and evaluate their performance against their main competitors. Governments are increasingly looking towards these comparisons as they develop and monitor education and training policies.

The United Kingdom participates in the continuing development of international comparisons of education and training. With help from the National Assembly for Wales, Scottish Executive, the Northern Ireland Department of Education and the Northern Ireland Department for Employment and Learning, DfES supply detailed statistics on education and training in the UK, drawn from this volume and other sources, to the Organisation for Economic Co-operation and Development (OECD), the Statistical Office of the European Union (EUROSTAT) and the United Nations Educational, Scientific and Cultural Organisation (UNESCO).

Based on information supplied by various countries to the international bodies, and the results of international studies, a range of 'indicators' is now available, seeking to compare different aspects of countries' education and training systems and their respective performance.

The comparative tables shown here draw from OECD's "Education at a Glance" (2001 Edition), which includes trends in international comparisons.

It is important to note however that international comparisons of education and training are very difficult and should therefore be treated with caution. In addition, some knowledge of the underlying systems in different countries is extremely useful in interpreting the data.

To ensure comparability, most educational activity in different countries has been assigned to 6 internationally-agreed "ISCED" (International Standard Classification of Education) levels of education. The best comparisons are based on such internationally agreed definitions and procedures, backed up by controls to ensure that each country meets these. Despite these efforts, there may still be comparability problems that persist – some of the more important ones are noted below:

Notes:

Classifying education
- Coverage of what is considered to be "education" may vary, especially at the pre-compulsory and post-compulsory level e.g. early childhood provision, apprenticeships, adult learning etc. The UK are participating in a revision of ISCED, attempting to address any inconsistencies between countries.

Expenditure on education
- Where institutions cover more than one of the education levels (e.g. "lower" (age 11-13) and "upper" (age 14+) secondary school education in the UK), estimates are often required to assign expenditure figures between levels.

- The range of public and private provision varies considerably between countries. In Japan and the United States, private expenditure on educational institutions is almost one-third of that from public sources.

- Public expenditure on education, as a percentage of GDP, is influenced by a number of factors. An obvious one is the proportion of the population of school age, which can vary widely between different countries.

- Expenditure coverage, especially at the HE level, differs according to the extent to which countries include elements such as student support and research and development.

Participation in education
- Many of the measures shown are on the basis of headcounts, no distinction being possible between full-time and part-time study. Some countries do not even recognise the concept of part-time study, although many of their students would be classified as "part-time" in the UK.

- When comparing expected years of schooling in different countries, the length of the school year and the quality of education offered is not necessarily the same.

- The reasons why adults in some countries are so much less likely than others to participate in university-level education are varied. One important factor may be the extensive provision of vocational education and apprenticeships in continental Europe, likely to have reduced the perceived need to enrol in formal university-level studies as preparation for work.

Teachers

- A clear definition of a "teacher", especially in higher education, has not been well established in international data collections. Some countries include professional staff such as guidance counsellors and school psychologists in their "teacher" counts.

CHAPTER 7: INTERNATIONAL COMPARISONS

Key Facts

- Public expenditure on all levels of education in the UK represented 4.9% of Gross Domestic Product in 1998, slightly below the OECD average. This was higher than in Germany (4.6%) and Japan (3.5%), but lower than France (6.0 %), the US (5.1%) and all the Scandinavian countries. **(Table 7.1)**

- Average expenditure per primary and secondary school pupil in the UK in 1998 (US$3,329 and US$5,230 respectively) was slightly below the OECD average (US$3,940 and US$5,294 respectively. **(Table 7.2)**

- Average expenditure per higher education student in the UK in 1998 (US$9,699) was slightly above the OECD average (US$9,063) – however, the US spent over twice the amount per higher education student as the UK. **(Table 7.2)**

- Over 90% of the population are enrolled in education in the UK, each year between the ages of 4 to 15. In most other OECD countries, compulsory education does not start until age 6 or 7, compared with age 5 in the UK. **(Table 7.3)**

- In 1999, given current conditions, a UK 5 year old could expect to enrol in 18.9 years of full-time and part-time education during their lifetime, compared with the OECD average of 16.7 years. Expected years in education in the UK increased by 10% between 1995 and 1999. They are currently highest in Sweden, where a 5 year old can expect to enrol in 20.3 years of full-time and part-time education. **(Table 7.3)**

- The ratio of students to teaching staff in the UK was above the OECD average at all levels of education in 1999. **(Table 7.4)**

- At age 16, 85% of the UK population were enrolled, full- or part-time, in educational institutions in 1999. Participation was near-universal in France (95%), Germany (97%), Japan (95%) and Canada (94%). At age 18, UK participation rates were 53%, compared with an OECD average of 68%. **(Table 7.5)**

- In 1999, the entry rate to university-level (first and higher degree) higher education was 45% in the UK, the same as the OECD average. "Expected years" of higher education in the UK (2.6 years) were slightly above the OECD average (2.5 years). **(Table 7.6)**

- In 1999, the graduation rate from first degrees in the United Kingdom was 37% compared with the OECD average of 19%. After New Zealand, the UK had the highest graduation rates from first degrees in the OECD. **(Table 7.6)**

- In 1999, the proportion of primary and lower secondary teachers in the United Kingdom aged 40-49 was above the OECD average. However, the proportion of teachers aged 50 and over was below the OECD average. **(Table 7.7)**

CHAPTER 7: INTERNATIONAL COMPARISONS – LIST OF TABLES

| | Public expenditure on education[1] as a percentage of GDP | | | |
| | 1998 | | | 1995 |
	Primary and Secondary Education	Higher Education	All levels[2]	All levels[2]
Australia	3.5	1.2	4.8	5.0
Austria	4.0	1.6	6.3	6.5
Belgium	3.5	1.1	5.2	..
Belgium (Flemish)	3.4	1.0	5.0	5.2
Canada	3.7	1.8	5.7	6.5
Czech Republic	2.9	0.8	4.3	4.9
Denmark	4.9	2.2	8.3	7.7
Finland	3.8	2.0	6.2	6.9
France	4.2	1.0	6.0	6.0
Germany	3.0	1.1	4.6	4.7
Greece	2.3	1.1	3.5	2.9
Hungary	2.9	0.9	4.6	5.0
Iceland	4.3	2.2	7.1	..
Ireland	3.3	1.1	4.5	5.1
Italy	3.5	0.8	4.9	4.6
Japan	2.8	0.4	3.5	..
Korea	3.1	0.4	4.1	..
Luxembourg	..	..	..	..
Mexico	3.0	0.8	4.2	4.6
Netherlands	3.1	1.4	4.9	5.0
New Zealand	4.9	1.8	7.2	5.7
Norway	4.6	2.0	7.7	9.1
Poland	3.5	1.2	5.4	5.5
Portugal	4.3	1.0	5.7	5.4
Spain	3.3	0.9	4.5	4.7
Sweden	5.3	2.1	8.0	..
Switzerland	4.1	1.1	5.5	..
Turkey	1.8	0.8	3.0	2.4
United Kingdom	**3.4**	**1.1**	**4.9**	**5.2**
United States	3.4	1.3	5.1	..
Country mean	**3.6**	**1.3**	**5.3**	**5.4**

Source: OECD, Education at a Glance, 2001

1 Direct expenditure for institutions and public subsidies to students e.g. for tuition fees and living costs. The definition of
   "education expenditure" used by OECD is different from the definition used in Chapter 1 of this Volume.
2 Includes expenditure for early childhood education and other miscellaneous expenditure.

	Expenditure per full-time equivalent student per year[1]				Cumulative expenditure per student over the average duration of higher education studies[2]
	(US$ converted using purchasing power parities)				
	Early childhood education	Primary education	Secondary education	Higher Education	
Australia	..	3,981	5,830	11,539	29,194
Austria[3]	5,029	6,065	8,163	11,279	72,184
Beligum[4]	2,726	3,743	5,970	6,508	..
Belgium (Flemish)[4]	2,601	3,799	6,238	6,597	..
Canada	4,535	..	..	14,579	27,419
Czech Republic	2,231	1,645	3,182	5,584	..
Denmark	5,664	6,713	7,200	9,562	40,065
Finland	3,665	4,641	5,111	7,327	45,413
France	3,609	3,752	6,605	7,226	33,830
Germany	4,648	3,531	6,209	9,481	46,078
Greece[4]	[5]	2,368	3,287	4,157	21,657
Hungary	2,160	2,028	2,140	5,073	20,545
Ireland	2,555	2,745	3,934	8,522	27,610
Italy[3]	4,730	5,653	6,458	6,295	34,559
Japan	3,123	5,075	5,890	9,871	..
Korea	1,287	2,838	3,544	6,356	21,800
Mexico	865	863	1,586	3,800	13,005
Netherlands	3,630	3,795	5,304	10,757	41,951
Norway[3]	7,924	5,761	7,343	10,918	..
Poland	2,747	1,496	1,438	4,262	15,685
Portugal	1,717	3,121	4,636	-	..
Spain	2,586	3,267	4,274	5,038	22,922
Sweden	3,210	5,579	5,648	13,224	60,928
Switzerland[3]	2,593	6,470	9,348	16,563	60,030
United Kingdom[4]	**4,910**	**3,329**	**5,230**	**9,699**	**34,348**
United States	6,441	6,043	7,764	19,802	..
Country Mean	**3,585**	**3,940**	**5,294**	**9,063**	**35,087**

Source: OECD, Education at a Glance, 2001

1 Calendar year 1998. Where the financial year and/or school year do not match the calendar year, corresponding weightings are made.

2 Calculated by multiplying the expenditure per full-time equivalent student per year by the average number of years of duration of higher education studies.
   Includes students who do not complete their course.

3 Public institutions only.

4 Public and Government-dependent private institutions only.

5 Included in primary education figure.

INTERNATIONAL COMPARISONS
Participation in education 1999

	Context			Expected years of education[1]	
	Compulsory school starting age[2]	Ending age of compulsory schooling[3]	Age range at which over 90% of the population are enrolled	Expected years of full-time and part time education from age 5	Index of change between 1995 and 1999 (1995 = 100)
Australia	6	15	6-16	19.9	103
Austria	6	15	5-16	16.0	103
Belgium	6	18	3-17	18.5	103
Canada	6	16	5-16	16.5	97
Czech Republic	6	15	5-16	15.1	106
Denmark[4]	7	16	4-16	17.7	105
Finland	7	16	7-17	18.3	107
France	6	16	3-17	16.5	100
Germany	6	18	6-17	17.2	105
Greece	6	14.5	6-19	15.6	112
Hungary	6	16	5-16	16.0	111
Iceland	6	16	4-15	17.7	..
Ireland	6	15	5-16	16.0	104
Italy	6	14	3-14	15.8	..
Japan	6	15	4-17	..	..
Korea	6	14	6-17	15.8	110
Luxembourg	6	15	4-15	..	..
Mexico	6	15	6-12	12.4	103
Netherlands[5]	5	18	4-17	17.1	..
New Zealand	6	16	4-15	17.2	..
Norway	7	16	6-17	17.9	102
Poland	7	15	6-16	16.0	111
Portugal	6	14	6-15	16.8	102
Slovak Republic	6	15	..	..	..
Spain	6	16	4-15	17.3	102
Sweden	7	16	6-18	20.3	..
Switzerland	6	15	6-16	16.3	..
Turkey	6	14	7-10	10.6	112
United Kingdom[6]	**5**	**16**	**4-15**	**18.9**	**110**
United States	6	17	6-15	17.2	..
Country mean	**6**	**16**	**.**	**16.7**	**105**

Sources: OECD, Education at a Glance, 2001; UNESCO Statistical Yearbook, 1999

1 Calculated as the sum of the net enrolment rates in education for each single year of age from age 5 onwards, divided by 100.
2 Age at start of academic year.
3 Age at end of academic year.
4 Adult education is excluded.
5 Only educational programmes lasting more than 12 months are included.
6 Coverage of enrolments in further education has been expanded from a "snapshot" to a "whole year" count. This has had an effect on "school expectancy" figures which are not directly comparable with earlier years.

INTERNATIONAL COMPARISONS
Ratio of students to teaching staff[1] by level of education (based on full-time equivalents) 1999

	Early childhood education	Primary education	Secondary education	Higher education
Australia[2, 3]	..	17.3	12.7	11.8
Austria	17.5	14.5	9.8	15.0
Belgium (Flemish)	17.7	13.9	8.8	18.1
Canada	15.1	18.7	19.3	..
Czech Republic	19.5	23.4	14.7	14.9
Denmark	6.5	10.6	12.4	..
Finland	12.3	17.4	13.5	15.7
France	19.3	19.6	12.8	16.9
Germany	23.7	21.0	15.2	12.3
Greece	15.9	13.5	10.6	26.0
Hungary	11.8	10.9	10.6	12.1
Iceland	5.7	13.3	13.5	8.0
Ireland	14.7	21.6	14.6	17.3
Italy	13.2	11.3	10.3	24.8
Japan	19.0	21.2	15.4	11.5
Korea	23.9	32.2	22.2	..
Luxembourg[4]	16.7	12.5	9.9	..
Mexico	24.4	27.2	32.2	14.8
Netherlands	[5]	16.6	17.7	12.0
New Zealand	6.6	20.5	16.1	14.8
Norway[6]	5.1	12.6	10.1	13.4
Slovak Republic	10.4	19.6	13.6	10.3
Spain	17.1	15.4	12.9	16.4
Sweden	..	13.3	14.5	9.5
Switzerland[4]	17.8	16.1	12.3	..
Turkey	15.3	30.0	16.1	21.5
United Kingdom[2]	**16.5**	**22.5**	**14.7**	**18.5**
United States	19.3	16.3	15.6	14.0
Country mean	**15.4**	**18.0**	**14.6**	**15.3**

Source: OECD, Education at a Glance, 2001

1 Includes head teachers and administrative personnel involved in teaching, pro-rata.
2 Includes only general secondary education programmes.
3 Higher education does not include sub-degree programmes.
4 Public institutions only.
5 Included in primary education figures.
6 Secondary education shows figure for lower secondary education only.

INTERNATIONAL COMPARISONS
Participation rates in education[1] of 16 to 18 year olds[2] 1999

	Age at end of compulsory education[3]	Age at graduation of upper secondary education[3]	Percentage		
			Age 16	Age 17	Age 18
OECD countries					
Australia	15	19	92	84	68
Austria	15	17-19	92	87	67
Belgium	18	18-19	98	96	85
Canada	16	18	94	84	54
Czech Republic	15	18-19	100	88	60
Denmark	16	19-20	93	82	76
Finland	16	19	94	96	85
France	16	18-20	95	91	80
Germany	18	19	97	92	85
Greece	14.5	18	92	65	69
Hungary	16	16-18	93	88	70
Iceland	16	20	90	77	67
Ireland	15	17-18	92	81	74
Italy	14	17-19	79	73	70
Japan	15	18	95	94	..
Korea	14	17-18	98	95	57
Luxembourg	15	18-19	87	81	66
Mexico	15	18	43	35	27
Netherlands[4]	18	18-19	107	95	80
New Zealand	16	18	90	75	54
Norway	16	19	94	93	88
Poland	15	18-20	90	89	74
Portugal	14	18	83	84	66
Spain	16	16-18	87	79	66
Sweden	16	19	97	97	95
Switzerland	15	18-20	91	85	80
Turkey	14	17	38	25	19
United Kingdom[5]	**16**	**16-18**	**85**	**74**	**53**
United States	17	18	89	83	62
Country Mean	**16**	**18**	**89**	**82**	**68**

Source: OECD, Education at a Glance, 2001

1 Includes all education taking place in educational institutions, so includes apprenticeships in countries which operate a dual
  system e.g. Austria, Germany. Age participation rates are based on a full-time and part-time headcount.
2 Age at start of academic year.
3 Age at end of academic year.
4 Only educational programmes lasting more than 12 months are included.
5 Coverage of enrolments in further education has been expanded from a "snapshot" to a "whole year" count. This has had an effect
  on participation rates which are not directly comparable with earlier years.

	Entry	Participation	Graduation rates[4]				
				University level[2]			
				First degree		Postgraduate	
	Net entry rate[1] to university-level higher education[2]	Expected years of higher education for all 17 year olds[3]	Non-university level[2]	Medium[5]	Long[6]	Masters or equiv.	Doctorate
OECD countries							
Australia	45	3.0	..	27.0	.	8.5	1.2
Austria	..	2.2	..	0.9	11.1	0.1	1.4
Belgium (Flemish)	30	2.7	25.4	10.9	6.9	5.1	0.6
Canada	..	2.7	12.6	26.9	2.4	4.7	0.8
Czech Republic[7, 8]	23	1.4	5.8	2.2	8.6	1.7	0.5
Denmark	34	2.5	23.3	..	..	..	0.6
Finland	67	3.9	22.3	16.4	17.5	0.7	1.7
France[8]	35	2.6	17.9	18.5	6.4	6.7	1.2
Germany[7]	28	2.0	11.8	5.2	10.8	.	1.8
Greece	..	2.5	..	..	..	..	..
Hungary	58	1.8	..	26.9	10	3.1	0.8
Iceland	55	2.0	8.4	26.0	2.9	1.8	-
Ireland[8, 9]	..	2.4	21.0	24.8	1.2	13.1	0.8
Italy	40	2.2	0.3	1.1	14.9	3.3	0.4
Japan[7, 8]	37	..	29.9	29.0	10	2.6	0.6
Korea[7, 8]	43	3.5	31.2	26.5	0.6	3.0	0.6
Luxembourg	..	..	..	..	..	..	..
Mexico	24	0.9	..	11.2	10	..	..
Netherlands	54	2.3	0.9	32.3	1.2	1.2	1.0
New Zealand	71	3.0	10.0	29.5	7.8	15.9	0.8
Norway	57	3.1	5.8	28.5	5.4	4.6	1.0
Poland[7, 8]	59	2.3	0.8	15.9	14.0	18.2	..
Portugal	..	2.3	..	..	..	..	..
Slovak Republic[7, 8]	35	..	2.5	5.3	14.4	-	0.5
Spain	46	2.8	5.4	12.8	17.5	11	0.5
Sweden	65	2.9	2.7	25.9	1.3	0.6	2.4
Switzerland[8]	29	1.7	19.0	7.8	12.7	5.1	2.6
Turkey	..	1.2	4.4	9.6	10	0.8	0.3
United Kingdom	**45**	**2.6**	**11.4**	**35.6**	**1.2**	**12.7**	**1.3**
United States[8]	45	3.6	8.6	33.2	.	14.3	1.3
Country Mean	**45**	**2.5**	**12.2**	**18.8**	**6.1**	**5.3**	**1.0**

Source: OECD, Education at a Glance, 2001

1 Calculated as the sum over all age groups of new university-level entrants within an age group divided by the total population for that age group.

2 "University-level" higher education refers to "largely theoretically based" courses with a minimum of 3 years full-time-equivalent duration. In the UK, this comprises first and higher degrees. "Non university-level higher education" courses are "more practically-oriented and occupationally specific". In the UK, this level comprises "sub-degree" higher education courses, such as HNCs, HNDs, Dip HEs.

3 Calculated as the sum of the net enrolment rates (full-time and part-time) in higher education for each single year of age from age 17 onwards, divided by 100.

4 Calculated as the sum over all age groups of graduates within an age group divided by the total population for that age group.

5 Three to less than 5 years duration.

6 Five or more years duration.

7 "Gross" entry rate.

8 "Gross" graduation rate.

9 Graduation rates refer to 1998.

10 Included in short first degree figure.

11 Included in long first degree figure.

Percentages

	Primary education					Lower secondary education				
	20 - 29	30 - 39	40 - 49	50 - 59	>= 60	20 - 29	30 - 39	40 - 49	50 - 59	>= 60
OECD countries										
Austria	16.0	30.7	38.0	14.4	0.9	9.2	30.7	43.2	16.3	0.5
Belgium (Fl.)[1]	20.2	31.2	27.9	20.4	0.3	13.8	22.6	35.9	25.8	1.9
Canada	11.8	24.4	38.7	24.0	1.1	11.8	24.4	38.7	24.0	1.1
Czech Republic	15.1	27.0	24.6	28.8	4.5	14.7	27.3	25.4	28.1	4.5
Finland	13.8	32.5	28.4	24.6	0.6	9.4	26.7	31.4	31.3	1.3
France	12.6	28.7	37.6	20.9	0.2	13.7	22.8	30.8	31.9	0.7
Germany	6.6	14.9	38.1	36.7	3.7	3.9	9.8	40.7	41.3	4.4
Iceland	16.0	29.9	31.8	16.7	5.6	[2]	[2]	[2]	[2]	[2]
Ireland[1]	13.3	28.5	33.6	19.0	5.7	10.7	25.8	34.9	23.5	5.2
Italy	4.7	27.0	39.7	24.7	3.9	-	9.0	46.4	41.4	3.2
Korea	22.0	31.2	29.8	15.1	2.0	14.4	49.0	23.1	10.9	2.6
Luxembourg[3]	26.8	21.0	29.4	22.5	0.4	8.6	26.3	32.3	29.6	3.2
Netherlands[1]	14.2	21.0	40.1	23.2	1.4	7.1	18.7	39.7	32.4	2.1
New Zealand	19.3	21.3	36.0	20.2	3.3	16.9	21.4	36.4	21.8	3.4
Norway	16.3	21.5	30.3	26.7	5.1	[2]	[2]	[2]	[2]	[2]
Slovak Republic	24.2	22.7	27.5	22.7	2.9	14.1	19.7	37.1	26.6	2.5
Sweden	11.6	14.5	32.9	35.0	6.0	14.2	19.0	25.1	34.7	6.9
Switzerland[3]	21.0	25.3	33.6	18.0	2.1	12.0	25.9	34.9	23.9	3.4
United Kingdom	**20.5**	**20.0**	**36.9**	**21.8**	**0.7**	**17.4**	**22.1**	**38.6**	**21.0**	**0.9**
Country mean	**16.1**	**25.1**	**33.6**	**22.7**	**2.5**	**11.7**	**23.8**	**34.3**	**27.0**	**4.0**

Source: OECD, Education at a Glance, 2001

1 Figures for lower secondary education include upper secondary education.
2 Included in primary education figure.
3 Public institutions only.

Annex A

SOURCES OF EDUCATION AND TRAINING STATISTICS

This section gives details of the current major sources of education and training statistics used in this publication. Previous editions of "Education and Training Statistics for the United Kingdom" and its predecessors, and "Training Statistics", give earlier sources used.

List of Sources

1   Education Expenditure

2   Further Education Statistics

3   Higher Education Statistics Agency (HESA)

4   Labour Force Survey (LFS)

5   Public Examinations: GCSE/GNVQ, GCE, SCE
    Standard Grade and National Qualifications (NQ)

6   School Leavers Destinations

7   Schools Statistics

8   TEC/LSC Delivered Government Supported
    Training

9   Vocational Qualifications

1 EDUCATION EXPENDITURE

HM Treasury provided education expenditure figures in Tables 1.1 and 1.2 from their Public Expenditure Statistical Analysis (PESA). The tables show Total Managed Expenditure (TME) on services, which is a definition of aggregate public spending on services based on the national accounts aggregate TME. It is the consolidated sum of current and capital expenditure, but excludes public sector debt interest, net public service pensions and other accounting adjustments. Gross Domestic Product (GDP) figures and deflators are based on the September 2001 National Accounts release. Table 1.3 reports identifiable Total Managed Expenditure on education services by country, and is also derived from PESA.

2 FURTHER EDUCATION STATISTICS

Statistical information on further education students in England, Scotland and Wales are produced by the respective Further Education Funding Councils. However in April 2001 the publication of data on further education in England became the responsibility of the Learning and Skills Council (LSC), which has taken over responsibility for funding the further education sector in England from the FEFC. Institutes of further education provide data for Northern Ireland to the Department for Employment and Learning (DELNI). The Higher Education Statistics Agency (HESA) provides data on FE students in higher education institutions in the UK.

3 HIGHER EDUCATION STATISTICS AGENCY (HESA)

From the academic year 1994/95 onwards, the Higher Education Statistics Agency (HESA) has collected information for HE students within UK HE institutions. The data collected include enrolment numbers, qualifiers and first destinations (home and EU students only from 1999/00) of qualifiers.

4 LABOUR FORCE SURVEY (LFS)

Please note that in the LFS tables some separate analyses will not sum to base figures shown because of unpaid family workers, those on government-supported training and employment programmes, or those who did not answer, who are excluded from the separate analyses (see below for details).

The Labour Force Survey (LFS) was first carried out in the United Kingdom in 1973, as part of the UK's obligations as members of the European Economic Community, and was repeated every two years until 1983. Between 1984 and 1991, the survey was carried out annually, with results published relating to the March to May quarter.

From spring (March to May) 1992 the survey was carried out in Great Britain on a quarterly basis. In Northern Ireland the LFS was conducted in spring 1992 and spring 1993, and was then carried out quarterly from winter (December to February) 1994-95. So for about the last seven years, there has been a quarterly survey covering the whole of the UK. The International Labour Organisation (ILO) – an agency of the United Nations – agrees the concepts and definitions used in the LFS.

The survey is based on a random sample throughout the whole of the United Kingdom. Every three months almost 65 thousand households are contacted and information is collected about the personal and work circumstances of everyone living in these households. As well as these private households, the survey covers two groups of people living in a type of accommodation called *communal establishments*. These two groups are students in halls of residence (whose parents usually answer the survey questions on the students' behalf) and people living in NHS accommodation (which used to be called nurses' homes). The survey does not sample people living in other forms of accommodation – for example, army camps, local authority homes, or hospitals.

The results of each survey are processed and 'grossed', to provide estimates that cover the whole population. This allows us to say that there are about 24 million people in employment, even though the sample itself has only identified about 70 thousand employed people.

ONS intends to undertake a re-grossing project to be completed in April 2002, which will revise LFS estimates back to the summer quarter 1998. This will be reflected in time series data used in the 2002 edition of *Education and Training Statistics for the United Kingdom*.

CONCEPTS AND DEFINITIONS

All People
This group includes everyone of working age (Males aged 16-64 and Females aged 16-59) and comprises; employees, the self-employed, those on government supported programmes, unpaid family workers, the ILO unemployed and the economically inactive.

Economically active – people aged 16 and over who are either in employment (did some paid work in the reference week) or ILO unemployed.

Employees/Self-employed – the division between employees and self-employed is based on survey respondents' own assessment of their employment status.

Full-time/part-time – the classification of full-time and part-time is on the basis of self-assessment. People on Government-supported training and employment programmes who are at college in the survey reference week are classified, by convention, as part-time.

Temporary employees – in the LFS these are defined as those employees who say that their main job is non-permanent in one of the following ways: fixed period contract; agency temping; casual work; seasonal work; other temporary work.

Government-supported training and employment programmes – This group comprises all people aged 16 and over participating in one of the Government's employment and training programmes administered by Learning and Skills Councils in England and Wales, local enterprise companies in Scotland, or the Training and Employment Agency in Northern Ireland. This group of people has been excluded from the separate economic analyses in the tables as the LFS generally undercounts the numbers involved. Administrative sources provide much more reliable information about this group (see separate source number 8).

Unpaid Family Workers – This group comprises persons doing unpaid work for a business they own or for a business that a relative owns. This group of people has been excluded from the separate economic analyses as it is relatively small (around 100,000) and when disaggregated many of the estimates fall below the publication threshold of 10,000.

ILO unemployment – the International Labour Office (ILO) measure of unemployment refers to people without a job who were available to start work in the two weeks following their LFS interview and who had either looked for work in the four weeks prior to interview or were waiting to start a job they had already obtained.

Economically inactive – people who are neither in employment nor unemployed on the ILO measure. This group includes, for example, all those who were looking after a home or retired (as well as those aged under 16).

Industry – the classification of respondents' industry of employment is based on the Standard Industrial Classification 1992, SIC (92).

Occupation – the classification of respondents' occupations are based on the Standard Occupational Classification (SOC), introduced in 1991.

5 PUBLIC EXAMINATIONS: GCSE/GNVQ, GCE, SCE STANDARD GRADE AND NATIONAL QUALIFICATIONS (NQ)

Data for England and Wales are produced from data provided by the GCSE and GCE examining boards and groups. GCSE and GCE data for Northern Ireland are derived from the School Performance Survey and Further Education examination results. In Scotland pupils study for the SCE Standard grade (a two-year course leading to examinations at the end of the fourth year of secondary schooling) and Higher grade, which requires at least a further year of secondary schooling. The data source is the Scottish Qualifications Authority (formerly Scottish Examination Board). From 1999/00 National Qualifications (NQ) were introduced in Scotland. NQ includes Intermediate 1 & 2 and Highers.

6 SCHOOL LEAVERS DESTINATIONS

From 1996, information on the early destinations of year 11 pupils in England has been collected via the Careers Service Activity Survey. This replaced the former School Leavers Destination Survey, which collected information on the destinations of year 11 pupils in England and Wales. It provides data about the choices of around half a million young people finishing compulsory education each year. School leaver data are collected for Scotland (but for leavers of all ages) and for Northern Ireland. However, data for Wales are no longer collected.

7 SCHOOLS STATISTICS

The Department for Education and Skills carries out an annual Census of schools in England on the third Thursday in January. Data are collected on the number of schools by type; number of pupils by age and sex; number of admissions; pupils' school meal arrangements; number of teaching and non-teaching staff; course of study followed by pupils aged 16 and over; number of classes as taught and number of pupils with statements of special educational needs. Data collected in January 2001 were published the following September in the publication *Statistics of Education: Schools in England*.

Corresponding annual schools census counts are also carried out in January for pupils in Wales, September for pupils in Scotland and October for pupils in Northern Ireland.

8 TEC/LSC DELIVERED GOVERNMENT SUPPORTED TRAINING

The main TEC/LSC delivered Government Supported Training programmes in England are Advanced Modern Apprenticeships (formerly Modern Apprenticeships), Foundation Modern Apprenticeships (formerly National Traineeships), Life Skills/Skill Build, and Other Training for Young People, plus Work-based Learning for Adults. The Department for Education and Skills funds these programmes in England, and in Wales the National Assembly for Wales. Until 25 March 2001, these programmes were delivered through the network of Training and Enterprise Councils (TECs), however, since 26 March 2001, work-based training for young people has been delivered through the Learning and Skills Council (LSC) and its Welsh counterpart. Since 1 April 2001, work-based learning for adults has been delivered through the Employment Service (ES) as an integral part of provision for long term unemployed adults. ES is now part of the newly formed Department for Work and Pensions (DWP). The programmes delivered in Wales are virtually identical, however because of a change in data reporting within DfES, the figures shown in this volume are for England only.

Until 25 March 2001, the statistics came from three sources: aggregate management information returns provided by TECs, certificates that training providers completed for each individual joining a programme (starts certificates) and a postal questionnaire sent to each trainee[1] six months[2] after leaving the programme, asking for information on whether they completed their training, usefulness of the training, their current activity and what qualifications they gained. While the questionnaires have changed several times since their introduction, the core questions have remained consistent. From 26 March 2001, the statistics for young people come from two sources: starts certificates and the postal questionnaire. Statistics for adult learning come from ES' labour market system (LMS).

Further details of the programmes and data sources can be obtained from the Statistical First Releases (SFRs) shown on the DfES Statistical Website (www.dfes.gov.uk/statistics).

9 VOCATIONAL QUALIFICATIONS

Information on awards of National Vocational Qualifications (NVQs)/Scottish Vocational Qualifications (SVQs), General National Vocational Qualifications (GNVQs)/General Scottish Vocational Qualifications (GSVQs), and Other Vocational Qualifications made by UK awarding bodies has been taken from the National Information System for Vocational Qualifications (NISVQ) held by DfES. As part of the NISVQ project the Qualifications and Curriculum Authority (QCA) provides annual totals (October-September) of NVQ awards by framework area and level, which are used for grossing up the more detailed NVQ award information, collected from the awarding bodies who participate in NISVQ, in order to produce UK NVQ estimates. QCA's totals are based on quarterly returns sent to QCA by all NVQ awarding bodies. UK NVQ/SVQ estimates are based on grossed-up numbers of NVQs plus all SVQs.

NISVQ receives detailed information on awards of NVQs/SVQs, GNVQs/GSVQs and Other VQs (made by four of the largest awarding bodies: City and Guilds, Edexcel, OCR and SQA). However, in 1999/00 the SQA were unable to supply information on their numbers of 'Other VQ' awards and have therefore been excluded. Information on GNVQs/GSVQs is complete, because all the relevant awarding bodies are included. SQA also provides complete information on SVQs.

More detailed statistical information on the awards of Vocational Qualifications is presented in the DfES Statistical Bulletin: Vocational Qualifications in the UK 1999/00, which can be found on the DfES Statistical Website. (www.dfes.gov.uk/statistics).

1 *Apart from those known to have ceased training as a result of serious injury, serious illness or death.*

2 *In the past, follow-up surveys have been carried out 3 months after leaving up to December 1990 leavers for Employment Training and up to September 1990 leavers for Youth Training.*

Annex B

UNITED KINGDOM EDUCATION AND TRAINING STATISTICS: OTHER REFERENCE MATERIAL

1 GENERAL

1.1 Various summaries of education and training statistics for all four parts of the United Kingdom are contained in the *Annual Abstract of Statistics*, *Regional Trends* and *Social Trends* publications prepared by the Office for National Statistics. Some education statistics also appear in the *Digest of Welsh Statistics*, *Scottish Social Statistics* and the *Annual Abstract of Statistics, Northern Ireland*.

1.2 Each of the home education departments also publish statistics in a variety of press notices, bulletins and statistical volumes. The relevant websites are as follows:

England: http://www.dfes.gov.uk/statistics
Wales: http://www.wales.gov.uk/
Scotland: http://www.scotland.gov.uk
N. Ireland: http://www.deni.gov.uk
       http://www.delni.gov.uk

2 OFFICE FOR NATIONAL STATISTICS (ONS) PUBLICATIONS

The Office for National Statistics publishes a quarterly journal entitled *Statistical News* (price £59.00 pa, or £16 per issue), which contains short articles and notes on the latest developments in all fields of government statistics, including education and training.

Social Trends is produced annually, No 31 2001 (£39.50. ISBN 0 11 621384 1) being the current edition. This publication brings together some of the more significant statistical series relating to social polices and conditions and presents a series of articles, followed by tables and charts. One chapter concentrates on education and training.

Regional Trends is also published annually, No 36 2001 (£39.50. ISBN 0 11 621464 3) being the current edition. This publication brings together detailed information highlighting regional variations in the United Kingdom and covering a wide range of social, demographic and economic topics. One chapter concentrates on education and training.

Guide to Official Statistics 2000 Edition (£32.00. ISBN 0 11 621 161 X) is a comprehensive guide to UK statistics, listing all the statistical censuses, surveys, administrative systems, press releases, publications, databases, CD-ROMs, and other services, by industry sector. The information is also available on StatBase at http://www.statistics.gov.uk.

Labour Market Trends (incorporating the Employment Gazette) is a monthly publication with over 70 pages of labour market statistical tables. It also contains regular analytical articles using Labour Force Survey data and every month includes an LFS Help Line feature, which presents information frequently requested by users of the LFS. The price per issue is £9.50 or £95.00 for annual subscription (UK). It is available from The Stationery Office Bookshops.

Social Focus on Men 2001 (£30.00. ISBN 0 11 621466 X) provides an overview of the changing lives and roles of men in the United Kingdom and brings together information from a wide range of sources to paint a social and economic picture of men, using charts, text and simple tables.

The Office for National statistics on behalf of The Government Statistical Service (GSS) has created StatBase® as an on-line access system for deposited official data. The data comes from a variety of individual sources throughout GSS. This can be accessed via the ONS website – the home page can be found at: www.ons.gov.uk.

3 INTERNATIONAL STATISTICS

A number of publications providing comparative statistics and indicators on education and training in different countries are now available – some of the most important are listed below.

Education at a Glance: OECD Indicators 2001. Organisation for Economic Co-operation and Development. Stationery Office, 2000. £30.00. ISBN 92 64 18668 9.

Key Data on Vocational Training in the European Union. European Commission, Eurostat, CEDEFOP. Stationery Office, 1999. ISBN 92 828 6215 1.

Key Data on Education in the European Union. Eurydice, Eurostat. Stationery Office, 1999. £20.00. ISBN 92 828 8537 2.

Education across the European Union: Statistics and Indicators 1999. European Commission, Eurostat. Stationery Office, 1999. £30.00. ISBN 92 827 9797 X.

UNESCO Statistical Yearbook 1999. United Nations Educational, Scientific and Cultural Organisation. UNESCO Publishing and Bernan Press. £65.00 + VAT. ISBN 92 3 003635 8.

T

V

W

Printed in the United Kingdom for The Stationery Office
TJ005748 C12 11/01 9385 16213